RECOVERY MONOGRAPHS

Volume I

RECOVERY MONOGRAPHS

Volume I

REVOLUTIONIZING THE WAYS THAT BEHAVIORAL HEALTH LEADERS THINK ABOUT PEOPLE WITH SUBSTANCE USE DISORDERS

WILLIAM L. WHITE

authorHOUSE

AuthorHouse™
1663 Liberty Drive
Bloomington, IN 47403
www.authorhouse.com
Phone: 1 (800) 839-8640

Published by AuthorHouse   09/15/2015

ISBN: 978-1-5049-0507-7 (sc)
ISBN: 978-1-5049-0506-0 (e)

Library of Congress Control Number: 2015905253

Print information available on the last page.

This publication was produced by the Addiction Technology Transfer Center (ATTC) Network with support
from a grant from the Substance Abuse and Mental Health Services Administration (SAMHSA) Center for
Substance Abuse Treatment (CSAT). All materials appearing in this publication except that taken directly form
copyrighted sources is in the public domain and may be reproduced or copied without permission from SAMHSA/
CSAT or the authors. Citation of the source is appreciated. Do not reproduce or distribute this publication
for a fee without specific, written authorization from the ATTC Network Coordinating Office.

At the time of publication, Pamela S. Hyde, JD, serves as the SAMHSA director. H. Westley
Clark as CSAT Director and Suzan Swanton as CSAT project officer.

The opinions expressed herein are the views of the authors and do not necessarily reflect the official position of CSAT,
SAMHSA, or DHHS. No official support of or endorsement by CSAT, SAMHSA, or DHHS for these opinions of for
particular instruments, software, or resources described in this document is intended or should be inferred. The guidelines
in this document should not be considered substitutes for individualized client care and treatment decisions.

TABLE OF CONTENTS

PREFACE

During the last three decades of the twentieth century, federal, state and local partnerships forged a national network of addiction treatment resources in the United States. This expanding network of local programs was supported by new federal and state agencies, new funding and regulatory structures, new educational and training resources and an addiction research industry that offered the promise of evidence-based treatment of substance use disorders. By the late 1990s, tremendous strides had been achieved in elevating the accessibility and quality of addiction treatment in the U.S., yet leaders in the field were beginning to suggest the need for a radical redesign of addiction treatment—a shift from acute and palliative care models of intervention to models of assertive and sustained recovery management (RM) nested within larger recovery-oriented systems of care (ROSC).

In 1998, I began work with Michael Boyle on the Illinois-based Behavioral Health Recovery Management (BHRM) project—a project specifically charged with exploring the potential of adapting chronic care models drawn from primary medicine to enhance the quality of addiction treatment. The papers on RM emanating from the Illinois project garnered considerable attention and led to early consultations with the State of Connecticut and the City of Philadelphia who were early pioneers in RM-focused systems transformation processes. The early BHRM work also led to an invitation by the Center for Substance Abuse Treatment's (CSAT) Great Lakes and Northeast Addiction Technology Transfer Centers (ATTCs) to author and co-author a series of monographs on RM and ROSC. Collaborations with Dr. Arthur Evans, Commissioner of Behavioral Health Services in Philadelphia and Dr. Michael Flaherty of the Institute for Research, Education and Training in Addictions also informed the work that became the RM/ROSC monograph series. I could not be more delighted that the most central of these monographs, described below, have now been assembled into two comprehensive volumes.

The first monograph, Recovery Management, was published in 2006 and contained four essays. Recovery: The Next Frontier, originally published in Counselor in

2004, described the emergence of recovery as a new organizing paradigm for addiction treatment and non-clinical recovery support services. The Varieties of Recovery Experience, co-authored with Dr. Ernest Kurtz and published in abridged form in the International Journal of Self Help and Self Care, summarized what could be gleaned from history and science about the pathways, stages and styles of long-term addiction recovery. Recovery Management: What if we Really Believed Addiction was a Chronic Disorder? was a preliminary attempt to outline the changes in service practices implicit within RM models of care. Recovery Management and People of Color, co-authored with Mark Sanders and originally published in Alcoholism Treatment Quarterly, was a first attempt to explore application of the RM/ROSC model to historically disempowered communities.

Wide dissemination of the Recovery Management monograph generated considerable interest from the field and led to two follow-up monographs in 2006 and 2007. Recovery: Linking Addiction Treatment and Communities of Recovery, co-authored with Dr. Ernest Kurtz, offered concrete suggestions for addiction counselors and recovery coaches on how to best link those they served with recovery mutual aid societies and other indigenous recovery support institutions. The third monograph, Perspectives on Systems Transformation: How Visionary Leaders are Shifting Addiction Treatment Toward a Recovery-Oriented System of Care, focused on the RM/ROSC implementation process through a collection of interviews offering national (Dr. H. Westley Clark), State (Dr. Thomas Kirk), municipal (Dr. Arthur Evans, Jr.), program (Michael Boyle), recovery community (Phil Valentine), and ATTC (Lonnetta Albright) perspectives on the implementation of RM/ROSC principles.

One central question loomed as RM/ROSC language and approaches spread through the field: What is the evidence-base for this proposed redesign of addiction treatment. The fourth monograph, Recovery Management and Recovery-Oriented Systems of Care: Scientific Rationale and Promising Practices, was released in 2008 to answer that question. It described promising practices in such critical treatment performance areas as attraction, access, screening/assessment, engagement/retention, team composition, service relationship, service dose/scope/quality, locus of service delivery, linkage to recovery communities, and post-treatment monitoring and support.

If there was a single area within RM/ROSC proposals that captivated the field's attention and often emerged as the most visible element of RM/ROSC transformation efforts, it was the reintegration of people in recovery into the addiction treatment arena in both volunteer and paid roles at all levels of the system. Such integration generated mountains of emails and calls about how to achieve such integration and the evidence-base approaches to such efforts. In response, the fifth monograph, Peer-based Addiction Recovery Support: History, Theory, Practice, and Scientific Evaluation, was published in 2009. This monograph achieved two goals. It addressed what was known at that time about peer-based recovery support services from the standpoint of history and science, and it described in considerable detail how peer-based recovery support services were being implemented within addiction treatment and recovery community organizations across the United States.

In 2010, a major question arose about the implications of RM/ROSC for medication-assisted treatment. This question prompted collaboration with Lisa Mojer-Torres (the "Rosa Parks of Medication-Assisted Treatment") in co-authoring the sixth monograph, Recovery-oriented Methadone Maintenance (ROMM). The ROMM monograph was widely disseminated and led to numerous follow-up presentations and papers.[1]

Other monographs[2] and a book[3] followed this first series, but I will always think of these first six monographs as my foundational writings on RM/ROSC.

The RM/ROSC monograph series was done in tandem with numerous other efforts to enhance long-term recovery outcomes in the U.S. Of particular note is the now iconic paper on addiction as a chronic disorder led by Tom McLellan that was published in the Journal of the American Medical Association in 2000.[4] There were also CSAT monographs[5]

---

[1]   White, W. (2012) Medication-assisted recovery from opioid addiction: Historical and contemporary perspectives *Journal of Addictive Diseases,* 31(3), 199-206.

[2]   White, W. (2011). *Narcotics Anonymous and the pharmacotherapeutic treatment of opioid addiction.* Chicago, IL: Great Lakes Addiction Technology Transfer Center and Philadelphia Department of Behavioral Health and Intellectual disability Services; White, W.L. (2012). *Recovery/Remission from Substance Use Disorders: An Analysis of Reported Outcomes in 415 Scientific Studies, 1868-2011.* Great Lakes Addiction Technology Transfer Center, Philadelphia Department of Behavioral Health and Intellectual disAbility Services Mental Retardation Services and Northeast Addiction Technology Transfer Center.

[3]   Kelly, J. & White, W. (Eds., 2011). *Addiction recovery management: Theory, science and practice.* New York: Springer Science

[4]   McLellan, A. T., Lewis, D. C., O'Brien, C. P., & Kleber, H. D. (2000). Drug dependence, a chronic medical illness: Implications for treatment, insurance, and outcomes evaluation. *Journal of the American Medical Association,* 284(13), 1689-1695.

[5]   Center for Substance Abuse Treatment (2006). Emerging Peer Recovery Support Services and Indicators of Quality: An RCSP Conference Report. Rockville, MD: Substance Abuse and Mental Health Services Administration, U.S. Department of Health and Human Services; Center for Substance Abuse Treatment, What are Peer Recovery Support Services? HHS Publication No. (SMA) 09-4454. Rockville, MD: Substance Abuse and Mental Health Services Administration, U.S. Department of Health and Human Services, 2009; Halvorson A., and Whitter M., (2009) *Approaches to recovery-oriented systems of care at the state and local levels: Three case studies.* HHS Publication No. (SMA) 09-4438. Rockville, MD: Center for Substance Abuse Treatment, Substance Abuse and Mental Health Services Administration, 2009. Sheedy C. K., and Whitter M. (2009). Guiding Principles and Elements of Recovery-Oriented Systems of Care: What Do We Know From the Research? HHS Publication No. (SMA) 09-4439. Rockville, MD: Center for Substance Abuse Treatment, Substance Abuse and Mental Health Services Administration.

and monographs from other ATTCs[6] during these same years that played an important role in promoting RM/ROSC system transformation efforts. Additionally, the increased focus on long-term recovery would not have been possible without the research studies of Michael Dennis, Mark Godley, Susan Godley, James McKay, Christy Scott and others focused on extending the effects of addiction treatment through assertive approaches to post-treatment continuing care.

There are many people to thank for their support of this monograph series, but none more important than Dr. Westley Clark, Lonnetta Albright, Dr. Michael Flaherty and Dr. Arthur Evans, Jr. whose leadership and support were beyond what words can adequately express. I am also deeply indebted to Stephanie Kerns for her assistance with literature searches and procuring the thousands of published research studies cited in the monographs. Stephanie and Pamela Woll also brought their incomparable editing skills to the final preparation of the monographs. Finally, I would like to thank the ATTC Network Coordinating Office for their support and for publishing these volumes.

RM/ROSC offered a new vision and new service technologies that promised to transform addiction treatment from an almost singular focus on recovery initiation to a system capable of supporting enhanced stability and quality of personal and family life in long-term addiction recovery. It will be up to future generations to judge how close we as a field came to fulfilling that vision.

William L. White
Emeritus Senior Research Consultant
Chestnut Health Systems
Punta Gorda, Florida

September, 2014

---

[6]   Flaherty, M. (2006). A unified vision for the prevention and management of substance use disorders building resiliency, wellness and recovery (A shift from an acute care to a sustained care recovery management model). Pittsburgh, PA: Institute for Research, Education and Training in Addictions (IRETA).

RECOVERY MANAGEMENT

WILLIAM L. WHITE, MA
ERNEST KURTZ, PHD
MARK SANDERS, LCSW, CADC

Published by the Great Lakes Addiction Technology Transfer Center (ATTC) Network.

Great Lakes Addiction Technology Transfer Center
Jane Addams College of Social Work
University of Illinois at Chicago
1640 W. Roosevelt Rd., Ste. 511 (M/C 779)
Chicago, Illinois 60608-1316

2006

PRODUCED UNDER A COOPERATIVE AGREEMENT FROM THE U.S. DEPARTMENT OF HEALTH AND HUMAN SERVICES, SUBSTANCE ABUSE AND MENTAL HEALTH SERVICES ADMINISTRATION, CENTER FOR SUBSTANCE ABUSE TREATMENT.
Center for Substance Abuse Treatment, 1 Choke Cherry Road
Rockville, MD 20857, 301.443.5700

Its contents are solely the responsibility of the authors and do not necessarily represent the official views of the agency.
Grant No. 6 UD1 TI13593-02-3

CSAT
Center for Substance
Abuse Treatment
SAMHSA

Recovery Management

PREFACE

Dear Colleague,

The Great Lakes Addiction Technology Transfer Center (Great Lakes ATTC) is part of a national network that includes 14 regional centers and a national office, funded by the Substance Abuse and Mental Health Services Administration's Center for Substance Abuse Treatment. Great Lakes' primary goal is to help elevate the quality of addiction treatment by designing and delivering culturally competent, research-based training, education, and systems-change programs for addiction treatment and other allied health professionals. Great Lakes ATTC is very pleased to be able to offer its professional constituents a new monograph on the topic of Recovery Management.

Many of the central ideas contained in this monograph were birthed over the past eight years inside the Behavioral Health Recovery Management project — a joint venture by Fayette Companies in Peoria, Illinois and Chestnut Health Systems in Bloomington, Illinois. Many of the core strategies outlined in this monograph have been and are being tested within the Lighthouse Institute (Chestnut Health Systems' research division) and within other addiction research centers around the country.

This monograph contains a synthesis of findings from scientific studies and recommendations from new grassroots recovery advocacy and support organizations that are collectively pushing a fundamental redesign of addiction treatment in the United States. Based on growing evidence of the chronicity and complexity of severe substance use disorders, we are faced with an increasing need to shift the current acute care model of treatment toward a model of assertive and sustained recovery management.

This monograph introduces the recovery management model through a collection of four papers.

- *The first paper, entitled "Recovery: The New Frontier," describes the historical shift in the addictions field from a pathology paradigm (knowledge derived from studies of the problem), through an intervention paradigm (knowledge derived from the clinical treatment of the problem), to an emerging recovery paradigm (knowledge derived from individuals, families, and communities that have solved the problem). It concludes with a discussion of ways in which this latter paradigm will reshape the future of treatment and recovery in the United States.*
- *The second paper, "The Varieties of Recovery Experience," describes what we as a country know from the standpoint of science and cultural experience about the long-term resolution of alcohol and other drug problems, as well as the implications of this knowledge for the design of addiction treatment.*
- *The third paper, "Recovery Management: What if we really believed addiction was a chronic disorder?" defines the core principles, changes in clinical practices, implementation obstacles, and potential pitfalls of the recovery management model.*
- *The final paper, "Recovery Management and People of Color: Redesigning Addiction Treatment for Historically Disempowered Communities," describes the special advantages the recovery management model offers to communities of color in the United States.*

Special thanks are due to Fayette Companies and Chestnut Health Systems, whose early pioneering work laid the foundation for this monograph; to the authors — William White, Ernest Kurtz, and Mark Sanders — for their work on these papers; and to the many addiction professionals in the states of Illinois, Indiana, Michigan, Ohio, and Wisconsin whose input in workshops over the past several years helped refine many of the ideas in these pages. Special gratitude is also extended to Herminio Rodriguez, whose brilliant and creative design and production work brought this publication to life; and to Pamela Woll, author and Great Lakes partner, who lent her magical "eyes" to the copy editing of this document.

Great Lakes ATTC is offering this monograph, not as the last word on this subject, but as a catalyst for renewed discussion about the future of addiction treatment and recovery in America. We invite you to be an active voice in these discussions. Recovery management is an idea whose time has come. It will be up to addiction treatment professionals and recovery support specialists across the country to bring that idea to life within the individuals, families, and communities we are committed to serve. The journey toward that goal will require courage and sustained commitment. Great Lakes ATTC and its staff look forward to sharing that journey with you.

Lonnetta Albright
Director
Great Lakes ATTC

Recovery: The Next Frontier

William L. White, MA

This article was originally published in *Counselor: The Magazine for Addiction Professionals* (2004, 5/1: 18-21) and is reprinted here with permission.

The history of the addictions field has been one of evolving paradigms (organizing constructs), evolving core technologies, and evolving definitions of the field's niche in the larger culture whose needs it must serve. This article traces the evolution of the field's organizing paradigms through three overlapping stages: a problem-focused stage, an intervention-focused stage, and an emerging solution-focused stage. These paradigms can be viewed as competing models but are best viewed as developmental stages, with each preparing for the emergence of the next.

The Pathology Paradigm

The first stage was launched by what Levine (1978) has christened "the discovery of addiction." This birthing stage in the late eighteenth century was sparked by a break from prevailing moral and religious frameworks of understanding and responding to chronic drunkenness. Compulsive and destructive AOD use became defined as a disease of the body and the will, a redefinition that has sustained more than 200 years of research on the nature of psychoactive drugs, their acute and chronic effects, the multiple sources of individual vulnerability to AOD problems, and the stages of AOD problem development. An enormous body of literature exists and continues to be generated on the psychopharmacology and epidemiology of AOD problems. Elaborate systems of data collection exist to measure the slightest shifts in drug-related attitudes, beliefs, and behaviors. A research industry exists whose sole mission is studying drugs, their patterns of consumption, and their personal and social costs. As a culture and a professional field, we have a knowledge of psychoactive drugs and drug addiction that is impressive. This cultural investment in studying the nature of AOD problems reflects a pathology paradigm — the assumption that knowledge of the sources of a problem will lead to its eventual solution.

Knowledge gained within this paradigm provided significant benefits and laid the foundation for policy, educational, and clinical responses to AOD problems.

THE INTERVENTION PARADIGM

Attempts to resolve AOD problems personally and socially also have a long history in America. These attempts span AOD-related social policies, education, and prevention efforts; early intervention programs; and addiction treatment. A voluminous body of knowledge and resources (including this journal) exists that focuses on when and how to intervene in these problems. The readers of this journal have been part of this country's unprecedented investment in the professionally directed treatment of AOD problems. Some readers are old enough to have witnessed the transition of treatment from an unfunded folk art to a highly professionalized and commercialized industry. We have learned within this modern era of treatment how to interrupt addiction careers. We know a lot about engagement, detoxification, problem stabilization, and recovery initiation. We know a lot about what people look like in the years before they were admitted to treatment. We know a lot about what people look like during treatment. And we know a little bit about what people look like in the months following treatment.

The knowledge gained from this intervention paradigm has advanced the field and allowed hundreds of thousands of individuals to initiate and sustain recovery. The majority of drug-dependent persons who achieve sustained recovery do so after participating in treatment (the percentage varies by substance: cannabis (43%), cocaine (61%), alcohol (81%), and heroin (92%) (Cunningham et al., 1999, 2000). That knowledge has also illuminated the limitations of our current treatment system. For persons with severe AOD problems, it often takes three to four episodes of acute treatment over a span of eight years to achieve stable and enduring recovery (Dennis, Scott, Funk, & Foss, under review). These findings challenge models of brief treatment; short-term aftercare; and follow-up studies whose designs, until recently, extended only several months following discharge from treatment. These shortcomings have led to calls for more recovery-sustaining models of intervention and support and more recovery-focused research and evaluation activities. In short, there is growing interest in extending the pathology and intervention paradigms into a more fully developed recovery paradigm.

AGITATION FOR CHANGE

For readers who think they and their programs and the larger field are already recovery-focused, it may be helpful to view this issue through the eyes of the recovery advocates (of the 1950s-1960s) who were the midwives of modern addiction treatment. It is among these advocates that the need and call for this recovery paradigm is most poignantly articulated. The advocacy leaders in local alcoholism and "drug abuse" councils were inspired by a vision of an ever-expanding recovery community. They championed the birth of professionally directed treatment as a special doorway of entry into that community for the many people who could not make the transition from addiction to recovery on their own. Decades later, these advocates see an ever-growing treatment industry that views recovery as an afterthought or adjunct to itself. While this view may seem harsh to the reader, consider the world through the advocates' eyes. They see "addiction studies" curricula in colleges and universities but no "recovery studies" curricula. They see scientific journals whose names reflect an interest in alcohol and other drugs (e.g., Journal of Studies on Alcohol, Journal of Psychoactive Drugs, Addiction, Contemporary Drug Problems) and professional intervention into AOD problems (e.g., Journal of Substance Abuse Treatment, Alcoholism Treatment Quarterly), but they see no peer-reviewed journals focused on the scientific study of addiction recovery. They read innumerable studies that meticulously describe who uses which psychoactive drugs and with what consequences, but see only a few recovery prevalence studies. They confront the public perception that people do not recover despite rarely acknowledged epidemiological studies finding that 58% of people with lifetime substance dependence eventually achieve sustained recovery (Kessler, 1994; see also Dawson, 1996; Robins & Regier, 1991). They see national institutes of "alcohol abuse and alcoholism" and "drug abuse" and national centers of "substance abuse prevention" and "substance abuse treatment" but they see no "national institute/center of addiction recovery." They see "addiction technology transfer centers" but no "recovery technology transfer centers." In short, they see a field that knows a lot about addiction and a lot about treatment, but which they perceive to have lost its focus on the goal and processes of long-term recovery. These advocates are joining with visionary policy leaders, treatment professionals, and addictions researchers to shift the field's kinetic ideas and slogans from the nature of the problem ("addiction is a disease") and the alleged effectiveness of its interventions ("treatment works") to the living proof of a permanent solution to AOD problems ("recovery is a reality"). Collectively, these voices are saying that it is time to use the foundations laid from the study of the problem and its treatment to build a fully developed recovery paradigm.

THE RECOVERY PARADIGM

The movement forward to a recovery paradigm is already underway. The evidence of this shift in grassroots communities includes the:

- growth and diversification of American communities of recovery (White, in press);
- emergence of a multi-branched new recovery advocacy movement (White, 2001);
- rapidly spreading Wellbriety movement in Indian Country (see www. whitebison.org);
- growth of faith-based recovery support structures, particularly within communities of color (see Sanders, 2002);
- organization of recovering ex-felons into mutual support networks, (e.g., the Winners Circle in Chicago);
- growth of self-managed recovery homes (see http://www.oxfordhouse.org) and recovery schools (e.g., the Association of Recovery Schools); and
- spread of recovery employment co-ops (e.g., Recovery at Work in Atlanta).

The shift to a recovery paradigm is evident at the federal level in President Bush's Access to Recovery Initiative, increased NIDA and NIAAA support for studies of long-term recovery, and CSAT's Recovery Community Support Program and Recovery Month initiatives. It is evident in state initiatives pushing treatment toward a "recovery-oriented system of care" (see http://www.dmhas.state.ct.us/policies/policy83. htm). It is evident in the research community's call to shift addiction treatment from serial episodes of acute intervention to models of sustained "recovery management" (McLellan, Lewis, O'Brien, & Kleber, 2000; White, Boyle, & Loveland, 2002, 2003). And it is evident in local experiments with peer-based models of recovery support, new recovery-focused service roles (recovery coaches, recovery support specialists), and the shift from traditional "aftercare" services to models of "assertive continuing care" (White & Godley, 2003; Dennis, Scott, & Funk, 2003).

RECOVERY MANAGEMENT

How will the transition toward a recovery-focused future differ from our past? The shift from acute intervention to recovery management for those persons with severe and persistent AOD problems will involve three changes in the continuum of care. First, it will intensify pre-treatment recovery support services to strengthen the engagement process, enhance motivation for change, remove environmental obstacles to recovery, and determine whether the individual/family can initiate and sustain recovery at this stage without additional professional intervention. (The latter may be quite possible for those with lower problem severity and indigenous supports for recovery.) Second, recovery management will intensify in-treatment recovery support services to enhance treatment retention and effects (by keeping treatment recovery focused). Traditional treatment methods will change in a number of important dimensions (e.g., from single-agency to multi-agency intervention, from categorical to global assessment, from institution-based to neighborhood- and home-based service delivery). Most important, it will differ in the nature and duration of the service relationship. Third, recovery management will shift the focus of treatment from acute stabilization to support for long-term recovery maintenance.

Professionally directed recovery management, like management of other chronic health disorders, shifts the focus of care from one of "admit, treat, and discharge" to a sustained health management partnership. This means that the traditional discharge process will be replaced with post-stabilization monitoring (recovery check-ups); stage-appropriate recovery education; recovery coaching; active linkage to communities of recovery; recovery community resource development; and, when needed, early re-intervention. Rather than cycling individuals through multiple self-contained episodes of acute treatment, recovery management provides an expanded array of recovery support services for a much greater length of time but at a much lower level of intensity and cost per service episode.

A New Language

New paradigms bring new ways of perceiving, thinking, and speaking. As we move deeper into this recovery paradigm, we will need to forge new concepts and a new language. We will need better words and concepts to:

- delineate the conceptual boundaries of recovery;
- describe types of recovery, e.g., partial versus full, serial recovery, solo versus assisted, medication-assisted recovery;
- evaluate recovery assets, e.g., Granfield and Cloud's (1999) concept of "recovery capital";
- chart the pathways of recovery, e.g., secular, spiritual, religious;

- distinguish styles of recovery initiation, e.g., incremental versus transformational change;
- depict variations in identity reconstruction, e.g., recovery-positive versus recovery-neutral identities; and
- describe variations in recovery relationships (with other recovering people, e.g., acultural, bicultural, and culturally enmeshed styles) (see White, 2002 for a detailed discussion of this new language).

We will all need to stretch our understanding of recovery and become multilingual as we expand the words and metaphors that reflect the growing varieties of recovery experiences in America.

A NEW VISION

Since its inception, the purpose of this column has been to enhance the addiction professional's understanding of the history of treatment and recovery in America. This article is about the living history that is unfolding before us in this moment. It is about the opportunity for recovery advocates, policy leaders, treatment professionals, and researchers to form a partnership that will write the future history of addiction treatment and recovery in America. Destiny will call some of you reading this to help lead this leap into the future. I wish you and your clients Godspeed on your journey from the problem we know so well to the recovery vision that lies ahead of us.

REFERENCES AND RECOMMENDED READING

Cunningham, J. A. (1999). Resolving alcohol-related problems with and without treatment: The effects of different problem criteria. *Journal of Studies on Alcohol*, 60, 463-466.

Cunningham, J. A. (2000). Remissions from drug dependence: Is treatment a prerequisite? *Drug and Alcohol Dependence*, 59, 211-213.

Dennis, M., Scott, C.K. & Funk, R. (2003). An experimental evaluation of recovery management checkups (RMC) for people with chronic substance use disorders. *Evaluation and Program Planning* 26(3), 339-352.

Dennis, M.L., Scott, C.K, Funk, R., & Foss, M.A. (under review). The Duration and correlates of addiction and treatment careers. *Journal of Substance Abuse Treatment*.

Dawson, D.A. (1996). Correlates of past-year status among treated and untreated persons with former alcohol dependence: United States, 1992. *Alcoholism: Clinical and Experimental Research*, 20, 771-779.

Granfield, R., & Cloud, W. (1999). *Coming clean: Overcoming addiction without treatment.* New York: New York University Press.

Kessler, R. (1994) The National Comorbidity Survey of the United States. *International Review of Psychiatry* 6:365-376.

Levine, H. (1978). The discovery of addiction: Changing conceptions of habitual drunkenness in America. *Journal of Studies on Alcohol*, 39(2), 143-174.

McLellan, A. T., Lewis, D. C., O'Brien, C. P, & Kleber, H. D. (2000). Drug dependence, a chronic medical illness: Implications for treatment, insurance, and outcomes evaluation. *Journal of the American Medical Association*, 284(13), 1689-1695.

Robins, L.N., & Regier, D.A. (1991). *Psychiatric Disorders in America: The Epidemiologic Catchment Area Study.* Free Press: New York.

Sanders, M. (2002). The response of African American communities to alcohol and other drug problems. *Alcoholism Treatment Quarterly*, 20(3/4), 167-174.

White, W. (2001). The new recovery advocacy movement: A call to service. *Counselor*, 2(6), 64-67.

White, W. (2002). An addiction recovery glossary: The languages of American communities of recovery. Retrieved from www.facesandvoicesofrecovery.org

White, W. (in press). Alcoholic mutual aid societies. In J. Blocker & I. Tyrell (Eds), *Alcohol and Temperance in Modern History.* Santa Barbara, CA: ABC-CLIO.

White, W., Boyle, M., & Loveland, D. (2002). Addiction as chronic disease: From rhetoric to clinical application. *Alcoholism Treatment Quarterly*, 3/4, 107-130.

White, W., Boyle, M., & Loveland, D. (2003). Recovery management: Transcending the limitations of addiction treatment. *Behavioral Health Management*, 23(3), 38-44 (http://www.behavioral.net/2003_05-06/featurearticle.htm).

White, W., & Godley, M. (2003). The history and future of "aftercare." *Counselor*, 4(1), 19-21.

Acknowledgement: Support for this article was provided by grants from the National Institute on Drug Abuse (Grant R01 DA15523) and the Illinois Department of Human Services (Office of Alcoholism and Substance Abuse Services) via the Behavioral Health Recovery Management Project.

The Varieties of Recovery Experience: A Primer for Addiction Treatment Professionals and Recovery Advocates

William White, MA and Ernest Kurtz, PhD Chicago, IL

Abstract

The study of alcohol and other drugs (AOD) is historically marked by three stages: 1) the investigation of AOD-related social and personal pathologies, 2) the development of personal and social interventions aimed at resolving AOD problems, and 3) a focus on the prevalence and patterns of long-term recovery from AOD problems. This essay honors this transition from addiction and treatment paradigms to a recovery paradigm by exploring the growing varieties of pathways and styles through which people are resolving serious and persistent AOD-related problems. A review of scientific and mutual aid literature is used to catalogue variations in:

- scope of recovery (primary and secondary chemical health and global health),
- depth of recovery (partial, full, and enriched),
- types of recovery (abstinence-based, moderation based, medication assisted),
- context of recovery initiation (solo, peer assisted, treatment assisted),
- frameworks of recovery initiation (religious, spiritual, secular),
- temporal styles of recovery initiation (transformative change, incremental change, drift),
- recovery identity (positive, neutral, negative),
- recovery relationships (acultural, bicultural, and enmeshed styles; virtual recovery),

- *recovery stability/durability (At what point does present remission predict future remission?), and*
- *recovery termination (Is recovery ever completed?).*

After exploring the wide diversity of recovery styles and experiences that exist within Twelve-Step fellowships and other recovery mutual aid societies, the article explores the implications of the wide diversity in recovery experiences to the design and conduct of addiction treatment.

Keywords: addiction recovery, natural recovery, transformative change, stages of change, virtual recovery, religion, spirituality, secularity.

ADDICTION, TREATMENT, AND RECOVERY PARADIGMS

Alcohol- and other drug-related (AOD) problems constitute a significant public health problem within American and world history (Lender & Martin, 1982; Musto, 1999; Courtwright, 2001). Responses to these problems over the past two centuries reflect three organizing paradigms. From the late eighteenth century through the era of alcohol prohibition, pathology provided an organizing framework, whether religiously or medically conceived. The pathology paradigm fueled the debate over whether alcoholism was a sin or a sickness; guided studies of the incidence, prevalence and personal/social costs of AOD problems; and sparked the sustained search for the etiological roots of these problems. The hope upon which the pathology model was built was that knowledge of the scope and sources of AOD problems would generate specific solutions to these problems in the same way isolating and attacking particular pathogens had earlier led to the elimination or control of many infectious diseases. While failing to achieve this ultimate goal to-date, the pathology model has made significant contributions to our understanding of the multi-dimensional processes that interact to initiate and sustain addiction.

The failure to find the singular pathogen underlying AOD problems led to the testing of numerous strategies and techniques of intervention, both social and personal. To this day, the intervention model buttresses multi-billion-dollar industries aimed at preventing drug use, controlling drug supplies, punishing drug offenders, and treating those with severe AOD problems. The intervention model assumes that the scientific evaluation of AOD-related social policies and biopsychosocial interventions will reveal the most effective prevention, intervention, and control strategies, and that those strategies that can be best matched to particular communities, demographic/

clinical subpopulations, and individuals. This model has generated significant new understandings that are sparking widespread calls to bridge the gap between clinical research and clinical practice in addiction treatment.

The historical intractability of AOD problems at a societal level has led to disillusionment with the pathology and intervention paradigms and a recent shift in focus toward resilience and recovery (Morgan, 1995a; Elise, 1999; White, 2000, 2004a). As early as 1984, Edwards was calling for the field to explore the "natural processes of recovery." This was followed by calls for "recovery-oriented psychotherapy" (Zweben, 1986) and "recovery-sensitive counseling" (Morgan, 1995b). The recovery paradigm focuses on at-risk individuals, families, and communities who have avoided the development of severe AOD problems and the lives of individuals, families, and communities with severe AOD problems who have successfully resolved or are resolving these problems. Advocates of this model suggest that studying the lived solutions to AOD problems will reveal principles and strategies upon which broader, more effective social policies and professional interventions can be built (Morgan, 1995a; White, 2005).

Knowledge about AOD problems is substantial, but comparatively little is known from the standpoint of science about the long-term solutions to these problems. In recent epidemiological studies of individuals who once met criteria for alcohol dependence, 63% to 75% no longer met dependence criteria at the time they were surveyed, suggesting a substantial long-term recovery rate (Helzer, Burnam, & McEvoy, 1991; Dawson, Grant, Stinson, Chou, Huang, & Ruan, 2005). The Workgroup on Substance Abuse Self-help Organizations (2003) estimates the total U.S. membership of recovery mutual aid groups at more than 1.6 million people and reports that more than six million adults each year have some contact with these groups. In spite of a substantial body of recovery experience in the U.S., the addictions field does not draw its primary knowledge base from this source. Today, addiction professionals routinely assert the existence of multiple pathways of recovery, but from the standpoint of science, we know little about such pathways. As addiction treatment interventions become ever briefer, treatment professionals have less and less contact and knowledge of the long-term recovery process.

AOD problems arise out of quite different personal, family, and cultural contexts and unfold in variable patterns and trajectories. These same forces generate heterogeneous recovery experiences. The goals of this paper are to: 1) conceptually map the diverse patterns and styles of AOD problem resolution, 2) introduce a lexicon through which such variations can be described, and 3) explore the implications of the diversity of recovery experience for the design and conduct of professional interventions into such problems. This conceptual map is based primarily on scientific studies on the course of AOD problems in community and in clinical samples. The literature of multiple recovery mutual aid societies and biographical and autobiographical depictions of recovery are also used to illustrate key findings. We hope this preliminary recovery map will spark new scientific studies of the prevalence, patterns, stages, and personal styles of long-term recovery from AOD problems.

RECOVERY DEFINITION

Recovery is the process through which severe alcohol and other drug problems (here defined as those problems meeting DSM-IV criteria for *substance abuse* or *substance dependence*) are resolved in tandem with the development of physical, emotional, ontological (spirituality, life meaning), relational, and occupational health.

AOD problems vary in their course, including adverse reactions to a single episode of AOD-intoxication, problems that span only a few months or years, and problems that span significant periods of one's life. Such problems also vary in their intensity and overall severity, including:

- subclinical problems (transient AOD problems that do not meet DSM-IV criteria for abuse or dependence);

- AOD problems meeting DSM-IV criteria for substance abuse — Clinically significant impairment marked by one or more of the following in a 12-month time period: repeated substance use that results in failure to perform major role obligations, repeated use in situations that are physically hazardous, repeated substance-related legal problems, and continued substance use in spite of adverse AOD-related problems; and

- AOD problems meeting DSM-IV criteria for substance dependence — Clinically significant impairment marked by at least three of the following in a 12-month period: tolerance, withdrawal, loss of control (erosion of volitional control over quantity and duration of use), failed efforts to cease or reduce use; significant time involved in drug procurement, drug use, and recovery from drug effects; social, occupational, or recreational activities forsaken or reduced due to drug use; and continued use in spite of adverse physical or psychological problems caused by substance use (American Psychiatric Association, 1994).

The term *recovery*, because of its medical connotations, is most applicable to the process through which severe and persistent AOD problems (meeting DSM-IV criteria for substance abuse or dependence) are resolved. Terms such as *quitting*, *cessation,* and *resolution* more aptly describe the problem-solving processes of individuals who have transient and less severe AOD problems. Recovery implies reversal of a greater level of debility and a more involved and enduring problem-solving process (White & Scott, draft manuscript). Our continued discussion of varieties of recovery experience will focus on these more severe forms of AOD problems.

The term *family recovery* conveys the processes through which family members impacted by severe and persistent AOD problems individually and collectively regain their health. Family recovery involves enhanced health across three dimensions: 1) individual family members, 2) family subsystems (adult intimacy relationships, parent-child relationships, and sibling relationships), and 3) the family as a system (redefinition of family roles, rules, and rituals; recovery-conducive boundary transactions with people and institutions outside the family) (White, 1996). The recovery of an addicted family member can destabilize and threaten the survival of the family unit if professional and social supports are not available to soften what Stephanie Brown and Virginia Lewis (1999) have christened the "trauma of recovery" (See also Rouhbakhsh, Lewis, & Allen-Byrd, 2004).

RECOVERY PREVALENCE

Elaborate systems exist to measure the subtlest of changes in the prevalence of AOD use and its consequences, but no similar system exists to measure the incidence and prevalence of recovery from AOD problems. However, individual researchers have conducted long-term treatment follow-up studies and community surveys over the past 25 years that reveal significant recovery rates: 41% (Ojesjo, 1981); 63% (Helzer, Burnam & McEvoy, 1991); 72% (Dawson, 1996); 30% (Schutte, Nichols, Brennan, & Moos, 2001); 59% (Vaillant, 2003); and 48% (Dawson, Grant, Stinson, Chou, Huang, & Ruan, 2005). Factors such as differing demographic and clinical characteristics of study participants and different definitions of recovery influence variations in reported recovery rates.

THE SCOPE AND DEPTH OF RECOVERY

Recoveries from addiction can differ in their scope (the range of measurable changes) and depth (degree of change within each measured dimension). Aborting a destructive relationship with a particular drug or combination of drugs is at the core of addiction recovery, but recovery experiences can range from complete cessation of AOD use in an otherwise unchanged life to a complete transformation of one's personal identity and interpersonal relationships.

There are quite varied trajectories in the relationship between primary and secondary drug use among people seeking recovery from substance use disorders. One pattern of drug dependence can be aborted while a co-occurring pattern continues. For example, there are high rates of nicotine dependence among adults and adolescents before and after treatment for dependence upon alcohol, opiates, cocaine, and cannabis (Maddux & Desmond, 1986; Myers & Brown, 1990; Hughes, 1995, 1996; Bien & Barge, 1990; Hoffman & Slade, 1993).

A second pattern involves the escalation of secondary drug use following cessation of primary drug use, e.g., an increase in alcohol or cocaine use following the cessation of heroin use. Such drug substitution is a common problem in treated adults and adolescents, particularly among those with a history of polydrug use (Vaillant, 1979; Edwards, Duckitt, Oppenheimer, Sheehan, & Taylor, 1983; Toneatto, Sobell, Sobell, & Rubel, 1999; Maddux & Desmond, 1980, 1981, 1992; Anglin, Almong, Fisher & Peters, 1989; Simpson & Sells, 1990; Carmelli & Swan, 1993).

A third pattern involves individuals who use secondary drugs therapeutically during early recovery to manage acute and post-acute withdrawal and to help ameliorate the psychological stresses of early recovery (e.g., heroin users consuming cannabis following opiate abstinence to prevent relapse) (Willie, 1978; Waldorf, 1983; Biernacki, 1986; Copeland, 1988). In this pattern, secondary drug use ceases or decelerates within the first two years of recovery (Waldorf, 1983; Vaillant, 1979; Copeland, 1988; Bachus, Strang, & Watson, 2000).

The ability to understand when drug substitution is an effective, time-limited strategy for managing early recovery (requiring professional understanding, if not tolerance) and when drug substitution is a mutation of the existing problem (requiring prevention, early intervention, or focused treatment) is an important research agenda. Some investigators have found that secondary drug use is more likely to be problematic for persons with family histories of AOD problems, those who begin AOD use at an early age, and those who experience problems with a secondary drug before developing their primary addiction (Simpson & Sells, 1990; Maddux & Desmond, 1992). Also needed is a greater understanding of how sequential drug problems are resolved over time. The factors that contribute to the cessation of co-occurring dependencies or secondary drug use may differ from those factors associated with the cessation of primary drug use (Downey, Rosengren, & Donovan, 2000).

The scope of recovery can extend far beyond altered patterns of primary and secondary drug use. Historically, the definition of recovery has shifted from a focus on what is deleted from one's life (alcohol and other drugs, arrests for criminal acts, hospitalizations) to what is added to one's life (the achievement of health and happiness). This shift is reflected in such terms as *mental sobriety* (Mental Sobriety, 1946) and *emotional sobriety* — a phrase A.A. co-founder Bill Wilson coined to describe a state of emotional health that far exceeds the achievement of not drinking. Wilson defined emotional sobriety as "real maturity . . . in our relations with ourselves, with our fellows and with God" (Wilson, 1958). This broadened vision of recovery is also reflected in the term *Wellbriety* that is currently being used within the Native American recovery advocacy movement to depict recovery as the pursuit and achievement of physical, emotional, intellectual, relational, and spiritual health, or "whole health" (Coyhis, 1999; *Red Road to Wellbriety*, 2002). Wellbriety within the Native American context is also related to a new set of core *recovery values*: honesty, hope, faith, courage, integrity, willingness, humility, forgiveness, justice, perseverance, spiritual awareness, and service (Coyhis, 2000).

Because severe and persistent AOD problems impact many areas of life functioning, recovery from such problems must be measured across multiple *zones* (or *domains*) *of recovery*: 1) the relationship(s) with the substance(s) for which one previously met DSM-IV criteria for abuse or dependence; 2) the presence, frequency, quantity, intensity, and personal and social consequences of secondary drug use; 3) physical health; 4) psychological/emotional/ontological health; 5) family/relational health; and 6) lifestyle health, e.g., a developmentally appropriate, pro-social style of work and leisure (White, 1996). Seen as a whole, the goal of recovery is what we refer to as *global health*.

Like that of other severe and potentially chronic health problems, the resolution of substance use disorders can be categorized in terms of levels of recovery, e.g., a state of *full recovery* (complete and enduring cessation of all AOD-related problems and the movement toward global health) or a state of *partial recovery* (Jorquez, 1983). The term *partial recovery* can convey two different conditions: 1) a reduced frequency, duration, and intensity of AOD use and reduction of related personal and social problems; or 2) the achievement of complete abstinence or stable moderation, but the failure to achieve parallel gains in physical, emotional, ontological, relational, or occupational health. Partial recovery can constitute a permanent state, a stage preceding full recovery, or a hiatus in AOD problems with eventual reversion to a previous or greater level of problem severity.

Falling between the parameters of no recovery and full recovery are individuals who cycle in and out of periods of moderate use, problematic use, and abstinence (Hser, Hoffman, Grella, & Anglin, 2001). A recent review of alcoholism treatment outcome studies drew three major conclusions: 1) treatment-related remissions (persons no longer meeting DSM-IV criteria for a substance use disorder following treatment) average about one-third of those treated, 2) substance use (measured by days of use and volume of use) decreases by an average of 87% following treatment, and 3) substance-related problems decrease by an average of 60% following treatment (Miller, Walters, & Bennett, 2001). People who are constitutionally incapable of permanent sobriety at particular points in their lives may achieve *partial recovery* — significant decreases in AOD-related problems, improved levels of health and social functioning, and significant reductions in the costs and threats they pose to the larger community (Zweben 1996).

Partial recovery is reflected in individuals who cycle through multiple episodes of treatment, recovery initiation, and relapse (Scott, Foss & Dennis, 2005; Dennis, Scott, Funk & Foss, 2005). Such cycling is evidence that recovery is not fully stabilized, but the continued help seeking within such cycles also suggests that addiction is no longer stable. Cycling in and out of recovery (with reduced frequency, intensity, and duration of use episodes) can be a precursor to stable recovery or a chronic state. Partial recovery can also refer to residual levels of impairment that continue after the cessation or deceleration of AOD use. While most recovering alcoholics establish levels of personal and family functioning comparable to non-alcoholics (Moos, Finney, & Cronkite, 1990; Chapman, 1987), early recovery can be marked by poor levels of adjustment, e.g., depression, anxiety, poor self-esteem, guilt, and impaired social functioning (Kurtines, Ball, & Wood, 1978; Polich, Armor, & Braiker, 1980; Gerard & Saenger, 1962; Behar, Winokur, & Berg, 1984). De Soto and colleagues (1985) distinguished recovery status by length of recovery in a study of 312 members of Alcoholics Anonymous. They concluded that: 1) the early months and years of recovery from alcoholism are marked by continued impairment of emotional and social functioning, 2) these symptoms continue to improve and remit over the first ten years of recovery, and 3) some residual symptoms of cognitive dysfunction may continue in long-term recovery. The achievement of only a partial reversal of alcohol-related cognitive impairments is most common in alcoholics who began their recoveries after long drinking careers (Goldman, 1983; Schutte, 1994, 2001). The principle that global health and functioning improve with earlier onset of recovery and length of sobriety is further confirmed in follow-up studies of persons recovering from cocaine addiction (Selby, Quiroga, Ireland, Malow, & Azrin, 1995).

Some individuals experience changes so profound across these zones of recovery that they come to view addiction and recovery as "gifts" that have brought a depth of experience and meaning far superior to their pre-addiction lives. Such individuals achieve an enriched *state of recovery*. This enriched state of recovery is evident across recovery traditions:

The walls crumpled — and the light streamed in. I wasn't trapped. I wasn't helpless. I was free, and I didn't have to drink to "show them." This wasn't "religion" — this was freedom! Freedom from anger and fear, freedom to know happiness and love. (From *Alcoholics Anonymous*, 1976, p. 228.)

It is impossible to put on paper all the benefits I have derived . . . physical, mental, domestic, spiritual, and monetary. This is no idle talk. It is the truth. (From *Alcoholics Anonymous*, 1976, p. 481.)

My life is well-rounded and I am becoming a more comfortable version of myself, not the neurotic, boring person that I thought I would be without drugs…I have a way to live cleanly, honestly and comfortably. I have all I need. (From *Narcotics Anonymous*, 1988, p. 262.)

It's been a very long, long struggle but worth every single minute of it. I'm really happy to be alive, and life is truly great and wonderful for me right now. (Women for Sobriety member, From Kirkpatrick, 1986, p. 258.)

Back in 1970 I found myself dying from the abuse of my body.…The Creator had something he had for me to learn. First, I had to learn who he was. Then I had to learn who I was. I began to visit with my Elders…I had to come to grips with who I am as an Indian, as being a castaway, as being an unloved person. The Creator has love for each of us but we have to find that foundation. (From *Red Road to Wellbriety*, 2002, p. 187.)

A final scope-and-depth dimension of recovery involves individuals who are engaged in concurrent or sequential recovery processes from two or more conditions or experiences, e.g., developmental trauma, psychiatric illness, AIDS. The overlapping processes involved in recovering from addiction and other physical or behavioral/ emotional disorders might be described as *serial recovery.*

Problem Severity And Recovery Capital

Recovery can occur at different stages of problem progression. There are patterns of *high-bottom recovery* among people who have not yet suffered severe losses related to their AOD use. There are also patterns of *low-bottom recovery* achieved by individuals in the latest stages of addiction who have experienced severe personal and social disintegration and anguish before achieving stable recovery (High Bottom, 1949).

In addition to the degree of problem severity, one's recovery capital influences one's prognosis for recovery. *Recovery capital* is the quantity and quality of internal and external resources that one can bring to bear on the initiation and maintenance of recovery (Granfield & Cloud, 1999). The interaction of problem severity and recovery capital shapes both the prospects of recovery and the intensity and duration of resources required to initiate and sustain recovery.

Pathways And Styles Of Recovery

The phrase *pathways of recovery* refers to different routes of recovery initiation. This phrase recognizes the varieties of ways people successfully resolve AOD problems. One of the earliest origins of this notion of paths and choices of recovery frameworks was A.A. co-founder Bill Wilson's 1944 observation that "The roads to recovery are many" (Wilson, 1944). *Cultural pathways of recovery* are culturally or subculturally prescribed avenues through which individuals can resolve alcohol and other drug problems. Such culturally prescribed avenues might be a product of:

- developmental consciousness (e.g., something to be resolved through maturation and assumption of adult role responsibilities),
- medical consciousness (e.g., response to an alcohol-related health problem),
- religious consciousness (e.g., conversion to and/or affiliation with an abstinence-based faith community), or
- political consciousness (e.g., rejection of alcohol as a "tool of genocide").

The phrase *styles of recovery* depicts variations in beliefs and recovery support rituals that exist within particular pathways of recovery. For example, Twelve-Step programs constitute one of the major pathways of recovery from addiction, but the close observation of several Twelve-Step groups would reveal wide variation in styles of "working the program," e.g., patterns of meeting attendance, approaches to "Step work," conceptualizations of "Higher Power," and utilization of sponsors.

ABSTINENCE-BASED, MODERATION-BASED, & MEDICATION-SUPPORTED RECOVERIES

One of the variations in recovery from substance use disorders involves differences in the ways in which one's relationship with psychoactive drugs is changed. The scientific literature on the resolution of AOD problems documents three such variations. *Abstinence-based recovery* has historically been the culturally prescribed approach to the resolution of severe AOD problems. This approach, which has guided mainstream addiction treatment in the United States in the modern era, calls for complete and sustained cessation of one's primary drug(s) and the non-medical use of other psychoactive drugs (with nicotine and caffeine historically excepted). Over the past several decades, scientific evidence has grown on moderated approaches to AOD problem resolution. *Moderation-based recovery* (the sustained deceleration of AOD use to a subclinical level — continued AOD use that no longer meets DSM-IV criteria for substance abuse or dependence) has triggered great debates in America, spanning the 1976 Rand Report[1], the extended controversies over Mark and Linda Sobell's research at Patton State Hospital[2], and later controversies surrounding Moderation Management, a moderation-based mutual support group (Kishline, 1994). There has also been growing interest in *medication-assisted recovery* (the use of medically monitored pharmacological adjuncts to support recovery from addiction, e.g., detoxification agents, stabilizing agents, aversive agents, antagonizing agents, anti-craving agents, or psychoactive drugs prescribed for the treatment of co-occurring physical or psychiatric disorders).

Discussion of these approaches is best grounded in the finding that substance-use problems exist across a continuum of problem severity and that problem severity influences pathways of problem resolution. Abstinence-based and medication-assisted styles of recovery predominate in patterns of severe alcohol and drug dependence, whereas moderation-based styles of recovery predominate in individuals with lower problem severity and greater recovery capital (younger, married, employed, higher socioeconomic status, higher social support and social stability, positive marital and work relationships) (Finney & Moos, 1981; Polich, et al., 1980; Vaillant, 1983; Armor & Meshkoff, 1983; Edwards et al., 1983; Rosenberg, 1993; Dawson, 1996; Cunningham, Lin, Ross, & Walsh, 2000; Vaillant, 1996).

The moderated resolution of substance use disorders is well documented in general population surveys. Dawson (1996), in a community survey of treated and untreated adults who previously met DSM-IV criteria for alcohol dependence, found that in the year prior to the survey 49.9% were drinking but no longer met criteria for abuse or dependence (27.8% met criteria for alcohol abuse or dependence, and 22.3% were abstinent). Two other studies (one a Canadian national study and the other an Ontario study) used a broader definition of "alcohol problems" and found that 38% and 62.7% (respectively) of those with alcohol problems had later resolved those problems via moderate drinking recoveries (Sobell, Cunningham, & Sobell, 1996). Moderated recovery at much lower rates of prevalence has also been noted in follow-up studies of those treated for alcohol dependence (Finney & Moos, 1981; Rosenberg, 1993; Vaillant 1996) and drug dependence (Levy, 1972; Willie, 1978; Harding, Zinberg, Stelmack, & Michael, 1980). Treatment outcome studies of adolescents have also found a subgroup of treated teens who "may evidence intermittent substance use, typically alcohol, but do not exhibit any ongoing alcohol-or-drug-related problems" (Brown, 1993).

Given the propensity for substance-related problems to wax and wane over time, one could rightly question whether subclinical use following addiction is sustainable. In the longest follow-up study of alcoholic men to-date (60 years), Vaillant (2003) found that 4% of inner-city men and 11% of college men sustained controlled drinking over the course of the follow-up. Most migrated from dependence to efforts at control to eventual abstinence. In the largest and most recent alcohol dependence and recovery prevalence survey (recovery defined as meeting DSM-IV alcohol dependence criteria prior to the last year but not meeting these criteria during the past year), 25% of those with prior alcohol dependence continued to meet dependence criteria, 27% were in partial remission (sub-clinical symptoms of dependence or presence of alcohol abuse), 12% were asymptomatic risk drinkers (drinking in a pattern predictive of risk for future relapse), 18% were low-risk drinkers, and 18% were abstainers (Dawson et al., 2005). As problem severity declines, the prevalence of moderated outcomes increases. This is most frequently noted in studies of people who develop alcohol and other drug-related problems during their transition from adolescence to adulthood but later moderate their substance use (Fillmore, Hartka, Johnstone, Speiglman, & Temple, 1988).

Early members of Alcoholics Anonymous made a clear distinction between themselves and other heavy drinkers and problem drinkers, suggesting that moderation was an option for some problem drinkers, but not for "alcoholics" like themselves.

The following two excerpts reflect their beliefs and attitudes about moderation-based recovery.

> *Then we have a certain type of hard drinker. He may have the habit badly enough to gradually impair him physically and mentally. It may cause him to die a few years before his time. If a sufficiently strong reason — ill health, falling in love, change of environment, or the warning of a doctor — becomes operative, this man can also stop or moderate, although he may find it difficult and troublesome and may even need medical attention* (Alcoholics Anonymous, 1939, p. 31).

> *If anyone, who is showing inability to control his drinking, can do the right-about-face and drink like a gentleman, our hats are off to him. Heaven knows we have tried hard enough and long enough to drink like other people!* (Alcoholics Anonymous,1939, p. 42).

Medication-assisted recovery continues to generate considerable controversy within the American culture, within communities of recovery, and within the professional addiction treatment community, in spite of evidence that attitudes toward medications as an adjunct to recovery may be softening (Rychtarik, Connors, Demen, & Stasiewicz, 2000). Influencing these shifts in attitudes are new pharmacological adjuncts in the treatment of alcohol dependence (e.g., naltrexone, acamprosate) and opiate dependence (e.g., clonidine, buprenorphine) (Vopicelli & Szalavitz, 2000).

One of the most widespread approaches to medication-assisted recovery is methadone maintenance treatment (MMT). There are an estimated 900,000 narcotic addicts in the United States and approximately 179,000 individuals enrolled in MMT (Kreek & Vocci, 2002). The major health policy authorities in the United States have weighed in on MMT and have universally concluded that optimal dosages of methadone combined with psychosocial supports and administered by competent practitioners: 1) decrease death rates of opiate addicts by as much as 50%; 2) reduce transmission of HIV, hepatitis B, hepatitis C and other infections; 3) eliminate or reduce illicit opiate use; 4) reduce criminal activity; 5) enhance productive behavior via employment and academic/vocational functioning; 6) improve global health and social functioning; and 7) are cost-effective (National Consensus Development Panel on Effective Medical Treatment of Opiate Addiction, 1998; White & Coon, 2003). In spite of such evidence, misunderstanding and social stigma attached to MMT (the perception that MMT simply substitutes one addictive drug for another) leave many in methadone-assisted recovery hiding their recovery status and stories from their employers and co-workers, their friends, and even their own family members (Murphy & Irwin, 1992).

THE CONTEXT OF RECOVERY INITIATION

The context in which people achieve remission from substance use disorders varies considerably and includes styles of solo recovery, treatment-assisted recovery, and peer-assisted recovery.

Solo (natural) recovery involves the use of one's own intrapersonal and interpersonal resources (family, kinship, and social networks) to resolve AOD problems without benefit of professional treatment or involvement in a recovery mutual aid community. This phenomenon is extensively documented in the professional literature under such descriptors as *maturing out* (Winick, 1962, 1964), *autoremission* (Vaillant, 1983; Klingeman, 1992), *self-initiated change* (Biernacki, 1986), *unassisted change* (McMurran, 1994), *spontaneous remission* (Tuchfield, 1981; Anthony & Helzer, 1991), *de-addiction* (Frykholm, 1985; Klingeman, 1991), *self-change* (Sobell, Sobell, & Toneatto, 1991), *self-managed change* (Copeland, 1988), and *natural recovery* (Havassey, Hall, & Wasserman, 1991). Natural recovery is, according to some studies, the most common recovery pathway (Fillmore, et al., 1988; Sobell, Sobell, Toneatto, & Leo, 1993; Cunningham, Sobell, Sobell, & Kapur, 1995; Cunningham, 1999; Sobell, et al., 1996), but the prevalence of this style declines as problem duration and severity increase. Natural recovery is a more viable pathway for people with shorter and less severe AOD problems and for those with higher incomes and more stable social and occupational supports (Sobell, et al., 1993; Sobell, et al., 1996; Larimer & Kilmer, 2000).
Natural recovery exists across the spectrum of drug choices (Biernacki, 1986; Waldorf, Reinarman, & Murphy, 1991; Klingeman, 1992; Shaffer & Jones, 1989; Cohen & Sas, 1994; Toneatto et al., 1999; Kandel & Raveis, 1989) and seems to be influenced by two age-related patterns: 1) a young adult pattern associated with maturation and the assumption of adult role responsibilities, and 2) a later-life pattern associated with cumulative consequences of alcohol and other drug use (Fillmore, et al., 1988; Sobell, Ellingstad, & Sobell, 2000).

Those who achieve natural recovery report multiple reasons for avoiding formal treatment institutions and mutual aid societies. These reasons include a desire to protect their privacy (aversion to sharing problems with others), a desire to avoid the stigma of being labeled, a belief that they can solve their problems without professional treatment, and a perception that treatment and mutual aid groups are ineffective or not personally suited for them (Tuchfield, 1981; Jordan & Oei, 1989; Cloud & Granfield, 1994; Burnam, 1997; Sobell, Ellinstad, & Sobell, 2000).

Treatment-assisted recovery involves the use of professional help in the initiation and stabilization of recovery. More than 1.5 million people are admitted to addiction treatment in the United States each year, but multiple factors complicate the relationship between treatment and recovery:

- Less than 10% of people with a substance use disorder in the U.S. seek professional treatment in a given year (SAMHSA, 2003), and only 25% of individuals with such disorders will receive treatment in their lifetime (Dawson et al., 2005).
- Addiction treatment in the United States is not a homogenous entity, but a network of service organizations with diverse philosophies and techniques that vary significantly in their effectiveness (Wilbourne & Miller, 2003).
- Those who seek professional treatment are characterized by high personal vulnerability (e.g., family history of AOD problems, lowered age of onset of use, traumatic victimization), greater problem severity and complexity, weaker social supports, fewer occupational opportunities, and less success (Polich, Armour, & Braiker, 1980; Room, 1989; Weisner, 1993; Tucker & Gladsjo, 1993; Cunningham et al., 1995).
- Recovery outcomes are compromised by high treatment attrition rates (more than 50%) (SAMHSA, 2002) and doses of treatment services (measured in days of care or number of sessions) that often fall below standards recommended for optimal effects (NIDA, 1999).
- Individuals may have experienced professional treatment, but such treatment may not have played a role in their later achievement of stable recovery.

In spite of such limitations, the vast majority of persons who suffer from substance dependence (in contrast to less severe AOD-related problems) enter recovery through the vehicle of professionally directed treatment (Cunningham 1999a,b, 2000). But this link is not as direct as one might think. Recent studies have shown that a significant portion of people with the most severe substance use disorders achieve stable recovery only after multiple treatment episodes spread over a number of years (Anglin, Hser, & Grella, 1997; Hser, Grella, Chou, & Anglin, 1998;

Dennis, Scott, & Hristova, 2002), suggesting a possible cumulative effect of such interventions.

Peer-assisted recovery involves the use of structured recovery mutual aid groups to initiate and/or maintain recovery from AOD problems. Addiction recovery mutual aid structures of many varieties exist in the United States (see discussion below). Alcoholics Anonymous is the most widely used community resource for the resolution of alcohol-related problems (Room, 1989; Weisner, Greenfield, & Room, 1995), with 3.1% of U.S. citizens reporting having attended A.A. meetings sometime in their life for an alcohol problem and 1.5% reporting attendance at A.A. meetings for an alcohol problem in the past year (Room & Greenfield, 1993). Mutual aid involvement, as measured by studies of A.A., can play a significant role in the movement from addiction to recovery (Timko, Moos, Finney, & Moos, 1994; Fiorentine, 1999; Fiorentine & Hillhouse, 2000; Emrick, Tonigan, Montgomery, & Little, 1993; Tucker, Vuchinich, & Gladsjo, 1994; Morgenstern, Labouvie, McCray, Kahler, & Frey, 1997; Humphreys, Wing, McCarty, Chappel, & Galant, 2004). This positive effect extends to:

- adolescents (Johnsen & Herringer, 1993; Margolis, Kilpatrick, & Mooney, 2000; Kelly, Myers, & Brown, 2002),
- women and cultural minorities (Denzin, 1987; Caetano, 1993; Humphreys, Mavis, & Stoffelmayr, 1994; Kessler, Mickelson, & Zhoa, 1997; Bischof, Rumpf, Hapke, Meyer, & John, 2000; Winzelberg & Humphreys, 1999),
- persons experiencing substance use and psychiatric disorders (Meissen, Powell, Wituk, Girrens, & Artega, 1999; Ouimette, Humphreys, Moos, Finney, Cronkite, & Federman, 2001),
- persons using medications to support their recovery (Rychtarik, Connors, Demen, & Stasiewicz, 2000), and
- agnostics and atheists (Winzelberg & Humphreys, 1999; Weiss, Griffin, Gallop, Onken, Gastfriend, Daley, Crits-Christoph, Bishop, & Barber, 2000).

For those seeking support from recovery mutual aid groups, there is a dose effect related to meeting participation. The probability of stable remission rises in tandem with the number of meetings attended in the first three years of recovery (Hoffmann, Harrison, & Belille, 1983; Pisani, Fawcett, Clark, & McGuire, 1993; Humphreys, Moos, & Cohen, 1997; Chappel, 1993). Recovery prospects also rise with the intensity of mutual aid involvement, as measured by active application of program concepts, meeting participation (speaking, interacting, leading), participation in pre- and post-meeting rituals, use of mutual aid networks for fellowship and leisure, reading program literature, being sponsored, sponsoring others, and involvement in other service work (Sheeren, 1988; Cross, Morgan, Moonye, Martin, & Rafter, 1990; Johnson & Herringer, 1993; Emrick et al., 1993; Caldwell & Cutter, 1998; Montgomery, Miller, & Tonigan, 1995; Humphreys, Moos, Cohen, 1997). This intensity of participation effect also applies to adolescents (Margolis, Kilpatrick, & Mooney, 2000).

Peer-assisted recovery is also reflected in the growing recovery home movement (most visibly in the Oxford Houses) (Jason, Davis, Ferrari, & Bishop, 2001) and the rapid growth of non-clinical, peer-based recovery support services (White, 2004c).

Natural recovery, treatment-assisted recovery, and peer-assisted styles of recovery are not mutually exclusive. A.A.'s 2004 membership survey reveals that 64% of A.A. members received some type of treatment or counseling prior to joining A.A. and that 65% received professional treatment or counseling after they entered A.A. (Alcoholics Anonymous, 2005). In a 2001 national survey of people who self-identified as "in recovery" or "formerly addicted to" alcohol and other drugs, 25% reported initiating and sustaining recovery without treatment or mutual aid (Faces & Voices of Recovery, 2001).

RECOVERY INITIATION FRAMEWORKS (RELIGIOUS, SPIRITUAL, SECULAR)

There are considerable differences in recovery styles based on the presence or absence of religion or spirituality as an important dimension of the recovery process. There are *religious frameworks of recovery* (sometimes referred to as *faith-based*) in which severe alcohol and other drug problems are resolved within the rubric of religious experience, religious beliefs, prescriptions for daily living, rituals of worship, and support of a community of shared faith. Within various religious traditions, the abandonment of addiction is viewed as a byproduct of the experience of religious conversion/affiliation and the reconstruction of a faith-based personal identity and lifestyle. In this framework, recovery is a divine gift of grace rather than something that one does. Religion is viewed, not as an enriching dimension of recovery, but as the catalytic agent that initiates and sustains recovery (White & Whiters, 2005). Religious pathways of recovery are marked by:

- a religious rationale for the roots of addiction (e.g., the Islamic interpretation of alcoholism as a fruit of the tree of *Jahiliyyah* (ignorance/idolatry) (Badri, 1976);

William L. White

- a mytho-magical personification/demonization of drugs and the addiction process, e.g., the Islamic interpretation of drink and drunkenness as an "infamy of Satan's handiwork" (Badri, 1976, pp. 3-5);
- a religious rationale for restraint and temperance (e.g., the body as the temple of God) (Bible, 1 Cr 3:16-17; Miller, 1995);
- rituals of confession, restitution, and forgiveness as tools of psychological reconstruction;
- the use of prayer, reading, and service to others (e.g., witnessing) as daily rituals of recovery; and
- enmeshment in a community of faith that meets needs once met within the culture of addiction.

Religious and spiritual frameworks of recovery can closely co-exist. For example, there are societies that help A.A. members who share a particular religious orientation pursue work on A.A.'s Step Eleven: "Sought through prayer and meditation to improve our conscious contact with God as we understood Him, praying only for knowledge of His will for us and the power to carry that out." Two of the oldest Eleventh Step groups are the Calix Society and Jewish Alcoholics, Chemically Dependent People and Significant Others (JACS). Eleventh Step groups usually serve as adjuncts rather than alternatives to A.A. participation (White, 1998).

Spiritual frameworks of recovery overlap with religious pathways of recovery in the sense that both flow out of the human condition of wounded imperfection (what William James, 1902, referred to as "torn-to-pieces-hood"), involve experiences of connection with resources within and beyond the self, and involve a core set of values (e.g., humility, gratitude, and forgiveness) (Kurtz & Ketcham, 1992). Spiritual frameworks of recovery such as Alcoholics Anonymous focus on defects of character (self-centeredness, selfishness, dishonesty, resentment, anger, preoccupation with power and control) as the root of addiction, and provide a means of reaching both into oneself (e.g., self-inventory, developing the traits of honesty, humility, and tolerance) and outside oneself (reliance on a Higher Power, prayer, confession, acts of restitution, acts of service, participation in a community of shared experience) (Miller & Kurtz, 1994; Green, Fullilove, & Fullilove, 1998). Spirituality as a framework of recovery involves the embrace of paradox (e.g., "sober alcoholic"), gaining a degree of control by admitting one's powerlessness, and becoming whole by accepting one's imperfection (Kurtz, 1999). Spirituality as a medium of recovery is rooted in the understanding that: 1) human beings are born with a vacuum inside themselves that craves to be filled with meaning, 2) we can artificially and temporarily fulfill this need through

26

the medium of drug intoxication, and 3) more authentic and lasting frameworks of meaning can displace the craving for intoxication. Religious and spiritual frameworks can overlap (e.g., religion as a vehicle of spirituality) or exist as distinct experiences (spirituality without religion, religion without spirituality). One of A.A.'s innovations was its emancipation of spirituality from its explicitly religious roots.

Secular recovery is a style of recovery that does not involve reliance on any religious or spiritual ideas (God or Higher Power), experiences (conversion), or rituals (prayer). Secular recovery rests on the belief in the ability of each individual to rationally direct his or her own self-change processes. Secular recovery groups view the roots of addiction more in terms of irrational beliefs about oneself and the world and ineffective coping strategies than in terms of biology, morality, character, or sin. Secular frameworks of recovery such as Secular Organization for Sobriety and LifeRing Secular Recovery reinforce the "Big Decision" or "Sobriety Priority" ("not using no matter what") through a variety of cognitive and behavioral self-change techniques. Where spiritual and religious frameworks of recovery involve a transcendence of self, secular frameworks of recovery involve an assertion of self (White & Nicolaus, 2005). Where spiritual frameworks of recovery emphasize wisdom (emphasis on experience, search for meaning, freedom rooted in the acceptance of limitation, self-transcendence by connection to a greater whole, strength flowing from limitation), secular frameworks of recovery emphasize knowledge (emphasis on scientific evidence, an assertion of control, self-mastery through knowledge of self and knowledge of one's problem, and strength flowing from personal competence).

All three recovery initiation frameworks share what Morgan (1995a) has described as a 1) re-visioning of self, 2) a re-visioning of one's life-context, and 3) a restructuring of life-stance and lifestyle. All three frameworks share a three-part story-style in which people in recovery report "in a general way what we used to be like, what happened, and what we are like now" (Alcoholics Anonymous, 1939, p. 70). And yet listening to these tales of "rescue and renewal" (Morgan, 1995b), one finds critical differences in the instrument of recovery (the grace/gift of having been changed versus personal ownership of that change), different metaphors and rituals used to initiate and sustain recovery, and different views of the role of a community of shared experience in the recovery process.

RECOVERY INITIATION STYLES

There are three styles of recovery initiation: *quantum change*, conscious *incremental change,* and a less conscious process that sociologists refer to as *drift.*

Quantum change, also referred to as *transformational change*, is distinguished by its vividness (emotional intensity), suddenness (lack of intentionality), positiveness, and permanence of effect (Miller and C'de Baca, 2001). Quantum change can occur as a breakthrough of self-perception or insight (an epiphany) or as a mystical or religious experience. Both experiences produce fundamental alterations in one's perception of self and the world. The liberation from alcohol and other drug problems and related changes flow from these core alterations of identity and values. Quantum change is sometimes experienced as a Damascus-type[3] conversion (religious, spiritual, or secular in nature) that precisely and forever demarks addiction and recovery. Such recovery conversion experiences are rooted in calamity — often referred to as "hitting bottom." Recovery-catalyzing breakthroughs have been described in the research literature as an "existential crisis" (Coleman, 1978), a "naked lunch experience" (Jorquez, 1993), a "rock bottom experience" (Maddux and Desmond, 1980), a "brief developmental window of opportunity" (White, 1996), a "crossroads" (Klingemann, 1991, 1992), an "epistemological shift" (Shaffer and Jones, 1989), and a "radical reorientation" (Frykholm, 1985). Quantum change as a pathway of addiction recovery has a long history and is often the ignition point of historically important abstinence-based healing and religious/cultural revitalization movements (White, 2004b). Quantum change occurs in religious, spiritual, and secular forms. Illustrative of this experience is the report of Samuel Hadley, whose religious conversion at the Water Street Mission in New York City marked the beginning of a lifetime of service to God and other alcoholics.

> *Although up to that moment my soul had been filled with indescribable gloom,*
> *I felt the glorious brightness of the noonday sun shine into my heart. I felt I was*
> *a free man....From that moment till now I have never wanted a drink of whiskey,*
> *and I have never seen money enough to make me take one. I promised God*
> *that night that if he would take away the appetite for strong drink, I would work*
> *for him all my life. He has done his part, and I have been trying to do mine*
> (Quoted in James, 1902, p. 203).

While there is a tendency to grant a special quality to these recovery conversion experiences, Bill Wilson cautioned against such glorification.

There is a very natural tendency to set apart those experiences or awakenings which happen to be sudden, spectacular or vision-producing….But as I now look back on this tremendous event [his own transformative change experience]*….it now seems clear that the only special feature was its electric suddenness and the overwhelming and immediate conviction that it carried to me. In all other respects, however, I am sure that my own experience was not different than that received by every AA member who has strenuously practiced our recovery program* (Wilson, 1962).

In contrast to the lightning strike of quantum change, incremental recovery involves a time-encompassing and stage-dependent process of metamorphosis. Researchers have described many stage models of addiction recovery, including:

- Frykholm's (1985) 3-stage model (ambivalence, lengthening periods of abstinence, and emancipation);
- Biernacki's (1986) four-stage model (a resolution to quit either through drift, rational decision, or "rock bottom" experience; a detachment from the physical and social worlds of addiction; managing cravings and impulses and staying clean (abstinent); and becoming ordinary);
- Waldorf's (1983, 1990) six-stage model (going through changes; forming a resolve; cessation experiments; becoming an ex-addict; learning to be "ordinary"; filling the physical, psychological, social, lifestyle void with family work, religion, politics, and mutual aid);
- Brown's (1985) four-stage model (drinking, transition, early recovery, and ongoing recovery);
- Shaffer and Jones' three-stage model (experiencing turning points, active quitting, and relapse prevention);
- Klingemann's (1991) three-stage model (motivation, action, maintenance); and
- Prochaska and colleagues' (1992) six-stage model (precontemplation, contemplation, planning, action, maintenance, and termination).

Stage models suggest that the process of recovery begins <u>before</u> AOD use is moderated or terminated and that, while linear movement through particular stages is possible, the more common experience is a recycling through these stages before permanent recovery is achieved. The repeated sequence that predates recovery stability might be constructed as follows: escalating AOD-related pain (I need to recover), the desire to change (I want to recover), belief in possibility of change (I can recover), commitment (I am going to recover), experiments in abstinence (I am recovering), and movement from sobriety experiments to sobriety identity (I am an ex-addict; I am a recovered/recovering alcoholic/addict; I no longer use or misuse alcohol or other drugs). Stages of change models are very popular among addiction professionals, but have come under attack for the lack of empirical evidence supporting them (Sutton, 2001; West, 2005).

Quantum change and incremental change have been described as two discrete phenomena, but we have listened to recovery stories in our travels that have dimensions of both. For example, we have seen individuals who repeatedly cycled through preparatory stages of recovery (what we have here referred to as recovery priming) but whose point of recovery stabilization was marked by a profound, life-altering quantum change experience.

The third style of recovery initiation is one of *drift* — the gradual cessation/reduction of AOD use and related problems as a matter of circumstance rather than choice. Here the addict simply "goes with the flow," only to find in retrospect that events and circumstances lead away from drugs and the culture in which his or her drug use was nested (see Waldorf, 1983; Biernacki, 1986, 1990; Granfield & Cloud, 1999). Developmental maturation and environmental change can elicit changes in alcohol and other drug use in some individuals in ways that do not follow the conscious, self-engineered styles of change depicted in stages of change models. For example, some studies of female heroin addicts depict recovery, not as a central goal, a but as an inadvertent outcome of severing contact with former drug-using environments and relationships (Gerstein, Judd, & Rovner, 1979). Some individuals drift out of addiction through processes similar to the processes by which they drifted into addiction, including finding an intense alternative pursuit that gives new meaning to one's life (Cloud & Granfield, 2001).

RECOVERY IDENTITY

Recovery styles also reflect different *recovery identity* patterns — variations in the extent to which AOD problems and the recovery process influence one's identity, and the degree to which one identifies with other people who share this recovery process. There are those with recovery-neutral identities (persons who have resolved severe AOD problems but who do not self-identify as "alcoholics," "addicts," or "persons in recovery"), those with recovery-positive identities (those for whom the status of recovery from addiction has become an important part of their personal identities), and those with recovery-negative identities (those whose addiction/recovery status is self-acknowledged but not shared with others due to a sense of personal shame derived from this status).

These identities, rather than being mutually exclusive, can constitute different points in a prolonged recovery career. For example, we have witnessed such evolution in the modern history of recovering people working as addiction counselors. Early addiction counselors boldly proclaimed their recovery status as their primary credential, but began withholding that recovery status in the 1980s and 1990s behind their accumulating credentials and the restigmatization of AOD problems. In the face of a new recovery advocacy movement calling upon recovering people to put a face and voice on recovery, many of those same addiction counselors are again going public with their recovery status. In our experience, evolution in identity is the norm in addiction recovery.

RECOVERY RELATIONSHIPS

There are acultural *styles of recovery* in which individuals initiate and sustain recovery from addiction without significant involvement with other people in recovery and without identification with a larger *recovery community* or *culture of recovery* (a social network of recovering people with their own recovery-based history, language, rituals, symbols, literature, and values). This is not to say that this style of recovery is void of social support, but that support usually comes from one's inner family and social circle rather than from a larger community of recovering people. Gerry Spense, the noted trial lawyer, describes this style of recovery:

> *We (Gerry and his new wife) sort of became each other's A.A. We quit together, and we hung on to each other. Although I have never attended an Alcoholics Anonymous session, we must have had the kind of experience that people have there.* (Quoted in *Wholey, 1984, p. 106.*)

In contrast, there are *bicultural styles of recovery,* in which individuals sustain their recovery through simultaneous involvement in a culture of recovery and the larger "civilian" culture (activities and relationships with individuals who do not have addiction/ recovery backgrounds). There are also *enmeshed styles of recovery,* in which one initiates and maintains recovery in almost complete sequestration within a culture of recovery (White, 1996).

These styles are not mutually exclusive and can change over the course of recovery, with some individuals exhibiting very enmeshed styles of early recovery, only to migrate toward a bicultural or acultural style of recovery later in their lives. Some individuals use recovery mutual aid groups for recovery initiation and maintenance, where others seem to initiate recovery through such resources, but then sustain that recovery through their own personal, family, and social resources. Some continue Twelve Step or other recovery maintenance practices without meeting participation, while others find other sources of long-term recovery support (Tonigan, Miller, Chavez, Porter, Worth, Westphal, Carroll, Repa, Martin, & Tracy, 2002). A relatively recent phenomenon is the advent of *virtual (Internet) recovery* — the achievement or maintenance of recovery through Internet support groups, with little or no participation in face-to-face support meetings. Web-based recovery support services include email and instant messaging systems, newsgroups, bulletin boards, chat rooms, self-assessment instruments, and recovery coaching (Walters, Hester, Chiauzzi, & Miller, 2005). The Internet seems to elicit a much higher degree of participation among women and individuals in high-status occupations than do either professional treatment or face-to-face recovery mutual aid groups (Hall & Tidwell, 2003).

Communities of recovery is a phrase coined by Ernest Kurtz to convey the existence of multiple recovery communities. Addiction treatment professionals should refer people to these communities with the goal of achieving reciprocity of fit between the individual and the group. Style differences based on the evolution in how one relates (or does not relate) to these communities of recovery are part of what could be described as one's *recovery career*. The concept of *career* has been applied to the process of addiction (Frykholm, 1985) and to conceptually link multiple episodes of treatment (Hser, Anglin, Grella, Longshore, & Prendergast, 1997; Timko, Moos, Finney, Moos, & Kaplowitz, 1999; Dennis, Scott, Funk, & Foss, 2005). *Recovery career* is an extension of this application and refers to the evolving stages of recovery stability and one's identity and recovery support relationships over time.

VARIETIES OF TWELVE-STEP EXPERIENCE

Peer-based support groups constitute a major resource for the resolution of alcohol and other drug problems (Room & Greenfield, 1993; Kessler, Mickelson, & Zhoa, 1997; Kissin, McLeod, & McKay, 2003). Such groups are attractive, are geographically accessible and affordable, require no formal admission procedures, and place no limits on length of participation (Humphreys, et al., 2004). Twelve-Step groups began with the founding of Alcoholics Anonymous in 1935. Although there were dozens of recovery mutual aid societies that pre-dated A.A. (White, 2001), A.A. continues to be the standard by which other mutual aid groups are measured due to its size (2.1 million members in 100,766 groups), geographical growth (150 countries), and longevity (Kurtz & White, 2003). Varieties of A.A. experience were evident from its inception (e.g., differences between A.A. in Akron and New York City) and have grown throughout A.A.'s history.

Varieties of A.A. experience are reflected in the diversity of A.A. meeting formats (e.g., open vs. closed meetings, speaker meetings vs. discussion meetings), in the trend to organize A.A. around special populations and special needs, and in the wide variance of styles of "working" the A.A. program. Local A.A. meeting lists reflect such specialization, e.g., meetings organized by age (young people's meetings, old-timers meetings), gender (women-only and men-only meetings), sexual orientation (lesbian, gay, bisexual, transgender), language (Spanish, Polish, no profanity), profession (physicians, lawyers, airline pilots), social status (off-the-books meetings for celebrities and those in high-status positions), relationship status (single, couples), co-occurring problems (psychiatric illness, HIV/AIDS), and smoking status (non-smoking), to name just a few. There are differences in A.A. that transcend filtering the A.A. program through particular types of categorical/ cultural experience. Significant differences can be found in A.A. meetings related to such factors as degree of religious orientation (from efforts to Christianize A.A. to A.A. groups for atheists and agnostics), meeting rituals, pre- and post meeting activities; and basic interpretations of the nature of the A.A. program (Kurtz & White, 2003). Such varieties multiply exponentially when one examines the range of adaptations of A.A.'s Twelve Steps to other drug problems (e.g., Narcotics Anonymous, Cocaine Anonymous, Marijuana Anonymous, Pills Anonymous, Methadone Anonymous) and to co-occurring problems (e.g., Dual Diagnosis Anonymous, Double Trouble in Recovery).

The explosive growth of A.A. in the 1970s and 1980s and the growing influence of the addiction treatment industry and the criminal justice system upon A.A. (via mandated A.A. attendance) led to concerns among A.A. old-timers that the core of A.A.'s program was being corrupted. This concern led to efforts to define and recapture the historical A.A. historian Ernest Kurtz (1999, pp. 131-138) proposed five criteria to distinguish "real A.A." from meetings that had taken on the flavor of treatment groups: 1) A.A. vocabulary (defects of character, self-inventory, Higher Power) rather than treatment vocabulary; 2) humor and the appreciation of paradox; 3) a story style that "describes in a general way what we used to be like, what happened, and what we are like now"; 4) respect for and adherence to A.A. traditions; and 5) a conviction by those attending meetings that they NEED rather than WANT to be there.

The growing varieties of A.A. experience triggered efforts in the scientific community to define the "active ingredients" of A.A. These scientists, confronted with the large menu of concepts and activities that make up the A.A. experience, attempted to define which aspects of the A.A. experience were the most potent in altering the course of alcoholism and strengthening the recovery experience. To-date, these studies have focused on such mechanisms as motivational enhancement, development of Twelve-Step cognitions (e.g., commitment to abstinence and continued A.A. participation), recovery coaching (advice), mastery of behavioral prescriptions for coping, exposure to recovery role models, enhanced self-efficacy, changes in friendship networks, and the therapeutic benefits of helping others (Morgenstern, et al., 1997; Humphreys, Mankowski, Moos, & Finney, 1999; Pagano, Friend, Tonigan, & Stout, 2004). Scientists have also plotted a continuum of response to Twelve-Step involvement across three populations: optimal responders, nonresponders, and partial responders (Morgenstern, Kahler, Frey, & Labouvie, 1996).

Other areas of diverse experience within Twelve-Step groups include patterns of co-attendance of Twelve Step and other groups, e.g., attending A.A. and Al-Anon, A.A. and N.A., A.A. and Women for Sobriety; patterns of primary affiliation (e.g., shifting primary allegiance from N.A. to A.A.); patterns of intensity of participation (frequency of meeting attendance and other Twelve-Step practices); and duration of participation over time (e.g., decreasing involvement or disengagement from regular involvement in meetings and rituals).

Still Other Varieties

The existence of those who did not respond or only partially responded to spiritually oriented Twelve-Step programs set the stage for the emergence of explicitly religious and secular frameworks of peer-based recovery support (Humphreys, 2004). Religious recovery support groups include (with their founding dates where available) Alcoholics Victorious (1948), Teen Challenge (1961), Alcoholics for Christ (1976), Overcomers Outreach (1977), Liontamers Anonymous (1980), Mountain Movers, High Ground, Free N' One, Victorious Lady, Celebrate Recovery, Millati Islami, and innumerable local recovery-support ministries. As noted earlier, these groups share a religious interpretation of the roots of addiction (e.g., as a sin of the flesh, idolatry, or demonic possession), recovery founded on total surrender to a religious deity, a religiously based reconstruction of personal identity and values, and immersion in a faith-based community (White & Whiters, 2005).

Secular recovery support groups (with their founding dates) include Women for Sobriety (WFS) (1975), Secular Sobriety Groups (later renamed Secular Organization for Sobriety — Save Our Selves (SOS) (1985), Rational Recovery (RR) (1986), Men for Sobriety (MFS) (1988), Moderation Management (MM) (1994), SMART Recovery® (1994), and LifeRing Secular Recovery (LSR) (1999). Secular groups are distinguished by their meeting locations (homes and religiously neutral sites); lack of reference to religious deities; discouragement of self-labeling ("alcoholic" and "addict"); emphasis on personal empowerment and self-reliance; openness to crosstalk (direct feedback and advice between members); lack of formal sponsorship; encouragement to complete a recovery process and move on to a full, meaningful life (rather than sustain meeting participation for life); and use of volunteer professional advisors (persons not in personal recovery) to facilitate and speak at meetings (White & Nicolaus, 2005).

Individuals who participate in Twelve-Step alternatives may do so exclusively, concurrently with A.A. meetings, or sequentially (using one framework to initiate recovery and another framework to maintain and enrich that recovery over time (Kaskutas, 1992; Connors, Dermen & Duerr, 1992; White & Nicolaus, 2005).

RECOVERY DURABILITY

Interest has grown over the past decade in the prospects and processes involved in long-term recovery stabilization (Morgan, 1995; Chappel, 1993), as it has become clear that short periods of sobriety or decelerated AOD use are not predictive of sustained recovery. Some researchers have claimed that stable remission can be predicted by as little as six months of sobriety (Armor, Polich, & Stambul, 1978). Vaillant (1983), in a prospective study of alcoholic men, found that the stability and durability of addiction recovery increases with length of sobriety, with no relapses in his study among those who had achieved six or more years of continuous sobriety. A growing number of studies are suggesting that the point at which most recoveries from alcohol dependence become fully stabilized is between four and five years of continuous remission (Vaillant, 1996; Nathan & Skinstad, 1987; De Soto, O'Donnel, & De Soto, 1989; Dawson, 1996; Jin, Rourke, Patterson, Taylor & Grant, 1998). Once attained, recovery from alcohol dependence is more stable for those with late-onset alcohol problems compared to those with early-onset alcohol problems (Schutte, Brennan & Moos, 1994).

Studies of heroin addicts further confirm the fragility of short periods of abstinence. Follow-up studies have demonstrated that only 42% percent of those abstaining from opiates in the community at two-year follow-up were still abstinent at five-year follow-up (Duvall, Lock, & Brill, 1963). One third of those who achieve three years of abstinence eventually relapse (Maddux & Desmond, 1981), and one quarter of heroin addicts with five or more years of abstinence later return to heroin use (Hser, Hoffman, Grella, & Anglin, 2001).

While recovery stability seems to vary somewhat across drugs used, the principle that recovery becomes more stable over time seems to apply to all patterns of addiction. In a 2001 national survey of people who self-identified as "in recovery" or "formerly addicted to alcohol or other drugs," half reported being in stable recovery more than five years, and 34% reported having achieved stable recovery lasting ten or more years (Faces & Voices of Recovery, 2001). The average length of continuous sobriety reported in the latest membership survey of Alcoholics Anonymous was 8 years, with 36% of A.A. members reporting continuous sobriety of more than 10 years (*A.A. Grapevine*, July, 2005).

Persons who achieve full, uninterrupted recovery for five years, like persons who have achieved similar patterns of symptom remission from other primary health disorders, can be described as *recovered*. In general, this means that the risk of future lifetime relapse has approached the level of addiction risk for persons without a history of prior addiction. Those who achieve full symptom remission for less than five years or who have achieved partial recovery (marked reduction of AOD use and related consequences) can best be described as *in recovery* or *recovering*. Use of the term *recovering* in later years (after five years) of recovery reminds the individual that recovery is an enduring process requiring sustained vigilance and recovery maintenance. However, such use, by inadvertently conveying the lack of a permanent solution for severe AOD problems, may contribute to the stigma and pessimism attached to these problems.

RECOVERY TERMINATION

One of the recent controversies related to recovery from addiction involves the question of whether addiction recovery is ever fully completed. The stage models of recovery summarized earlier collectively portray four broad stages of recovery: 1) *recovery priming* (experiences that open a doorway of entry into recovery), 2) *recovery initiation* (discovering a workable strategy of problem stabilization), 3) *recovery maintenance* (achieving recovery stability and sustaining and refining broader strategies of problem resolution with a continued focus on the recovery process), and

4) *recovery termination* (achievement of global health with diminished preoccupation with recovery). This last stage, referred to as *Stage II Recovery* ("rebuilding the life that was saved in Stage I") (Larsen, 1985, p. 15), transcends the early concern with the addictive behavior and focuses on a reconstruction of personal character, identity, beliefs, and interpersonal relationships. This stage is also referred to as *completed recovery* or the *real thirteenth step*[4] — an "advanced state" of recovery marked by global health and a heightened capacity for intimacy, serenity, self-acceptance, and public service (Picucci, 2002; Tessina, 1991).

IMPLICATIONS FOR THE PROFESSIONAL TREATMENT OF AOD PROBLEMS

This review contains critical understandings that could help shape recovery-oriented systems of care. Some of the most important of these include the following.

Paradigmatic Shift: There will be increasing calls to shift addiction treatment and addiction counseling from a problem-focused or intervention-focused paradigm to a recovery paradigm. This will shift the emphasis of treatment from one of brief biopsychosocial stabilization to one of sustained recovery management (pre-recovery engagement; recovery initiation; sustained monitoring; stage-appropriate recovery education and coaching; assertive linkage to communities of recovery; and, when needed, early re-intervention) (White, Boyle & Loveland, 2003).

Recovery Definition and Scope: The shift to a recovery paradigm will require considerable discussion between the professional addictions field and diverse communities of recovery about the very definition of recovery. These discussions will be contentious, but we would make the following predictions:

1. Abstinence will shift from its status as a *goal* and definitional requirement of recovery to the status of *one method* of achieving recovery (and the preferred method for those with the most severe AOD problems). The goal will shift to the resolution of AOD problems by any means possible — a goal that will legitimize moderated outcomes for those with less severe AOD problems.

2. The focal point of recovery (changes in one's primary drug relationship) will broaden to include a healthy relationship or non-relationship with all psychoactive drugs and the achievement of global health. Addiction treatment programs will increasingly be held accountable for multiple recovery outcomes, e.g., changes in primary and secondary drug use as well as changes in physical, emotional, family/relational, and occupational/ academic health and

functioning. There will be a shift in focus from what recovery eliminates (AOD use and related problems) to what recovery adds to individuals, families, and communities (global health, occupational and academic productivity, active citizenship)(http://www.samhsa.gov/Matrix/SAP_treatment.aspx).

3. Re-elevating the concept of *family recovery* will exert pressure for new technologies of family assessment, intervention, and sustained monitoring as well as impetus for a family-oriented recovery research agenda.

4. The concept of *partial recovery* will receive greater elucidation and legitimacy within the addictions treatment field, and cases of *enriched recovery* (dramatically elevated health, functioning, and community service) will be documented and culturally elevated to help ameliorate the social stigma that continues to be attached to AOD problems.

Recovery Capital: The pathology and intervention paradigms that have guided addiction treatment have shaped assessment and placement protocol so that they focus almost exclusively on problem severity and complexity. The resiliency/recovery paradigm calls for measuring recovery capital; distinguishing the role of recovery capital in *natural*, *treatment-assisted*, and *peer-assisted* recoveries; and giving prominence to an individual's/ family's recovery capital within the process of clinical decision-making. The most important implication of the concept of recovery capital is the premise that not all individuals experiencing AOD problems need professional treatment. Individuals with lower problem severity and high recovery capital can be encouraged to explore natural and peer-based resources as less restrictive, less expensive, and less stigma-laden alternatives to addiction treatment. Monitoring responses to such resources can be used to determine if and when professional services are necessary.

Medication-Assisted Recovery: Tension is growing between an anti-medication bias within the field of addiction treatment (and within American communities of recovery and the larger American culture), the growing availability of a wide variety of pharmacological adjuncts in the treatment of addiction, and the growth in scientific evidence supporting their effectiveness. We anticipate a day when the legitimacy of such pharmacological adjuncts will be widely recognized in professional and recovery communities and integrated within the large spectrum of treatment and recovery support services. If such legitimacy is not achieved, we would anticipate a schism within the field in which more scientifically and medically based treatments split off into a separate field within primary medicine. We would consider this further splitting of body from mind and soul a tragic event in the history of the field.

Recovery Frameworks: Religious, spiritual, and secular frameworks of recovery must be more completely charted and evaluated, with a particular focus on their applicability to particular cultural and clinical populations. For example, researchers have extensively studied (some would say over-studied) AOD problems in Native American and African American communities, but no comparable quantity of literature exists on the varieties of recovery experience within these communities. How many African Americans initiate and sustain recovery through the historical Black church? How many African Americans initiate recovery through A.A. or N.A. and then migrate into the Black church to sustain their recoveries? How many Native Americans use indigenous cultural or religious revitalization movements as a framework for long-term sobriety? In the same vein, how do members of secular frameworks of recovery differ from those in religious or Twelve-Step frameworks of recovery? What mechanisms of change are shared across religious, spiritual, and secular frameworks of recovery; and what mechanisms of change distinguish such frameworks from each other? Definitive, scientifically researched answers to such questions do not yet exist.

Recovery Styles: Variations in how recovery is initiated and how recovery shapes personal identity and interpersonal relationships illustrate the diversity of experiences that constitute recovery from AOD problems. Further documentation of such styles and their relative prevalence across cultural and clinical subpopulations is needed to guide the delivery of treatment and recovery support services. The elucidation of recovery styles is part of a larger recovery research agenda that is currently gaining prominence.

Varieties of Recovery Mutual Support Societies: The numerical expansion and growing diversity of peer-based recovery support groups suggests the need for all addictions professionals to become students of such groups, develop relationships with these groups, provide clients information about such groups, and develop a style of active linkage to these groups. The diversity of recovery support groups has prompted calls for matching individual clients to particular groups by such factors as age, gender, socioeconomic status, drug of choice, smoking status, and attitudes toward religion and spirituality (Forman, 2002; White & Nicolaus, 2005). Celebration of the growing diversity of recovery pathways and a philosophy of choice permeate the philosophies of the best treatment programs. Recent reviews of treatment effectiveness have linked this philosophy of choice to enhanced motivation and treatment outcomes (Hester & Miller, 2003). All recovery support structures, like all treatments, will have optimal responders, partial responders, and non-responders. This calls for continued monitoring and support to get the best possible fit between each individual and a particular method of treatment or recovery support. Combinations of natural resources, peer recovery networks, and professional treatment may generate amplified recovery outcomes for those individuals and families with the greatest problem severity and complexity.

SUMMARY AND CONCLUSIONS

The extension of the pathology and intervention paradigms toward a recovery paradigm will generate significant new understandings about the varieties of recovery experience. However, our understanding of those varieties is in its infancy. It is time the recognition of multiple pathways and styles of recovery moved beyond the level of superficial rhetoric. It is time the field aggressively pursued a recovery research agenda. It is time that the recognition of multiple pathways and styles of recovery fully permeated the philosophies and clinical protocols of all organizations providing addiction treatment and recovery support services.

REFERENCES AND RECOMMENDED READING

Alcoholics Anonymous: The Story of How Many Thousands of Men and Women Have Recovered from Alcoholism. (1939). New York: Works Publishing Company.

Alcoholics Anonymous: The Story of How Many Thousands of Men and Women Have Recovered from Alcoholism. (1976) New York: A.A. World Services, Inc.

Alcoholics Anonymous (2005). Survey profiles today's AA members. *About AA: A Newsletter for Professionals*, Fall, p. 1.

American Psychiatric Association. (1994). Diagnostic and statistical manual of mental disorders (4th ed.). Washington, DC: Author.

Anglin, M. D., Almong, I. J., Fisher, D. G. & Peters, K. R. (1989). Alcohol use by heroin addicts: Evidence for an inverse relationship. A study of methadone maintenance and drug free treatment samples. *American Journal of Drug and Alcohol Abuse*, 15(2), 191-207.

Anglin, M. D., Hser, Y., & Grella C. E. (1997). Drug addiction and treatment careers among clients in DATOS. *Psychology of Addictive Behaviors*, 11(4), 308-323.

Anglin, M. D., Hser, Y., & Grella C. E. (1997). Drug addiction and treatment careers among clients in DATOS. *Psychology of Addictive Behaviors*, 11, 308-323.

Anthony, J. C., & Helzer, J. E. (1991). Syndromes of drug abuse and dependence. In L.N. Robins, & D. A. Regier. (Eds.). *Psychiatric Disorders in America: The Epidemiologic Catchment Area Study* (pp. 116-154). New York, NY: The Free Press.

Armor, D. J. and Meshkoff, J. E. (1983). Remission among treated and untreated alcoholics. In N. K. Mello. (Ed.), *Advances in Substance Abuse: Behavioral and Biological Research: Volume 3* (pp. 239-269). CN: JAI Press.

Armor, D. J., Polich, J. M., & Stambul, H. B. (1978). *Alcoholism and Treatment.* New York: Wiley.

Bacchus, L, Strang, J, and Watson, P. (2000). Pathways to abstinence: Two-Year follow-up data on 60 abstinent former opiate addicts who had been turned away from treatment. *European Addiction Research*, 6(3),141-147.

Badri, M. B. (1976). *Islam and alcoholism.* Tacoma Park, MD: Muslim Students Association of the U.S. and Canada.

Behar, D., Winokur, G. & Berg, C. J. (1984). Depression in the abstinent alcoholic. *American Journal of Psychiatry*, 141(9),1105-1107.

Bien, T. & Barge, R. (1990). Smoking and drinking: A review of the literature. *International Journal of the Addictions*, 25(12), 1429-1454.

Biernacki, P. (1986). *Pathways from Heroin Addiction: Recovery Without Treatment.* Philadelphia, PA: Temple University Press.

Bischof, G., Rumpf, H., Hapke, U., Meyer, C. & John, U. (2000). Gender differences in natural recovery from alcohol dependence. *Journal of Studies on Alcohol*, 61(6),783-786.

Borkman, T. (1997). Is recovery planning any different from treatment planning? *Journal of Substance Abuse Treatment*, 15(1), 37-42.

Brown, S. (1985). *Treating the Alcoholic: A Developmental Model of Recovery.* New York: Wiley.

Brown, S., & Lewis, B. (1999). *The Alcoholic Family in Recovery: A Developmental Model.* New York, NY: Guilford.

Burman, S. (1997). The challenge of sobriety: Natural recovery without treatment and self-help programs. *Journal of Substance Abuse*, 9, 41-61.

Caetano, R. (1993). Ethnic minority groups and Alcoholics Anonymous: A review. In B. McCrady and W. Miller (Eds.), *Research on Alcoholics Anonymous: Opportunities and Alternatives* (pp.209-231). New Brunswick, NJ: Rutgers Center of Alcohol Studies.

Caldwell, P. E., & Cutter, H. S. G. (1998). Alcoholics Anonymous affiliation during early recovery. *Journal of Substance Abuse Treatment*, 15(3), 221-228.

Carmelli, D. & Swan, G. (1993). The relationship between quitting smoking and changes in drinking in World War II veteran twins. *Journal of Substance Abuse*, 3(5), 103-116.

Chapman, R. E. (1987). Personality characteristics of alcoholics in long-term recovery. *Dissertation Abstracts International*, 48(2), 338-A.

Chappel, J. N. (1993). Long-term recovery from alcoholism. *Psychiatric Clinics of North America*, 16(1), 177-187.

Cloud, W. & Granfield, R. (1994). Terminating addiction naturally: Post-addict identity and the avoidance of treatment. *Clinical Sociology Review*, 12:159-174.

Cloud, W. & Granfield, R. (2001). Natural recovery from substance dependency: Lessons for treatment providers. *Journal of Social Work Practice in the Addictions*, 1(1), 83-104.

Cohen, P. & Sas, A. (1994). Cocaine use in Amsterdam in non-deviant subcultures. *Addiction Research*, 2(1), 71-94.

Coleman, J. (1978) *A theory of narcotic abstinence*. Paper presented at the 1978 Conference of the Society for the Study of Social Problems, San Francisco, California.

Connors, G. J., Dermen, K. H. & Duerr, M. (1992). SOS membership survey: Preliminary results. In J. Christopher (Ed.), *SOS Sobriety* (pp. 61-65). Buffalo, NY: Prometheus Books,

Copeland, J. (1988). A qualitative study of self-managed change in substance dependence among women. *Contemporary Drug Problems*, 25(2), 321-345.

Courtwright, D. (2001). *Forces of Habit: Drugs and the Making of the Modern World*. Cambridge: Harvard University Press.

Coyhis, D. (1999). *The Wellbriety Journey: Nine Talks by Don Coyhis*. Colorado Springs, CO: White Bison, Inc.

Coyhis, D. (2000). Culturally specific addiction recovery for Native Americans. In: Krestan, J. (Ed.), *Bridges to Recovery* (pp. 77-114). New York: The Free Press.

Cross, G., Morgan, C., Moonye, A., Martin, C., & Rafter, J. (1990). Alcoholism treatment: A ten-year follow-up study. *Alcoholism Clinical and Experimental Research*, 14(2), 169-173.

Cunningham, J. A. (1999a). Resolving alcohol-related problems with and without treatment: The effects of different problem criteria. *Journal of Studies on Alcohol*, 60(4), 463-466.

Cunningham, J. A. (1999b). Untreated remissions from drug use: The predominant pathway. *Addictive Behaviors*, 24(2), 267-270.

Cunningham, J. A. (2000). Remissions from drug dependence: Is treatment a prerequisite? *Drug and Alcohol Dependence*, 59(3), 211-213.

Cunningham, J. A., Lin, E., Ross, H. E., & Walsh, G. W. (2000). Factors associated with untreated remissions from alcohol abuse or dependence. *Addictive Behaviors*, 25(2), 317-321.

Cunningham, J., Sobell, L. Sobell, M. & Kapur, G. (1995) Resolution from alcohol problems with and without treatment: Reasons for change. *Journal of Substance Abuse*, 7(3), 365-372.

Dawson, D. A. (1996). Correlates of past-year status among treated and untreated persons with former alcohol dependence: United States, 1992. *Alcoholism: Clinical and Experimental Research*, 20(4), 771-779.

Dawson, S. A., Grant, B. F., Stinson, F. S., Chou, P. S. Huang, B. & Ruan, W. J. (2005). Recovery from DSM-IV alcohol dependence: United States, 2001-2002. *Addiction*, 100(3), 281-292.

Dennis, M. L., Scott, C. K, & Hristova, L. (2002). The duration and correlates of substance abuse treatment careers among people entering publicly funded treatment in Chicago [Abstract], *Drug and Alcohol Dependence*, 66(Suppl. 2), 44.

Dennis, M.L., Scott, C.K., Funk, R. & Foss, M.A. (2005). The duration and correlates of addiction and treatment careers. *Journal of Substance Abuse Treatment*, 28, S51-S62.

Denzin, N. K. (1987). *The Recovering Alcoholic.* Newbury Park, CA: Sage.

De Soto, C. B., O'Donnell, W. E., Allred, L. J. & Lopes, C. E. (1985). Symptomatology in alcoholics at various stages of abstinence. *Alcoholism Clinical and Experimental Research,* 9(6),505-512.

De Soto, C. B., O'Donnel, W. E. & De Soto, J. L. (1989). Long-term recovery in alcoholics. *Alcoholism: Clinical and Experimental Research*, 13(5),693-697.

Dickens, B.M., Doob, A.N., Warwick, O.H., & Winegard, W.C. (1982). *Report of the Committee of Inquiry into Allegations Concerning Drs. Linda and Mark Sobell.* Toronto, Canada: Addiction Research Foundation.

Downey, L., Rosengren, D. B., & Donovan, D. M. (2000). To thine own self be true: Self-concept and motivation for abstinence among substance abusers. *Addictive Behaviors*, 25(5), 743-757.

Duvall, H. J., Lock, B. Z. & Brill, L. (1963). Follow-up study of narcotic drug addicts five years after hospitalization. *Public Health Reports*, 78(3),185-193.

Edwards, G. (1984). Drinking in longitudinal perspective: Career and natural history. *British Journal of Addiction*, 79, 175-183.

Edwards, G., Duckitt, A., Oppenheimer, E., Sheehan, M. & Taylor, C. (1983). What happens to alcoholics? *The Lancet*, 2(8344), 269-271.

Elise, D. (1999) Recovering recovery. *Journal of Ministry in Addiction And Recovery*, 6(2),11-23.

Emrick, D. C., Tonigan, J. S., Montgomery, H. & Little, L. (1993). Alcoholics Anonymous: What is currently known? In B. McCrady and W. R. Miller (Eds.),

Research on Alcoholics Anonymous: Opportunities and Alternatives (pp. 41-78). Brunswick, NJ: Rutgers Center of Alcohol Studies.

Faces & Voices of Recovery (2001). *The Road to Recovery: A Landmark National Study on the Public Perceptions of Alcoholism and Barriers to Treatment.* San Francisco, CA: Peter D. Hart Research Associates, Inc./The Recovery Institute.

Fillmore, K. M., Hartka, E., Johnstone, B. M., Speiglman, R., & Temple, M. T. (1988). *Spontaneous Remission of Alcohol Problems: A Critical Review.* Washington, D.C.: Institute of Medicine.

Finney, J. & Moos, R. (1981). Characteristics and prognosis of alcoholics who become moderate drinkers and abstainers after treatment. *Journal of Studies on Alcohol*, 42(1), 94-105.

Fiorentine, R. (1999). After drug treatment: Are 12-step programs effective in maintaining abstinence? *American Journal of Drug and Alcohol Abuse*, 25(1), 93-116.

Fiorentine, R., & Hillhouse, M. (2000). Drug treatment and 12-step program participation: The additive effects of integrated recovery activities. *Journal of Substance Abuse Treatment*, 18(1), 65-74.

Forman, R.F. (2002). One AA meeting doesn't fit all: 6 keys to prescribing 12-step programs. *Psychiatry Online*, 1(10), 1-6.

Frykholm, B. (1985). The drug career. *Journal of Drug Issues*, 15(3), 333-346.

Gerard, D., Sanger, G. & Wile, R. (1962). The abstinent alcoholic. *Archives of General Psychiatry*, 6, 83-95.

Gerstein, D., Judd, L.L., & Rovner, S.A. (1979) Career dynamics of female heroin addicts. *American Journal of Drug and Alcohol Abuse*, 6(1), 1-23.

Goldman, M. S. (1983). Cognitive impairment in chronic alcoholics: Some causes for optimism. *American Psychologist*, 38(10),1045-1054.

Granfield, R., & Cloud, W. (1999). *Coming Clean: Overcoming Addiction Without Treatment.* New York, NY: New York University Press.

Green, L. L., Fullilove, M. T. & Fullilove, R. E. (1998). Stories of spiritual awakening: The nature of spirituality in recovery. *Journal of Substance Abuse Treatment*, 15(4), 325-331.

Hall, M. J. & Tidwell, W. C. (2003). Internet recovery for substance abuse and alcoholism: An exploratory study of service users. *Journal of Substance Abuse Treatment*, 24(2), 161-167.

Harding, W. M., Zinberg, N. E., Stelmack, S. M. & Michael, B. (1980). Formerly-addicted-now-controlled opiate users. *International Journal of the Addictions* 15(1), 47-60.

Havassy, B. E., Hall, S. M., & Wasserman, D. A. (1991). Social support and relapse: Commonalities among alcoholics, opiate users, and cigarette smokers. *Addictive Behaviors*, 16(5), 235-246.

Helzer, J. E., Burnam, A. & McEvoy, L. T. (1991). Alcohol abuse and dependence. In L.N. Robins & D. A. Regier (Eds.), *Psychiatric Disorders in America: The Epidemiologic Catchment Area Study* (pp. 81-115). New York: The Free Press.

Hester, R. K., & Miller, W. R. (Eds.) (2003). *Handbook of Alcoholism Treatment Approaches: Effective Alternatives* (3rd ed.). Boston, MA: Allyn & Bacon.

High Bottom. (1949). *A.A. Grapevine*, October.

Hoffman, A. & Slade, J. (1993). Following the pioneers: Addressing tobacco in chemical dependency treatment. *Journal of Substance Abuse Treatment*, 10(2), 153-160.

Hoffmann, N., Harrison, P. & Belille, C. (1983). Alcoholics Anonymous after treatment: Attendance and abstinence. *International Journal of the Addictions*, 18(3), 311-318.

Hser, Y. (2000). Substance Abuse and Aging Project: Drug Use Careers: Recovery and Mortality. Retrieved on March 24, 2005 from http://www.oas.samhsa.gov/aging/chap3.htm.

Hser, Y., Anglin, M., Grella, C., Longshore, D., & Prendergast, M. (1997). Drug treatment careers: A conceptual framework and existing research findings. *Journal of Substance Abuse Treatment*, 14(3), 1-16.

Hser, Y., Grella, C., Chou, C. & Anglin, M.D. (1998) Relationship between drug treatment careers and outcomes: Findings from the National Drug Abuse Treatment Outcome Study. *Evaluation Review*. 22(4):496-519.

Hser, Y., Hoffman, V., Grella, C. & Anglin, D. (2001) A 33-year follow-up of narcotics addicts. *Archives of General Psychiatry*, 58(5), 503-508.

Hughes, J.R. (1996). Treating smokers with current or past alcohol dependence. *American Journal of Health Behavior*, 20(5), 286-290.

Hughes, J. R. (1995). Clinical implications of the association between smoking and alcoholism. In J. B. Fertig & J. P. Allen (Eds.), *Alcohol and Tobacco: From Basic Science to Clinical Practice*. (NIAAA Research Monograph No. 30, NIH Publication No 95-3931, pp. 171-185). Washington, Government Printing Office.

Humphreys, K. (2004). *Circles of Recovery: Self-Help Organizations for Addictions*. Cambridge: Cambridge University Press.

Humphreys, K., Mankowski, E., Moos, R. & Finney, J. (1999). Do enhanced friendship networks and active coping mediate the effect of self-help groups on substance abuse? *Annals of Behavioral Medicine*, 21(1), 54-60.

Humphreys, K., Mavis, B. E., & Stoffelmayr, B. E. (1994). Are twelve-step programs appropriate for disenfranchised groups? Evidence from a study of posttreatment mutual help group involvement. *Prevention in Human Services*, 11, 165-180.

Humphreys, K., Moos, R. J., & Cohen, C. (1997). Social and community resources and long-term recovery from treated and untreated alcoholism. *Journal of Studies on Alcohol*, 58(3), 231-238.

Humphreys, K., Wing, S., McCarty, D., Chappel, J., Galant, L., et al, (2004). Self-help organizations for alcohol and drug problems: Toward evidence-based practice and policy. *Journal of Substance Abuse Treatment*, 26(3), 151-158.

James, W. (1902, 1982). *The Varieties of Religious Experience*. New York: Penguin.

Jason, L.A., Davis, M.I., Ferrari, J.R. And Bishop, P. D. (2001) Oxford House: A review of research and implications for substance abuse recovery and community research. *Journal of Drug Education*, 31(1):1-27.

Jin, H., Rourke, S. B., Patterson, T. L., Taylor, M. J. & Grant, I. (1998). Predictors of relapse in long-term abstinent alcoholics. *Journal of Studies on Alcohol*, 59(6), 640-646.

Johnson, E. & Herringer, L. (1993). A note on the utilization of common support activities and relapse following substance abuse treatment. *Journal of Psychology*, 127(1), 73-78.

Jordan, C. M. & Oei, T. P. S. (1989). Help-seeking behavior in problem drinkers: A review. *British Journal of Addiction*, 84, 979-988.

Jorquez, J. (1983). The retirement phase of heroin using careers. *Journal of Drug Issues*, 18(3), 343-365.

Kandel, D. B. & Raveis, V. H. (1989). Cessation of drug use in young adulthood. *Archives of General Psychiatry*, 46(2), 109-116.

Kaskutas, L. (1992). Beliefs on the source of sobriety: Interactions of membership in Women for Sobriety and Alcoholics Anonymous. *Contemporary Drug Problems*, 19(4), 631-648.

Kelly, J. F., Myers, M. G., & Brown, S. A. (2002). Do adolescents affiliate with 12-step groups? A multivariate process model of effects. *Journal of Studies on Alcohol*, 63(3), 293-304.

Kessler, R. C., Mickelson, K. D. & Zhoa, S. (1997). Patterns and correlates of self-help group membership in the United States. *Social Policy*, 27(3), 27-45.

Kessler R. C., Nelson, C. B., McGonagle, K. A., Edlund, M. J., Frank, R. G., & Leaf, P. (1996). The epidemiology of co-occurring addictive and mental disorders: Implications for prevention and service utilization. *American Journal of Orthopsychiatry*, 66(1), 17-31.

Kirkpatrick, J. (1986). *Goodbye Hangovers, Hello Life*. New York: Ballantine Books.

Kishline, A. (1994). *Moderate Drinking*. Tucson, Arizona: See Sharp Press.

Kissin, W., McLeod, C. & McKay, J. (2003). The longitudinal relationship between self-help group attendance and course of recovery. *Evaluation and Program Planning*, 26, 311-323.

Klingemann, H. K. H. (1991). The motivation for change from problem alcohol and heroin use. *British Journal of the Addictions,* 86(6), 727-744.

Klingemann, H. K. H. (1992). Coping and maintenance strategies of spontaneous remitters from problem use of alcohol and heroin in Switzerland. *International Journal of the Addictions*, 27(12), 1359-1388.

Kreek, M. & Vocci, F. (2002). History and current status of opioid maintenance treatments. *Journal of Substance Abuse Treatment*, 23(2), 93-105.

Kurtines, W. M., Ball, L. R.& Wood, G. H. (1978). Personality characteristics of long-term recovered alcoholics: a comparative analysis. *Journal of Consulting and Clinical Psychology*, 46(5), 971-977.

Kurtz, E. (1999). *The Collected Ernie Kurtz.* Wheeling, WV: The Bishop of Books.

Kurtz, E. & Ketchum, K. (1992). *The Spirituality of Imperfection: Modern Wisdom from Classic Stories.* New York: Bantam Books.

Kurtz, E. & White, W. (2003). Alcoholics Anonymous. In J .Blocker and I. Tyrell (Eds.), *Alcohol and Temperance in Modern History* (pp. 27-31). Santa Barbara, CA: ABC-CLIO.

Larimer, M. E. & Kilmer, J. R. (2000). Natural history. In G. Zernig, A. Saria, M. Kurz, & S.S. O'Malley, (Eds.), *Handbook of Alcoholism* (pp. 13-28). Boca Raton, FL: CRC Press.

Larsen, E. (1985). *Stage II Recovery: Life Beyond Addiction.* New York, NY: HarperCollins Publishers.

Lender, M & Martin, J. (1982). *Drinking in America.* NY: The Free Press.

Levy, B. S. (1972) Five years later: A follow-up study of 50 narcotic addicts. *American Journal of Psychiatry*, 128(7),102-106.

Maddux, J. & Desmond, D. (1986). Relapse and recovery in substance abuse careers. In F. Tims & C. Leukefeld, (Eds.), *Relapse and Recovery in Drug Abuse. (NIDA Monograph Series* 72, pp. 49-72).

Maddux, J. F. & Desmond, D. P. (1980). New light on the maturing out hypothesis in opioid dependence. *Bulletin on Narcotics*, 32(1),15-25.

Maddux, J. F. & Desmond, D. P. (1981). *Careers of Opioid Users.* New York: Praeger.

Maddux, J. F. & Desmond, D. P. (1992). Ten-year follow-up after admission to methadone. *American Journal of Drug and Alcohol Abuse*, 18(3),289-303.

Margolis, R., Kilpatrick, A., & Mooney, B. (2000). A retrospective look at long-term adolescent recovery: Clinicians talk to researchers. *Journal of Psychoactive Drugs*, 32(1), 117-125.

McMurran, M. (1994). The Psychology of Addiction. Washington, D.C.: Taylor and Francis.

Meissen, G., Powell, T. J., Wituk, S. A., Girrens, K. & Artega, S. (1999). Attitudes of AA contact persons toward group participation by person with mental illness. *Psychiatric Services,* 50(8), 1079-1081.

Mental sobriety means spotting danger signals. (1946). *AA Grapevine,* March.

Miller, W. R. (1995). Toward a Biblical perspective on drug use. *Journal of Ministry in Addiction & Recovery,* 2(2), 77-86.

Miller, W. & C'de Baca, J. (2001). *Quantum Change: When Epiphanies and Sudden Insights Transform Ordinary Lives.* New York, NY: Guilford Press.

Miller, W. & Kurtz, E. (1994). Models of alcoholism used in treatment: contrasting AA and other perspectives with which it is often confused. *Journal of Studies on Alcohol,* 55(2), 159-166.

Miller, W. R., Walters, S. T., & Bennett, M. E. (2001). How effective is alcoholism treatment in the United States? *Journal of Studies on Alcohol,* 62(2), 211-220.

Montgomery, H. A., Miller, W. R., & Tonigan, J. S. (1995). Does Alcoholics Anonymous involvement predict treatment outcome? *Journal of Substance Abuse Treatment,* 12(4), 241-246.

Moos, H., Finney, M., & Cronkite, R.C. (1990). *Alcoholism treatment: Context, process and outcome.* New York: Oxford University Press.

Morgan, O.J. (1995a). Extended length sobriety: The missing variable. *Alcoholism Treatment Quarterly,* 12(1), 59-71.

Morgan, O.J. (1995b). Recovery-sensitive counseling in the treatment of alcoholism. *Alcoholism Treatment Quarterly,* 13(4), 63-73.

Morgenstern, J., Kahler, C. W., Frey, R. M. & Labouvie, E. (1996). Modeling therapeutic response to 12-step treatment: Optimal responders, nonresponders, partial responders. *Journal of Substance Abuse,* 8(1), 45-59.

Morgenstern, J., Labouvie, E., McCray, B. S., Kahler, C. W., & Frey, R. M. (1997). Affiliation with Alcoholics Anonymous after treatment: A study of its therapeutic effects and mechanisms of action. *Journal of Consulting and Clinical Psychology,* 65, 768-777.

Murphy, S. and Irwin, J. (1992). "Living with the dirty secret": Problems of disclosure for methadone maintenance clients. *Journal of Psychoactive Drugs,* 24(3), 257-264.

Musto, D. (1999). *The American Disease: Origins of Narcotic Control.* New York: Oxford University Press.

Myers, M. & Brown, S. (1990). *Cigarette smoking and health in adolescent substance abusers.* Paper presented at the Society of Behavioral Medicine, Chicago, IL.

Narcotics Anonymous. (1988). Van Nuys, CA: NA World Service Office, Inc.

Nathan, P. & Skinstad, A. (1987). Outcomes of treatment for alcohol problems: Current methods, problems and results. *Journal of Consulting and Clinical Psychology.* 55(3), 332-340.

National Consensus Development Panel on Effective Medical Treatment of Opiate Addiction (1998). Effective medical treatment of opiate addiction. *Journal of the American Medical Association*, 280(22):1936-1943. (See http://odp.od.nih.gov/consensus/cons/108/108_statement.htm)

National Institute on Drug Abuse. (1999). *Principles of Drug Addiction Treatment* (NIH Publication No. 00-4180). Rockville, MD: NIDA.

Ojesjo, L. (1981). Long-term outcome in alcohol abuse and alcoholism among males in Lundby general population, Sweden. *British Journal of Addiction*, 76, 391-400.

Ouimette, P., Humphreys, K., Moos, R., Finney, J. Cronkite, R. & Federman, B. (2001). Self-help participation among substance use disorder patients with posttraumatic stress disorder. *Journal of Substance Abuse Treatment*, 20(1), 25-32.

Pagano, M. E., Friend, K. B., Tonigan, J. S., & Stout, R. L. (2004). Helping other alcoholics in Alcoholics Anonymous and drinking outcomes: Findings from Project MATCH. *Journal of Studies on Alcohol,* 65(6), 766-773.

Pendery, M., Maltzman, I., West, L. (1982). Controlled drinking by alcoholics? New findings and a reevaluation of a major affirmative study. *Science*, 217, 169-175.

Picucci, M. (2002). An Interview with Dr. Michael Picucci; *Terms and Definitions.*

Pisani, V. D., Fawcett, J., Clark, D. C., & McGuire, M. (1993). The relative contributions of medication adherence and AA meeting attendance to abstinent outcome of chronic alcoholics. *Journal of Studies on Alcohol*, 54,115-119.

Polich, J. M., Armor, D. J., & Braiker, H. B. (1980). *The Course of Alcoholism: Four Years after Treatment.* New York: Wiley.

Prochaska, J., DiClimente, C., & Norcross, J. (1992). In search of how people change: Applications to addictive behaviors. *American Psychologist*, 47(9),1102-1114.

The Red Road to Wellbriety. (2002). Colorado Springs, CO: White Bison, Inc.

Room, R. (1989) The U.S. general population's experiences of responding to alcohol problems. *British Journal of Addiction*, 84(11), 1291-1304.

Room, R. & Greenfield, T. (1993). Alcoholics Anonymous, other 12-step movements, and psychotherapy in the U.S. Population, 1990. *Addiction*, 88(4), 555-562.

Rosenberg, H. (1993). Prediction of controlled drinking by alcoholics and problem drinkers. *Psychological Bulletin*, 113(1), 129-139.

Rouhbakhsh, P., Lewis, V., & Allen-Byrd, L. (2004). Recovering Alcoholic Families: When is normal not normal and when is not normal healthy? *Alcoholism Treatment Quarterly*, 22(2), 35-53.

Rychtarik, R. G., Connors, G. J., Demen, K. H. & Stasiewicz, P. R. (2000). Alcoholics Anonymous and the use of medications to prevent relapse: An anonymous survey of member attitudes. *Journal of Studies on Alcohol*, 61(1), 134-138.

Schutte, K., Brennan, P. & Moos, R. (1994). Remission of late-life drinking problems: A 4-year follow-up. *Alcoholism: Clinical and Experimental Research*, 18(4), 835-844.

Schutte, K. K., Nichols, K. A., Brennan, P. L., & Moos, R. H. (2001). Successful remission of late-life drinking problems. *Journal of Studies on Alcohol*, 64(3), 367-374.

Scott, C.K., Foss, M.A. & Dennis, M.L. (2005). Pathways in the relapse—treatment—recovery cycle over 3 years. *Journal of Substance Abuse Treatment*, 28, S63-S72.

Selby, M., Quiroga, Ireland, S, Malow, R. & Azrin, R. (1995). Neuropsychological recovery in alcoholics and cocaine users. In L. Harris (Ed.), *Problems of Drug Dependence, 1994: Proceedings of the 56th Annual Scientific Meeting, the College on Problems of Drug Dependence, Inc.* Volume 2 (NIDA Research Monograph 153). Rockville, MD: National Institute on Drug Abuse.

Shaffer, H. J. & Jones, S. B. (1989). *Quitting Cocaine: The Struggle Against Impulse.* Lexington, MA: Lexington Books.

Sheeren, M. (1988). The relationship between relapse and involvement in Alcoholics Anonymous. *Journal of Studies on Alcohol*, 49(1), 104-106.

Simpson, D. D. & Sells, S. B. (1990). *Opioid Addiction and Treatment: A 12-year Follow-up.* Malabar, FL.: Krieger.

Sobell, M.B. & Sobell, L.C. (1973). Individualized behavior therapy for alcoholics. *Behavior Therapy*, 4, 49-72.

Sobell, M.B. & Sobell, L.C. (1976). Second year treatment outcome of alcoholics treatment by individualized behavior therapy: Results. *Behavior Research and Therapy*, 14, 195-215.

Sobell, M.B. & Sobell, L.C. (1978). *Behavioral Treatment of Alcohol Problems.* New York: Plenum.

Sobell, M. B., Sobell, L. C. & Toneatto, T. (1991). Recovery from alcohol problems without treatment. In N. Heather, W. R. Miller and J. Greeley (Eds.) *Self Control and the Addictive Behaviors* (pp. 198-242). New York: Maxwell Macmillan. Sobell, L. C., Cunningham, J. A., & Sobell, M. B. (1996). Recovery from alcohol problems with and without treatment: Prevalence in two population surveys. American Journal of Public Health, 86(7), 966-972.

Sobell, L. C., Ellingstad, T., & Sobell, M. B. (2000). Natural recovery from alcohol and drug problems: Methodological review of the research with suggestions for future directions. *Addiction*, 95(5), 749-764.

Sobell, L.C., Sobell, M.C., Toneatto, T., & Leo, G.I. (1993). What triggers the resolution of alcohol problems without treatment? *Alcoholism: Clinical and Experimental Research*, 17, 217-224.

Substance Abuse and Mental Health Services Administration, Office of Applied Studies (2002). *Treatment Episode Data Set (TEDS): 1992-2000. National Admissions to Substance Abuse Treatment Services.* (DASIS Series: S-17, DHHS Publication No. (SMA) 02-3727). Rockville, MD: Substance Abuse and Mental Health Services Administration.

Substance Abuse and Mental Health Services Administration. (2003). *Results from the 2002 National Survey on Drug Use and Health: National Findings* (Office of Applied Studies, NHSDA Series H-22, DHHS Publication No. SMA 033836). Rockville, MD.

Sutton, S. (2001). Back to the drawing board? A review of the applications of the transtheoretical model of substance use. *Addiction*, 96, 175-186.

Tessina, T. (1991). *The Real Thirteenth Step: Discovering Confidence, Self-reliance and Autonomy beyond the 12-Step Programs.* Los Angeles, CA: Jeremy P. Tarcher, Inc.

Timko, C., Moos, R., Finney, J. & Moos, B. (1994). Outcome of treatment for alcohol abuse and involvement in Alcoholics Anonymous among previously untreated drinkers. *The Journal of Mental Health Administration*, 21(2),145-160.

Timko, C., Moos, R. H., Finney, J. W., Moos, B. S., & Kaplowitz, M. S. (1999). Long-term treatment careers and outcomes of previously untreated alcoholics. *Journal of Studies on Alcohol*, 60(4), 437-447.

Toneatto, A., Sobell, L. C., Sobell, M. B., & Rubel, E. (1999). Natural recovery from cocaine dependence. *Psychology of Addictive Behaviors*, 13(4), 259-268.

Tonigan, J. S., Miller, W. R., Chavez, R., Porter, N., Worth, L., Westphal, V, Carroll, L., Repa, K., Martin, A & Tracy, L. A. (2002). *AA participation 10 years after Project MATCH treatment: Preliminary findings.* Poster presentation, Research Society on Alcoholism, San Francisco, July.

Trachtenberg, R.L. (1984). *Report of the Steering Group to the administrator Alcohol, Drug Abuse and Mental Health Administration regarding its attempt to investigate allegations of scientific misconduct concerning Drs. Mark and Linda Sobell.* Alcohol, Drug Abuse and Mental Health Administration. Rockville, MD.

Tuchfeld, B. S. (1981). Spontaneous remission in alcoholics: Empirical observations and theoretical implications. *Journal of Studies on Alcohol*, 42, 626-641.

Tuchman, B. (1981). *Practicing History.* New York: Alfred A. Knopf.

Tucker, J. A., & Gladsjo, J. A. (1993). Help-seeking and recovery by problem drinkers: Characteristics of drinkers who attended Alcoholics Anonymous or formal treatment or who recovered without assistance. *Addictive Behaviors*, 18(5), 529-542.

Tucker, J. A., Vuchinich, R. E. & Gladsjo, J. A. (1994). Environmental events surrounding natural recovery from alcohol-related problems. *Journal of Studies on Alcohol*, 55(4), 401-411.

Vaillant, G. (1983). *The Natural History of Alcoholism: Causes, Patterns, and Paths to Recovery*. Cambridge, MA: Harvard University Press.

Vaillant, G. (2003). 60 year follow-up of alcoholic men. *Addiction*, 98(8), 1043-1051.

Vaillant, G. E. (1979). Paths out of alcoholism. In *Evaluation of the Alcoholic: Implications for Research, Theory and Treatment* (Research Monograph No. 5, pp. 383-394). Rockville, MD: National Institute of Alcohol Abuse and Alcoholism.

Vaillant, G. E. (1996). A long-term follow-up of male alcohol abuse. *Archives of General Psychiatry*, 53(3). 243-249.

Volpicelli, J. & Szalavitz, M. (2000). *Recovery Options*. New York: Wiley.

Waldorf, D. (1983). Natural recovery from opiate addiction: Some social-psychological processes of untreated recovery. *Journal of Drug Issues*, 13(2), 237-80.

Waldorf, D., Reinarman,C. & Murphy, S. (1991). *Cocaine Changes: The Experience of Using and Quitting*. Philadelphia, PA: Temple University.

Walters, S., Hester, R., Chiauzzi, E. & Miller, E. (2005). Demon rum: High-tech solutions to an age-old problem. *Alcoholism: Clinical & Experimental Research*, 29(2), 270-277.

Weiss, R.D., Griffin, M.L., Gallop, R., Onken, L., Gastfriend, D.R., Daley, D., Crits-Christoph, P., Bishop, S. & Barber, J. (2000). Self-help group attendance and participation among cocaine dependent patients. *Drug and Alcohol Dependence* 60(2), 169-177.

Weisner, C. (1993). Toward an alcohol treatment entry model: A comparison of problem drinkers in the general population and in treatment. *Alcoholism Clinical and Experimental Research*, 17(4), 746-752.

Weisner, C, Greenfield, T & Room, R. (1995). Trends in the treatment of alcohol problems in the U.S. population. *American Journal of Public Health*, 85(1), 55-60.

West, R. (2005). Time for a change: Putting the transtheoretical (stages of change) model to rest. *Addiction*, 100, 1036-1039.

White, W. (1996). *Pathways from the Culture of Addiction to the Culture of Recovery: A Travel Guide for Addiction Professionals* (2nd ed.). Center City, MN: Hazelden.

White, W. (1998). *Slaying the Dragon: The History of Addiction Treatment and Recovery in America*. Bloomington, IL: Chestnut Health Systems.

White, W. (2000). *Toward a new recovery movement: Historical reflections on recovery, treatment and advocacy*. Presented at Recovery Community Support Program (RCSP) Conference, April 3-5, 2000. Retrieved July 31, 2004 from http://www. facesandvoicesofrecovery.org/pdf/toward_new_recovery.pdf.

White, W. (2001) Pre-AA Alcoholic Mutual Aid Societies. *Alcoholism Treatment Quarterly* 19(1), 1-21.

White, W. (2004a). Recovery: The next frontier. *Counselor*, 5(1), 18-21.

White, W. (2004b). Transformational Change: A Historical Review. IN SESSION: *Journal of Clinical Psychology*, 60(5), 461-470.

White, W. (2004c). The history and future of peer-based addiction recovery support services. Prepared for the SAMHSA Consumer and Family Direction Initiative 2004 Summit, March 22-23, Washington, DC. Retrieved on September 19, 2005 from http://www.facesandvoicesofrecovery.org/pdf/peer-based_recovery.pdf

White, W. (2005). Recovery: Its history and renaissance as an organizing construct. *Alcoholism Treatment Quarterly*, 23(1), 3-15.

White, W., Boyle, M. & Loveland, D. (2002). Alcoholism/addiction as a chronic disease: From rhetoric to clinical reality. *Alcoholism Treatment Quarterly*, 20(3/4),107-130.

White, W. & Coon, B. (2003). Methadone and the anti-medication bias in addiction treatment. *Counselor*, 4(5), 58-63.

White, W. & Nicolaus, M. (2005). Styles of secular recovery. *Counselor*, 6(4), 58-61.

White, W. & Scott, C. (Draft Manuscript) Addiction recovery: Its definition and conceptual boundaries.

White, W. & Whiters, D. (2005). Faith-based recovery: Its historical roots. *Counselor*, 6(5), 58-62.

Wholey, D. (1984). *The Courage to Change: Personal Conversations about Alcoholism with Dennis Wholey*. New York: Warner Books.

Wilbourne, P., & Miller, W. (2003). Treatment of alcoholism: Older and wiser? *Alcoholism Treatment Quarterly*, 20(3/4), 41-59.

Willie, R. (1978). Preliminary communication--cessation of opiate dependence: processes involved in achieving abstinence. *British Journal of Addiction*, 73(4), 381-384.

Wilson, B. (1944). Bill's comments on Wylie ideas, hunches. *A.A. Grapevine*, 1(4), 4.

Wilson, B. (1958). The next frontier: Emotional sobriety. *A.A. Grapevine*, January, 2-5.

Wilson, B. (1962). Spiritual Experiences. *A.A. Grapevine*, July, 2-3.

Winick, C. (1962). Maturing out of narcotic addiction. *U.N. Bulletin on Narcotics*, 14,1-7 (January-March).

Winick, C. (1964). The life cycle of the narcotic addict and of addiction. *U.N. Bulletin on Narcotics*, 16(1),1-11.

Winzelberg, A. & Humphreys, K. (1999). Should patients' religiosity influence clinicians' referral to 12-step self-help groups? Evidence from a study of 3,018 male substance abuse patients. *Journal of Counseling and Clinical Psychology*, 67(5), 790-794.

Workgroup on Substance Abuse Self-Help Organizations (2003). *Self-Help Organizations for Alcohol and Other Drug Problems: Towards Evidence-based Practice and Policy.* (February 2003 Technical Report). SAMHSA.

Zweben, J. E. (1996). Psychiatric problems among alcohol and other drug dependent women. *Journal of Psychoactive Drugs,* 28(4), 345-366.

Zweben, J.E. (1986). Recovery oriented psychotherapy. *Journal of Substance Abuse Treatment,* 3, 255-262.

Acknowledgement: Financial support for the preparation of this paper was provided by the Great Lakes Addiction Technology Transfer Center (ATTC), which is funded by the Substance Abuse and Mental Health Services Administration/Center for Substance Abuse Treatment (SAMHSA/CSAT). The ideas expressed here are those of the authors and should not be interpreted as reflecting the opinions or policies of the Great Lakes ATTC and SAMHSA. The authors would like to extend their appreciation to Earl Harrison, whose comments and suggestions on our first draft of this paper were particularly helpful.

RECOVERY MANAGEMENT:
WHAT IF WE <u>REALLY</u> BELIEVED THAT ADDICTION WAS A CHRONIC DISORDER?

A quiet revolution is unfolding within the worlds of addiction treatment and recovery support. This revolution is founded on new understandings of the nature of substance use disorders and their management. It calls for shifting the treatment of severe and persistent alcohol and other drug (AOD) problems from an emergency room model of acute care (AC) to a model of sustained recovery management (RM). The RM model wraps traditional interventions in a continuum of recovery support services spanning the pre-recovery (recovery priming), recovery initiation and stabilization, and recovery maintenance stages of problem resolution. Particularly distinctive is the model's emphasis on post-treatment monitoring and support; long-term, stage-appropriate recovery education; peer-based recovery coaching; assertive linkage to communities of recovery; and, when needed, early re-intervention.

PROMOTIONAL FORCES

There are several forces pushing the addiction field toward a redesign of its treatment processes. Frontline addiction professionals are articulating (and a growing number of scientific studies are confirming) the limitations of addiction treatment as currently practiced. Grassroots recovery advocacy organizations are calling upon the treatment industry to reconnect professional treatment to the larger and more sustained process of addiction recovery. Pioneer states (e.g., Connecticut) are building research, clinical, and recovery advocacy coalitions to infuse the recovery management model into new "recovery-oriented systems of care." And finally, technological advances in the management of primary chronic health care problems (e.g., diabetes, heart disease, asthma, arthritis, cancer, chronic lung disease, glaucoma, irritable bowel syndrome) are suggesting alternative approaches through which severe and complex behavioral health disorders might be managed more effectively.

PREMISES

The shift from acute care to sustained recovery management models rests upon six propositions.

1. *Alcohol and other drug problems present in transient and chronic forms.* The transient forms vary in intensity, from the clinical (*substance abuse* and *substance dependence*) to the subclinical (problems not meeting DSM-IV criteria for abuse or dependence). Transient forms share a short duration (a single episode or period of problematic use) and a propensity for natural resolution or resolution through brief professional intervention. Transient AOD problems are common in community populations, but are more rarely represented among populations entering addiction treatment. Compared to community populations, clients entering addiction treatment are distinguished by:

   - greater personal vulnerability (e.g., family history of substance use disorders, early age of onset of AOD use, developmental trauma),
   - greater severity and intensity of use and related consequences,
   - high concurrence of medical/psychiatric illnesses,
   - greater personal and environmental obstacles to recovery, and
   - less "recovery capital" (the internal and external resources required to initiate and sustain recovery).

2. *The evidence is overwhelming that the course of severe substance use disorders and their successful resolution (addiction, treatment, and recovery careers) can span years, if not decades.* Alcohol and other drug dependencies resemble chronic disorders (e.g., type 2 diabetes mellitus, hypertension, and asthma) in their etiological complexity (interaction of genetic, biological, psychological, and physical/social environmental factors), onset (gradual), course (prolonged waxing and waning of symptoms), treatment (management rather than cure), and clinical outcomes. To characterize addiction as a chronic disorder is not to suggest that recovery is not a possibility. There are millions of people in stable, long-term recovery from addiction. The notion of addiction as a chronic disorder does, however, underscore the often-long course of

such disorders and the sustained "treatment careers" that can precede stable recovery. Recent studies have confirmed that the majority of people with severe and persistent substance use disorders (e.g., substance dependence) who achieve a year of stable recovery do so following 3-4 treatment episodes over a span of eight years.

3. *Severe and persistent AOD problems have been collectively depicted as a "chronic, progressive disease" for more than 200 years, but their historical treatment more closely resembles interventions into acute health conditions (e.g., traumatic injuries, bacterial infections).* If we (the practitioners of addiction treatment) really believed addiction was a chronic disorder, we would not:

*   view prior treatment as a predictor of poor prognosis (and grounds for denial of treatment admission);
*   convey the expectation that all clients should achieve complete and enduring sobriety following a single, brief episode of treatment;
*   punitively discharge clients for becoming symptomatic;
*   relegate post-treatment continuing care services to an afterthought;
*   terminate the service relationship following brief intervention; or
*   treat serious and persistent AOD problems in serial episodes of self-contained, unlinked interventions.

4. *Acute models of treatment are not the best frameworks for treating severe and persistent AOD problems.* The limitations of the acute model of addiction treatment as currently practiced include:

*   Failure to Attract: Less than 10% of U.S. citizens who meet DSM-IV criteria for substance abuse or dependence currently seek treatment, and most of those admitted to treatment arrive under coercive influences.
*   Failure to Engage/Retain: More than half of the people admitted to addiction treatment in the U.S. do not successfully complete treatment, and 18% of people admitted to addiction treatment are administratively discharged from treatment.
*   Inadequate Service Dose: A significant percentage of individuals completing treatment receive less than the optimum dose of treatment recommended by the National Institute on Drug Abuse.
*   Lack of Continuing Care: Post-discharge continuing care can enhance recovery outcomes, but only one in five clients actually receives such care.

- <u>Recovery Outcomes</u>: The majority of people completing addiction treatment in the U.S. resume AOD use in the year following treatment, most within 90 days of discharge from treatment.
- <u>Revolving Door</u>: Of those admitted to publicly funded addiction treatment, 60% already have one or more prior treatment admissions, and 24% have three or more prior admissions. Between 25% and 35% of clients who complete addiction treatment will be re-admitted to treatment within one year, and 50% will be re-admitted within 2-5 years.

A large number of people are undergoing repeated episodes of brief interventions whose designs have little ability to fundamentally alter the trajectory of substance dependence and its related consequences. This failure does not result from client foibles or the inadequate execution of clinical protocol by service professionals. It flows instead from a fundamental flaw in the design of the intervention — an acute-care model of treating addiction that is analogous to treating diabetes or asthma through a single, self-contained episode of inpatient stabilization. In the AC model, brief symptom stabilization is misinterpreted as evidence of sustainable recovery.

5. *Most people discharged from addiction treatment are precariously balanced between recovery and re-addiction in the weeks, months, and years following treatment. Recent studies have confirmed the fluidity of post-treatment adjustment.* One such study conducted quarterly monitoring interviews of 1,326 clients over three years following an index episode of addiction treatment. Each client was categorized each quarter as 1) in the community using, 2) incarcerated, 3) in treatment, or 4) in the community not using. More than 80% of the clients changed status one or more times over the course of the three years. Beyond the groups of clients who categorically succeed or do not succeed stands a larger body of clients who vacillate between periods of recovery and periods of re-addiction. The precarious nature of early recovery is further confirmed by longer-term studies finding that stable recovery from alcoholism (the point at which the future risk of lifetime relapse drops below 15%) is not achieved until 4-5 years of continuous recovery, and that stable recovery from opiate addiction takes even longer. Such findings beg for models of sustained post-treatment monitoring and support.

PROMISES AND PROSPECTS

Recovery management models hold great promise in treating severe and complex substance use disorders. Chronic disorders are disorders that resist cure via brief intervention but can often be successfully managed (the achievement of full or partial recovery). Such management entails care and sustained support aimed at enhancing the strength, quality, and durability of remission periods and shortening the frequency, duration, and intensity of relapse episodes. This longer-term vision of the treatment and recovery process is based on several critical assumptions:

- A single brief episode of treatment rarely has sufficient effect for those with the most severe substance use disorders to sustain recovery following the intervention.
- Multiple episodes of treatment, if they are integrated within a recovery management plan, can constitute incremental steps in the developmental process of recovery.
- Treatment episodes over time may generate cumulative effects.
- Particular combinations and sequences of professional treatment interventions and peer-based recovery support services may generate synergistic effects (dramatically elevated long-term recovery outcomes).

RM models are focusing initially on the power of post-treatment monitoring and recovery support services. Early studies are confirming the potential utility of such approaches. One study of recovery management checkups (RMC) and early re-intervention over 24 months following treatment found that members of the RMC group had significantly fewer post-treatment days of substance use, were more likely to return to treatment, were more likely to return to treatment sooner, received treatment on a greater number of days following discharge from the index episode, and experienced fewer quarters during follow-up in which they were in need of treatment.

Treating alcohol and other drug dependence solely through repeated episodes of detoxification and brief stabilization is clinically ineffective and constitutes a poor stewardship of personal and community resources. It contributes to the pessimism of clients, service providers, policy makers, and the public regarding the prospects for permanent resolution of alcohol and other drug problems. It is time we acted as if we really believed addiction was a chronic disorder. Today millions of people are reaping the fruits of recovery while others continue to suffer. It is time we widened the doorway of entry into recovery for those with the most severe and persistent substance use disorders. To achieve that will require changes in our thinking, changes in our clinical technologies, and changes in systems of service reimbursement.

MODEL DEFINITION

The recovery management model of addiction treatment shifts the focus of care from professional-centered episodes of acute symptom stabilization toward the client-directed management of long-term recovery. It wraps traditional interventions within a more sustained continuum of:

- pre-recovery support services to enhance recovery readiness,
- in-treatment recovery support services to enhance the strength and stability of recovery initiation, and
- post-treatment recovery support services to enhance the durability and quality of recovery maintenance.

The influence of this emerging model is evident in many quarters. It is evident in the research community's exploration of addiction as a chronic disease (O'Brien & McLellan, 1996; McLellan, Lewis, O'Brien, & Kleber, 2000). It is reflected in the work of the Behavioral Health Recovery Management project in Illinois (White, Boyle, & Loveland, 2003a/b) and other pioneer state efforts to reshape addiction treatment into a "recovery-oriented system of care" (e.g., see http://www.dmhas.state.ct.us/recovery.htm). Interest in recovery management at the federal level is revealed in the move toward a more recovery-oriented research agenda at NIAAA and NIDA, in SAMHSA and CSAT's growing interest in peer-based models of recovery support services (particularly within CSAT's Recovery Community Support Program), and in the White House-initiated Access to Recovery program funded and administered by CSAT. Private sector interest in recovery-focused treatment system enhancements is reflected in the Robert Wood Johnson Foundation's Paths to Recovery Initiative (http://www.pathstorecovery.org). The shift from acute intervention models to models of sustained recovery support are further reflected in the policy agendas of new grassroots recovery advocacy organizations across the country (see http://www.facesandvoiceofrecovery.org).

Describing the emerging "model" of recovery management is a bit like describing a painting while it is being created, but there are broad principles and early changes in clinical practices that are becoming visible. There may be no single program in the country that reflects all the changes described below, but these changes do collectively represent what is increasingly being characterized as a model of *recovery management*.

MODEL PRINCIPLES

There are several cornerstone beliefs that distinguish the recovery management model from acute models of addiction treatment. These principles and values include:

- emphasis on resilience and recovery processes (as opposed to pathology and disease processes),
- recognition of multiple long-term pathways and styles of recovery,
- empowerment of individuals and families in recovery to direct their own healing,
- development of highly individualized and culturally nuanced services,
- heightened collaboration with diverse communities of recovery, and
- commitment to best practices as identified in the scientific literature and through the collective experience of people in recovery. (http://www.bhrm. org/papers/principles/ BHRMprinciples.htm and http://www.dmhas.state.ct.us/ corevalues.htm)

MODEL PRACTICES

White, Boyle, and Loveland's (2003a/b) review of recovery management (RM) pilot programs reveals several critical differences between the RM models and traditional acute care (AC) models of intervention. These differences span seven broad areas of clinical practice.

Engagement and Motivational Enhancement: RM models place great emphasis on engagement and motivational enhancement. This emphasis is reflected in low thresholds of engagement (inclusive recruitment and admission processes), an investment in outreach and pre-treatment support services, and high retention and low post-admission extrusion (administrative discharge) rates. Within the RM model, motivation is viewed as an important factor in long-term recovery, but is viewed as something that emerges within the service relationship rather than a precondition for service initiation. This emphasis is based on two premises: 1) chronic disorders increase in complexity and severity over time, and 2) recovery outcomes are enhanced by the earliest possible point of recovery initiation and stabilization. AC models of addiction treatment are essentially reactive in their wait for individuals to enter states of crisis that bring them to treatment. RM models reach out to people prior to such crises and sustain contact with them to re-nurture motivation for recovery following such crises.

Assessment and Service Planning: In traditional treatment, the clinical assessment is categorical (focused on substance use and its consequences), is pathology-based (focused on the identification and elucidation of problems), and is an intake activity. Problem severity dictates level of care, and the problems list drives the development of the treatment plan. In recovery management models, assessment is global (focused on the whole life of the recovering person), asset-based (focused on recovery capital — internal and external assets that can help initiate and sustain recovery), and is continual over the span of the service relationship. This altered view of the assessment process is based on three propositions:

1. Chronic disorders beget other acute and chronic problems; therefore, all aspects of the life of the recovering person must be assessed and incorporated into an integrated recovery process.
2. Service intensity and duration are dictated by the interaction of problem severity and recovery capital; therefore, problem severity alone is an inadequate and disempowering framework for service planning.
3. There are developmental stages of long-term recovery, and service and support needs can shift dramatically in the transition from one stage to another; therefore, stage-dependent service needs must be continually reevaluated.

The traditional professionally directed, short-term treatment plan of the acute care model is replaced in the RM model by long-term and short-term recovery plans prepared by the person seeking recovery. The former focuses primarily on reducing pathology; the latter focuses on building recovery capital and a meaningful life.

Service Duration and Emphasis: Acute care models do an excellent job of biopsychosocial stabilization, but often fail to facilitate the transition between recovery initiation and recovery maintenance. The evidence of such failure can be found in post-treatment relapse and treatment re-admission rates (see previous article in this series). Recovery management models rest on the assumption that the factors required to sustain recovery over a lifetime are different than those factors that spark brief sobriety experiments. The recovery management model emphasizes four post-treatment service activities: sustained post-stabilization monitoring; stage-appropriate recovery education and coaching; assertive linkage to local communities of recovery; and, when needed, early re-intervention. Detoxification and traditional treatment exist within

RM models, but the focus of service shifts from crisis intervention to post-treatment recovery support services.

Locus of Services: The institutional focus of the acute care model ("How do we get the addicted person into treatment?") shifts within the RM model to the larger community ("How do we nest the process of recovery within the client's natural environment?"). With this shift, there is a greater emphasis on home- and neighborhood-based services and indirect monitoring technology (e.g., telephone, mail, Internet), as well as an emphasis on organizing indigenous recovery support services within the client's physical and social environment. The RM model also pushes treatment agencies toward greater advocacy responsibilities related to stigma and discrimination, the removal of environmental obstacles to recovery, and the development of needed recovery support resources within local communities.

Role of the Client: In acute care models of intervention, the person entering treatment is viewed as the major obstacle to his or her own recovery, and thus is dependent upon an expert who assumes fiduciary responsibility for diagnosis and treatment. RM models champion the necessity and right of the person who is seeking recovery to self-manage his or her own recovery process. Each client must become an expert on his or her condition and its management. This emphasis is reflected in the client's role in service planning and evaluation, as well as in the RM model's inclusion of recovering people and family members in policy-making positions and as volunteers and paid service providers.

Service Relationship: The service relationship within the RM model shifts from one that is hierarchical, time-limited, and highly commercialized (the AC model) to one that is less hierarchical, more time-sustained, and more natural. In the RM model, the service provider role is more that of a teacher and ally within a long-term health care partnership. RM models are also pioneering new approaches to peer-based recovery support services that utilize new service roles, e.g., peer counselors, recovery coaches, recovery support specialists (White, 2004). The RM model emphasizes the importance of sustained continuity of contact in a primary recovery support relationship. This relationship would be analogous to the long-term alliance between a primary care physician and his or her diabetic patient or the long-term support that exists within addiction recovery mutual aid societies.

Model Evaluation: The evaluation of acute care models of addiction treatment focuses on measuring the short-term effects of a single, brief episode of intervention.

Evaluation within the RM model focuses on measuring the long-term effects of multiple service interventions. The goal is to identify particular combinations or sequences of clinical and recovery support services that generate dramatically elevated (cumulative or synergistic) effects upon recovery outcomes within particular populations. The RM model also balances science-based evaluations of service outcomes with consumer and community/ tribal evaluations of service processes and recovery outcomes.

Today, elements of the RM model exist within many traditional treatment programs that have evolved toward more client-responsive clinical policies and practices. Elements of the model exist within CSAT's Recovery Community Support Program and RWJ's Paths to Recovery grantee sites. The model is being tested within research studies that are evaluating elements of the RM model. It exists within the growing network of recovery homes and recovery support centers. The recovery management model of intervening with severe substance use disorders marks a dramatic change in the design of addiction treatment in the United States. Time will tell whether this model will struggle as a loosely attached appendage to the existing system of addiction treatment or whether it will transform addiction treatment in the United States into a truly recovery-oriented system of care and long-term support.

IMPLEMENTATION CHALLENGES

The scientific evidence documenting the need to shift addiction treatment from an acute model of intervention to a model of sustained recovery management is so overwhelming it leaves one wondering why this model is not yet fully implemented. The roots of this failure are historical, conceptual, financial, organizational, and technical.

The first barriers to treating addiction as a chronic disorder are the forces of historical and conceptual momentum. The modern field of addiction treatment is rooted in an acute biopsychological model of intervention. Addiction treatment programs were created in the image of the acute care hospital (via the profound influence of hospital-derived accreditation standards). The central service role in addiction treatment was similarly modeled after the therapy disciplines of psychiatry, psychology, and social work (via addiction counselor certification and licensure standards). For those of us steeped in the modern world of addiction treatment, it is almost impossible to think of treatment in terms other than number of days or number of sessions, and hard to think about continuing care as anything beyond the availability of a short regimen of "aftercare" sessions. We have viewed addiction treatment in terms of multiple levels of care and theory-based modalities, but have failed to recognize that all of

William L. White

these approaches are nested within an acute care model of assess, admit, treat, and discharge. To escape this closed conceptual world, programs exploring the RM model are re-educating their service workers and are conducting a rigorously honest, recovery-focused inventory of their current service practices.

All of the reimbursement and regulatory systems that govern addiction treatment are based on the acute care model. These structures, originally designed to elevate the consistency and quality of addiction treatment, now constitute a major barrier to shifting to more recovery-oriented systems of care. When programs embracing the RM philosophy seek to admit families rather than individuals, create multi-agency service teams that include indigenous institutions and cultural healers, utilize long-term recovery plans rather than short-term treatment plans, incorporate peer-based recovery support roles/teams, develop non-clinical recovery support systems in local communities, and provide long-term monitoring and early re-intervention services, they find themselves facing almost insurmountable fiscal and regulatory barriers. It is tragic and ironic that the major challenges of recovery management are posed, not by the complex needs of individuals and families seeking recovery, but by the systems originally set up to help facilitate that recovery. The mainstream implementation of recovery management will require a major overhaul of the reimbursement and regulatory systems governing addiction treatment. States like Connecticut that have begun this overhaul process are making a significant contribution to the future of addiction treatment and recovery in America (http://www.dmhas.state.ct.us/recovery.htm).

Slowing the development and implementation of RM models are the weak organizational infrastructures and high staff turnover rates that pervade the world of addiction treatment (McLellan, Carise, & Kleber, 2003). RM is founded on the continuity of relationship between an organization and the communities it serves and the capacity for sustained continuity of contact between each organization's front-line service professionals and the individuals and families within those communities who suffer from severe and persistent AOD problems. If there is an Achilles heel of the RM model, it is in the combined effects of organizational instability and staff turnover within the addictions field (Roman, Blum, Johnson, & Neal, 2002). If the process of RM is to parallel that of the long-term relationship between a primary care physician and a patient/family impacted by a chronic disease, that instability and turnover must be reversed.

The lack of a <u>science-based understanding of long-term recovery</u> constitutes a significant obstacle to the design of RM programs. As a field, our scientific knowledge about addiction and brief models of treatment has grown exponentially in recent decades, but our science has yet to connect the problem and the intervention to the process of long-term recovery. We know comparatively little from the standpoint of science about the prevalence, pathways, and styles of long-term recovery. The ability to find potent combinations and sequences of professionally directed treatment interventions and peer-based recovery support services rests on the emergence of a recovery research agenda at the federal level. Without scientific data, RM pioneers will lack a reliable compass to navigate the recovery frontier.

A fifth obstacle in implementing RM models of care involves the <u>integration of professional-directed treatment services and peer-based recovery support services</u> (particularly within the newly emerging role of recovery coach). Questions abound related to such integration. Are recovery support services best provided by addiction treatment organizations or by free-standing recovery support and recovery advocacy organizations? Should recovery support services be added to the role of addiction counselor or segregated within a new specialized role? What are the best ways to recruit, train and supervise recovery support specialists? What are the boundaries of competence of these new recovery support specialist roles, and how do they fit into larger multidisciplinary teams? Which models of integrating or coordinating professional and peer-based recovery support services are associated with the best long-term recovery outcomes? Answers to such questions are crucial to the future evolution of the RM model, and their absence constitutes a major implementation obstacle.

The <u>service capacity</u> of an organization or service professional within the RM model has yet to be clearly defined. If, for example, an addiction counselor is responsible for providing ongoing monitoring and support, stage-appropriate recovery education, assertive linkage to communities of recovery, and early re-intervention services for those leaving traditional inpatient or outpatient treatment, what is a reasonable caseload for such a counselor? The answer is that we do not know. RM will require a significant reallocation of resources — a shift that will de-emphasize expensive, high-intensity acute care and emphasize lower-intensity, lower-cost, and more enduring recovery support services. Service capacities for organizations and individual workers will have to be redefined in that transition.

The <u>ethical guidelines</u> that have guided addiction treatment agencies and addiction counselors for the past three decades grew out of the acute care service relationship and were closely modeled after the ethical guidelines for psychologists and social workers (e.g., discouragement or prohibition of self-disclosure, prohibition of all dual relationships, prohibition of gifts, etc.). These guidelines, which presupposed a short-term, expert-based fiduciary service relationship, do not easily fit the less hierarchical and more enduring service relationships that characterize the RM model. It is crucial that ethical standards evolve to guide the provision of professionally delivered and peer-based recovery support services. The lack of current ethical guidelines for recovery support services raises the ethical vulnerability of service organizations and service professionals.

POTENTIAL PITFALLS

This three-part series on the recovery management model of addiction treatment and recovery support would be incomplete without an exploration of some of the potential pitfalls of the RM model. Experience to-date suggests three potential pitfalls beyond the implementation challenges noted above.

Not everyone with an AOD-related problem needs RM services. Many individuals with such problems will resolve these problems on their own or will do so through mutual aid or brief professional intervention. Misapplying an RM model to persons with low problem severity and high recovery capital could generate iatrogenic effects within the RM model. Such misapplication could injure persons with transient AOD problems by inappropriately attaching a stigma-laden diagnosis and delivering services that are ineffective, a financial burden, and potentially harmful.

The emphasis on addiction as a chronic disorder within the RM model could inadvertently contribute to cultural pessimism about the resolution of AOD problems and heighten the stigma and discrimination attached to those problems (Brown, 1998). To counter such effects, RM models must constantly emphasize the reality of full recovery in the lives of millions of people who have suffered from severe and prolonged AOD problems.

The 1980s witnessed a period of institutional profiteering in which persons with alcohol and other drug problems were viewed as a crop to be harvested for financial profit. A too-rapid shift to RM models of reimbursement could unleash the same forces. Profiteers could garner large, capitated contracts for recovery support services, but then minimize the services delivered through such contracts to maximize institutional and personal profit. These profiteers could escape accountability for recovery outcomes behind the rhetoric that addiction is a chronic disease. To avoid this, RM models of reimbursement must include a high level of accountability for recovery outcomes. This will require clinical information systems that can track clinical outcomes and other performance indicators across multiple episodes of care.

Attempts to shift addiction treatment from a revolving emergency room door (via unending cycles of brief intervention) to a model of sustained recovery management face many implementation obstacles and potential pitfalls. These obstacles and pitfalls are offset by the potential of the RM model to align the design of addiction treatment with the growing body of scientific evidence documenting the chronicity of severe AOD problems and the complexity of long-term recovery. That potential and what it means for millions of people suffering from addiction will inspire many addiction professionals and addiction treatment organizations to experiment with this fundamental redesign of addiction treatment.

References and Recommended Reading

Anglin, M. D., Hser, Y. I., & Grella, C. E. (1997). Drug addiction and treatment careers among clients in the Drug Abuse Treatment Outcome Study (DATOS). *Psychology of Addictive Behaviors,* 11(4), 308-323.

Brown, B.S. (1998). Drug use: Chronic and relapsing or a treatable condition? *Substance Use and Misuse*, 33(12), 2515-2520.

Brown, S., Mott, M. & Stewart, M. (1992) Adolescent alcohol and drug abuse. In: Walker, C.E. Ed., *Handbook of Clinical Child Psychology* (2nd ed.), pp. 677-693.

Dawson, D.A. (1996). Correlates of past-year status among treated and untreated persons with former alcohol dependence: United States, 1992. *Alcoholism: Clinical and Experimental Research*, 20, 771-779.

Dennis, M. L., Scott, C. K., & Funk, R. (2003). An experimental evaluation of recovery management checkups (RMC) for people with chronic substance use disorders. *Evaluation and Program Planning*, 26(3), 339-352.

Dennis, M.L., Scott, C.K., & Hristova, L. (2002). The duration and correlates of substance abuse treatment careers among people entering publicly funded treatment in Chicago. (Abstract). *Drug and Alcohol Dependence*, 66(Suppl. 2).

Dennis, M.L., Scott, C.K., Funk, R.R., & Foss, M.A. (2005). The duration and correlates of addiction and treatment. *Journal of Substance Abuse Treatment*, 28 (Supplement 1), S51-S62.

Finney, J. & Moos, R. (1995). Entering treatment for alcohol abuse: a stress and coping model. *Addiction*, 90:1223-1240.

Godley, M.D., Godley, S.H., Dennis, M.L., Funk, R.R., & Passetti, L.L. (2004). Findings from the assertive continuing care experiment with adolescents with substance use disorders. In W. Dewey *Problems of Drug Dependence, 2003: Proceedings of the 65th Annual Scientific Meeting, The College on Problems of Drug Dependence, Inc.* (NIDA Research Monograph Series 184. pp. 123-124).

Godley, S. H., Godley, M. D., & Dennis, M. L. (2001). The assertive aftercare protocol for adolescent substance abusers. In E. Wagner, & H. Waldron (Eds.), *Innovations in Adolescent Substance Abuse Interventions* (pp. 311-329). New York: Elsevier Science.

Grella, C.E. and Joshi, V. (1999) Gender differences in drug treatment careers among the National Drug Abuse Treatment Outcome Study. *American Journal of Drug and Alcohol Abuse*, 25(3), 385-406.

Hser, Y., Hoffman, V., Grella, C. & Anglin, D. (2001). A 33-year follow-up of narcotics addicts. *Archives of General Psychiatry*, 58:503-508.

Hubbard, R. L., Flynn, P. M., Craddock, S. G. & Fletcher, B. W. (2001). Relapse after drug abuse treatment. In F. M. Tims, C. G. Leukefeld, & J. J. Platt (Eds.), *Relapse and Recovery in Addictions* (pp. 109-121). New Haven: Yale University Press.

Hubbard, R.L., Marsden, M.E., Rachal, J.V., Harwood, H.J. Cavanaugh, E.R. & Ginzburg, H.M. (1989). *Drug Abuse Treatment: A National Study of Effectiveness.* Chapel Hill, NC: University of North Carolina Press.

Humphreys, K. (2004). *Circles of Recovery: Self-Help Organizations for Addictions.* Cambridge: Cambridge University Press.

Jin, H., Rourke, S.B., Patterson, T.L., Taylor, M.J. & Grant, I. (1998) Predictors of relapse in long-term abstinent alcoholics. *Journal of Studies on Alcohol*, 59:640-646.

Johnson, E. & Herringer, L. (1993). A note on the utilization of common support activities and relapse following substance abuse treatment. *Journal of Psychology*, 127:73-78.

McKay, J.R. (2001). Effectiveness of continuing care interventions for substance abusers: Implications for the study of long-term effects. *Evaluation Review*, 25, 211-232.

McLellan, A. T., Lewis, D. C., O'Brien, C. P., & Kleber, H. D. (2000). Drug dependence, a chronic medical illness: Implications for treatment, insurance, and outcomes evaluation. *Journal of the American Medical Association*, 284(13), 1689-1695.

McLellan, A.T., Carise, D. & Kleber, H.D. (2003). Can the national addiction treatment infrastructure support the public's demand for quality care? *Journal of Substance Abuse Treatment*, 25:117-121.

McLellan, A.T., Carise, D., and Kleber, H.D. (2003). Can the national addiction treatment infrastructure support the public's demand for quality care? *Journal of Substance Abuse Treatment*, 25:117-121.

NIDA (1999). Principles of Drug Addiction Treatment. Rockville, MD: National Institute on Drug Abuse (NIH Publication No. 00-4180) (available at http://www.nida.nih.gov/PODAT/PODATIndex.html)

O'Brien, C. & McLellan, T. (1996). Myths about the Treatment of Addiction. *Lancet*, 347:237-240.

Roman, P.M., Blum, T.C., Johnson, J.A., & Neal, M. (2002). *National Treatment Center Study Summary Report* (No 5). Athens, GA: University of Georgia.

Roman, P.M., Blum, T.C., Johnson, J.A., & Neal, M. (2002). *National Treatment Center Study Summary Report* (No 5). Athens, GA: University of Georgia.

Ross, H. E., Lin, E., & Cunningham, J. (1999). Mental health service use: A comparison of treated and untreated individuals with substance use disorders in Ontario. *Canadian Journal of Psychiatry*, 44, 570-577.

Scott, C. K, Foss, M. A., & Dennis, M. L. (2003). Factors influencing initial and longer-term responses to substance abuse treatment: A path analysis. *Evaluation and Program Planning*, 26(3), 287-295.

Scott, C. K, Foss, M. A., & Dennis, M. L. (2005). Pathways in the relapse-treatment-recovery cycle over three years. *Journal of Substance Abuse Treatment*, 28(Supplement 1), S63-S72.

Simpson, D.D., Joe, G.W., & Broome, K.M. (2002). A national 5-year follow-up of treatment outcomes for cocaine dependence. *Archives of General Psychiatry*, 59, 539-544.

Substance Abuse and Mental Health Services Administration Office of Applied Studies. (2001). Treatment Episode Data Set (TEDS) *1994-1999: National Admissions to Substance Abuse Treatment Services*. Table (4.16.01). DASIS Series S14, DHHS Publication No. (SMA) 01-3550. Rockville, MD: Substance Abuse and Mental Health Services Administration.

Substance Abuse and Mental Health Services Administration Office of Applied Studies (2002). Treatment Episode Data Set (TEDS): 1992-2000. *National Admissions to Substance Abuse Treatment Services*, DASIS Series: S-17, DHHS Publication No. (SMA) 02-3727, Rockville, MD, 2002. http://wwwdasis.samhsa.gov/teds00/TEDS_2K_Highlights.htm; http://wwwdasis.samhsa.gov/teds00/TEDS_2K_Chp6.htm#Length of Stay).

Substance Abuse and Mental Health Services Administration. (2003). *Results from the 2002 National Survey on Drug Use and Health: National Findings* (Office of Applied Studies, NHSDA Series H-22, DHHS Publication No. SMA 03–3836). Rockville, MD.

White, W. (2004). The history and future of peer-based addiction recovery support services. Prepared for the SAMHSA Consumer and Family Direction Initiative 2004 Summit, March 22-23, Washington, DC. (Available at http://www.bhrm.org).

White, W., Boyle, M. & Loveland, D. (2003a) Addiction as chronic disease: From rhetoric to clinical application. *Alcoholism Treatment Quarterly*, 3/4:107-130.

White, W., Boyle, M. & Loveland, D. (2003b) Recovery Management: A model to transcend the limitations of addiction treatment. *Behavioral Health Management* 23(3):38-44. (http://www.behavioral.net/2003_05-06/featurearticle.htm).

White, W., Boyle, M. And Loveland, D. (2003). Addiction as chronic disease: From rhetoric to clinical application. *Alcoholism Treatment Quarterly*, 3/4:107-130.

Wilbourne, P and Miller, W. (2003). Treatment of alcoholism: Older and wiser? In T. McGovern & W. White (eds.), *Alcohol Problems in the United States: Twenty Years of Treatment Perspective*. New York: Haworth Press, pp. 41-59.

White, W., Boyle, M. And Loveland, D. (2003). Recovery Management: Transcending the Limitations of Addiction Treatment. *Behavioral Health Management* 23(3):38-44.

White, W. (2004). The history and future of peer-based addiction recovery support services. Prepared for the SAMHSA Consumer and Family Direction Initiative 2004 Summit, March 22-23, Washington, DC.

Recovery Management and People of Color: Redesigning Addiction Treatment for Historically Disempowered Communities.

William L, White, MA and Mark Sanders, LCSW, CADC

Abstract

Communities of color have been ill-served by acute care models of treating severe alcohol and other drug (AOD) problems that define the source of these problems in idiopathic (biopsychological) terms and promote their resolution via crisis-elicited episodes of brief, individual interventions. This article explores how approaches that shift the model of intervention from acute care (AC) of individuals to a sustained recovery management (RM) partnership with individuals, families, and communities may be particularly viable for historically disempowered peoples. The advantages of the RM model for communities of color include: a broadened perspective on the etiological roots of AOD problems (including historical/cultural trauma); a focus on building vibrant cultures of recovery within which individual recoveries can be anchored and nourished; a proactive, hope-based approach to recovery engagement; the inclusion of indigenous healers and institutions with the RM team; an expanded menu of recovery support services; culturally grounded catalytic metaphors and rituals; and a culturally nuanced approach to research and evaluation.

Introduction

Addiction has been characterized as a "chronic, progressive disease" for more than 200 years (White, 2000a), but interventions into severe alcohol and other drug (AOD) problems continue to be based on serial episodes of self-encapsulated, acute intervention (O'Brien & McLellan, 1996; Kaplan, 1997). Recent research has confirmed the chronic nature of severe AOD problems (Simpson, Joe, & Lehman, 1986; Hser, Anglin, Grella, Longshore, & Pendergast, 1997) and compared such problems to other chronic health disorders (e.g., type 2 diabetes mellitus, hypertension, and asthma) in terms of their etiological complexity, variability of course, and recovery and relapse rates (McLellan, Lewis, O'Brien, & Kleber, 2000). Calls for shifting addiction treatment from an acute care (AC) model to a model of sustained recovery management (RM) are increasing (White, Boyle, & Loveland, 2002, 2003; Compton, Glantz, & Delaney, 2003; Edwards, Davis, and Savva, 2003; Moore & Budney, 2003), and components of such models are currently being evaluated with adolescents (Godley, Godley, Dennis, Funk, & Passetti, 2002) and adults (Dennis, Scott & Funk, 2003). The emerging model of recovery management has been defined as:

> ...the stewardship of personal, family and community resources to achieve the highest level of global health and functioning of individuals and families impacted by severe behavioral health disorders. It is a time-sustained, recovery-focused collaboration between service consumers and traditional and non-traditional service providers toward the goal of stabilizing, and then actively managing the ebb and flow of severe behavioral health disorders until full remission has been achieved or until recovery maintenance can be self-managed by the individual and his or her family (White, Boyle, Loveland and Corrigan, 2003).

This article contrasts the application of AC and RM models of intervention into severe AOD problems within communities of color[5]. We will focus specifically on those American Indian/Alaskan Native[6], African American, Hispanic/Latino, and Asian and Pacific Islander communities whose members present unique challenges and resources as they enter publicly funded treatment for severe AOD problems. Our contrast of AC and RM models is drawn from the pioneering work of McLellan, Lewis, O'Brien, and Kleber (2000) and from the descriptions of the RM model set forth by White, Boyle, and Loveland (2002, 2003). We argue that historically disempowered persons, and, in particular, communities of color, have been ill-served by acute, biomedical models of intervention into AOD problems, and that models of recovery management hold great promise in providing more effective solutions to AOD problems within communities of color. We will explore elements of RM that tap deep historical traditions within communities of color and that are highly congruent with contemporary, abstinence-based religious and cultural revitalization movements within communities of color.

Great care must be taken that discussions of the needs of ethnic communities do not inadvertently contribute to stereotypes about communities of color. To determine whether RM models of intervention hold greater promise than AC models within communities of color, we will need to explore those characteristics of communities of color that have relevance to the viability of these models. Given the enormous differences within and between ethnic communities and the changes in communities over time, we would ask readers to keep all observations, ideas, and strategies set forth in this article on probation pending their validation within particular communities and with particular individuals and families. "People of color" and "communities of color" do not constitute a monolithic group to which any single explanatory or intervention model can be indiscriminately applied. We also recognize that the concepts set forth here may not be limited to communities of color and may also apply to particular white communities. Testing of components of the RM model will need to be conducted in all ethnic communities and across multiple subpopulations within those communities. To achieve this will require redesigning addiction treatment in light of new recovery management models and doing this within the larger framework of cultural competence.[7] We hope this introductory paper will stand as an invitation for such sustained exploration. Our vision is the development of culturally competent models of recovery management within all communities and the dynamic evolution of RM principles and practices based on experience within and dialogue between communities.

We will begin by contrasting how AC and RM models conceptualize the sources and solutions to AOD problems and then explore the RM model's emphasis on proactive engagement, the use of indigenous healers and institutions, catalytic rituals and metaphors, new technologies of monitoring and recovery support, a sustained recovery management partnership, and the need for culturally nuanced approaches to recovery research and evaluation.

AC AND RM MODELS: THE SOURCE OF AOD PROBLEMS

American Indians experienced massive losses of lives, land, and culture from European contact and colonization resulting in a long legacy of chronic trauma and unresolved grief across generations. This phenomenon…contributes to the current social pathology of high rates of suicide, homicide, domestic violence, child abuse, alcoholism and other social problems among American Indians.

—Brave Heart & DeBruyn, 1998

When people are taught to hate themselves, they will do bad things to themselves.

—Sanders, 1993.

Acute care (AC) models of intervention have assumed that the sources of and solutions to AOD problems reside within the individual, and that brief interventions to alter an individual's physical, cognitive, and emotional vulnerabilities can produce a permanent resolution of these problems. When the AC model fails to resolve AOD problems, the root of that failure is viewed as residing inside the individual. The professional response, in practice if not in theory, is to prescribe additional repetitions of the failed intervention. Of people admitted to publicly funded addiction treatment in the U.S., 60% have been in treatment before (including 23% 1 time, 13% 2 times, 7% 3 times, 4% 4 times, and 13% 5 or more times) (OAS, 2000). An aggressive system of managed behavioral health care has lowered the intensity and duration of these treatment episodes, further lessening the viability of addiction treatment for persons within communities of color who present with high problem severity and chronicity. Awareness of this inadequacy has triggered the rise of indigenous recovery movements, including the Wellbriety Movement in Indian Country (see www. whitebison.org) and Afrocentric frameworks of recovery, e.g., faith-based recovery ministries (Glide Memorial Church, One Church — One Addict, Free N' One, African American Survivors Organization, Turning Point) (Sanders, 2002). Recovery within these movements is seen, not as a singular goal, but as a therapeutic byproduct of participation in larger cultural and religious revitalization processes.

The premises of the RM model contrast sharply with those of the AC model. RM models posit that AOD problems spring from multiple, interacting etiologies; unfold (suddenly or progressively) in highly variable patterns; ebb (remission) and flow (relapse) in intensity over time; and are resolved at different levels (from full to partial) via multiple long-term pathways of recovery. This opening proposition has particular relevance to communities of color. It suggests that people of color may be at risk for AOD problems but that these risk factors differ between and within ethnic groups (Matsuyoshi, 2001). It suggests that historical, political, economic, and socio-cultural circumstances can also serve as etiological agents in the rise of AOD problems. Client discussions about cultural pain (e.g., slavery, the loss of land, attempted extermination, epidemic diseases, the purposeful break-up of tribes and families, the loss of families and culture via immigration or forced deportation, forced internment as prisoners of war, other forms of physical sequestration, immigration distress, acculturation pressure, racism, and discrimination) are viewed, not as defocusing or acting out, but as a medium of a consciousness raising and catharsis that can open doorways to personal and community healing and transformation (Green, 1995). This approach is much more congruent with beliefs within communities of color that their AOD problems result as much from historical trauma[8], economic and political disempowerment, and cultural demoralization as from biological vulnerability (Manson, 1996; Brave Heart & DeBruyn, 1998; Brave Heart, 2003). This view recognizes that historical trauma and cultural oppression elevate risk factors for substance use problems and erode resiliency factors that operate as a protective shield against AOD problems and speed their natural resolution (Brave Heart, 2003). Culturally nuanced models of RM reflect an understanding of the effects of intergenerational trauma (grief, rage, self-hatred, self-medication) upon whole communities. Positing multiple pathways of long-term recovery also opens up the potential for culturally prescribed frameworks of AOD problem resolution (abstinence-based religious and cultural revitalization movements, e.g., Nation of Islam) as well as cultural adaptations of existing recovery support structures (e.g., the "Indianization" of Alcoholics Anonymous and the adaptation of A.A. within Hispanic/Latino communities) (Womak, 1996; Hoffman, 1994).

RM models assume that severe AOD problems constitute complex, chronic disorders that require sustained individual, family, community, and cultural interventions for their long-term resolution. In this view, treating severe and persistent AOD problems via AC models of intervention is as ineffective as treating a bacterial infection with half the effective dose of antibiotics. While providing temporary symptom suppression, such treatment results in the subsequent return of the problem, often in a more virulent and treatment-resistant form. In the RM model, the treatment of severe and persistent AOD problems is best done within a sustained recovery management partnership that provides ongoing recovery support and consultation and anchors the recovery process in indigenous supports within the client's natural environment.

Chronic disorders such as diabetes and heart disease take an undue toll on communities of color, but substantial efforts are underway within communities of color for the prevention, early intervention, and sustained management of such chronic health problems. People of color are learning that the successful management of these disorders requires an understanding of:

- personal/family vulnerability;
- the influence of environmental conditions on the ebb and flow of these disorders;
- the propensity for these disorders to generate collateral health and family problems; and
- the role of daily lifestyle decisions (eating, sleeping, exercise, etc.), and the need for sustained self-vigilance, in the management of these disorders.

As communities of color learn more about the nature and treatment of chronic primary health disorders, that knowledge base can be extended to severe AOD problems. There is already some recognition of addiction as a chronic disorder via people of color sustaining hope for a family member or friend's recovery, long after the rest of the world has lost such hope. That capacity for patience, compassion, and forgiveness is not a sign of pathology (codependency), but an unheralded resource of hope and support within communities of color upon which the RM model seeks to build.

The acute model rests on the assumption that AOD problems are self-contained and that individuals have the internal and external resources to sustain recovery and assume full social functioning following detoxification and brief treatment. It assumes a foundation of pre-morbid skills and social functioning. This rehabilitation model promises the client that he or she will regain prior levels of functioning and status lost via the accelerating severity of AOD problems. This model is poorly suited to individuals who have not achieved such prior levels of successful functioning and who have no significant support for recovery within their family and social networks. The model is particularly unsuited to those poor communities of color whose members often present with high AOD problem severity, numerous co-occurring problems, and low "recovery capital" (internal and external resources that help to initiate and maintain recovery) (Granfield and Cloud, 1999).

In contrast, the RM model assumes that clients have widely varying degrees of problem severity and recovery capital and that the degree and duration of need for recovery support services requires differential allocation of services across these levels of functioning. Where levels of care within traditional treatment are dictated primarily by problem severity, RM models set service intensities and duration based on the unique interaction of problem severity and recovery capital. For example, the African American business executive with high AOD problem severity but high recovery capital would be viewed as needing less intensive and sustained recovery support than an African American adolescent with low AOD problem severity but with many co-occurring problems and low recovery capital. For those with little recovery capital, RM provides a framework for sustained habilitation.[9] The RM shift in emphasis is from recovery initiation to recovery maintenance (the movement toward global physical and emotional health; a reconstruction of personal identity and interpersonal relationships; and the development of a recovery-based, pro-social lifestyle). This habilitation emphasis is one of the driving forces behind the expanded menu of recovery support services (described below). This same habilitation emphasis is also extended to the families and communities within which AOD problems are enmeshed.

THE RM SOLUTION: PERSONAL, FAMILY, AND COMMUNITY RENEWAL

Ultimately, it is the community that cures...To cure the wounded, one need only return them to their community or construct a new one.

— Philip Rieff, 1987

Community healing along with individual and family healing are necessary to thoroughly address historical unresolved grief and its present manifestations.

— Brave Heart & DeBruyn, 1998

The unit of service within the AC model is the individual with an AOD problem. Professional interventions are designed to lower the biological vulnerability and alter the beliefs and behaviors thought to sustain addiction. Within the RM model, individuals with AOD problems are viewed as being nested within a complex web of family, social, and cultural relationships. Each level of this social ecosystem can contribute to the development of, help resolve, or sabotage the solution of these problems. As a result, it is the whole ecosystem rather than the individual that is the target of the RM intervention. RM moves beyond the clinical skills of assessment, diagnosis, and treatment of individuals to encompass the skills of family reconstruction, community resource development, and nation-building (see the work of White Bison for examples of the latter).[10] RM in communities of color is premised on the belief that the community — experienced through group solidarity with a historical and geographical community — is an essential dimension of personal healing (Murphy, Personal Communication).

In the AC model, the family is a stimulus for help-seeking, a source of emotional and financial support for treatment retention, and a target for brief education and referral to peer-support (e.g., Al-Anon). The assumption is that whatever wounds the family suffered through the addiction experience will naturally and quickly reverse themselves following the addicted family member's recovery initiation. In contrast, the RM model assumes the following:

- Addiction is but one wound families of color have suffered via the intergenerational transmission of historical trauma (e.g., the forced breakup of family units in slavery, the Indian boarding schools and their prolonged aftermath, traumatic separation via immigration), and the family unit itself needs a sustained process of recovery from these wounds (Brave Heart & DeBruyn, 1998).

- The addiction-related transformation of family roles, relationships, rules, and rituals is deeply imbedded within family members and habitual patterns of family interaction and will not spontaneously remit with recovery initiation.
- There are developmental stages of family recovery that entail personal healing, a realignment of family subsystems (adult intimate relationships, parent-child relationships, and sibling relationships), and the family's relationship with the outside environment — tasks that consume the first 3-5 years of stable recovery (See Brown, 1994; Brown & Lewis, 2002).
  Families who do not have sufficient supports to make these difficult transitions are at high risk for disintegration — in spite of their having remained intact through years of addiction (Brown & Lewis, 2002).
- Sustained recovery monitoring and support for family members is as crucial as it is for the individual recovering from severe AOD problems.
- RM services for families must be refined based on the unique family and kinship patterns that exist within particular ethnic communities.

A major focus of RM is to create the physical, psychological, and social space within local communities in which recovery can flourish. The ultimate goal is not to create larger treatment organizations, but to expand each community's natural recovery support resources. The RM focus on the community and the relationship between the individual and the community are illustrated by such activities as:

- initiating or expanding local community recovery resources, e.g., working with A.A./N.A. Intergroup and service structures (Hospital and Institution Committees) to expand meetings and other service activities; African American churches "adopting" recovering inmates returning from prison and creating community outreach teams;
- educating contemporary recovery support communities about the history of such structures within their own cultures, e.g., Native American recovery "Circles," the Danshukai in Japan;
- introducing individuals and families to local communities of recovery;
- resolving environmental obstacles to recovery;
- conducting recovery-focused family and community education;
- advocating pro-recovery social policies at local, state, and national levels;
- seeding local communities with visible recovery role models;

- recognizing and utilizing cultural frameworks of recovery, e.g., the Southeast Asian community in Chicago training and utilizing monks to provide post-treatment recovery support services; and
- advocating for recovery community representation within AOD-related policy and planning venues.

The importance of community in understanding AOD problems within communities of color is perhaps most evident within the rising Wellbriety movement in Indian Country. A central idea within this movement is the "Healing Forest" metaphor developed by Don Coyhis (1999). In Coyhis' work, the AC model of treatment is analogous to removing a sick tree from diseased soil, nursing it back to health in well fertilized and well watered soil, and then returning it to the diseased soil from which it came. Coyhis suggests that we would need fewer tree hospitals if we treated the trees AND the soil in which the trees suffer or thrive. He calls for the creation of a "healing forest" to nurture sobriety and wellness. This broader vision of creating healthy communities that resist AOD problems and within which recovery can thrive is pervasive in communities of color but is markedly absent within the professional field of addiction treatment.

In communities of color, the individual, the family, and the community are inseparable. To wound one is to wound the other; to heal one is to heal all (Red Road to Wellbriety, 2002). When asked how the Shuswap tribe in Alkali Lake, British Columbia successfully reduced its alcoholism rate from nearly 100% to less than 5%, Chief Andy Chelsea declared simply, "the community is the treatment center" (quoted in Abbot, 1998; See also Chelsea and Chelsea, 1985 and Taylor, 1987). Frameworks of recovery within communities of color have always been, and continue to be, defined in terms of an inextricable link between hope for the individual and hope for a community and a people. The most effective and enduring solutions to AOD problems among people of color are ones that emerge from within the very heart of communities of color. The RM model seeks to tap this vein of resistance and resilience by recognizing and enhancing the recovery support capacities of families, kinship networks, indigenous institutions (e.g., mutual aid groups, churches, clans), and whole communities and tribes. The focus of RM interventions is not restricted to the individual, the family, or the community, but is focused on all levels of this recovery ecosystem and their inter-relationships.

PROACTIVE ENGAGEMENT

My clients don't hit bottom; they live on the bottom. If we wait for them to hit bottom, they will die. The obstacle to their engagement in treatment is not an absence of pain; it is an absence of hope.

— Outreach Worker (Quoted in White, Woll, & Webber, 2003)

The AC model of intervention is essentially crisis oriented. It relies on internal pain or external coercion to bring individuals to treatment, and places the responsibility for motivation for change squarely and solely on the individual. It assumes that people move from addiction to recovery when the pain of the former state reaches a point of critical mass. The AC model is also characterized by a high threshold of engagement (extensive admission criteria and procedures), high rates of client disengagement (terminating services against staff advice) and high rates of client extrusion ("administrative discharge" for non-compliance). In contrast, the RM model is characterized by assertive models of community outreach, pre-treatment recovery support services, and the resolution of personal and environmental obstacles to recovery. Motivation for recovery is not assumed to be static — a dichotomous ("you have it or you don't") entity — but is an entity that emerges out of and is sustained by an empowering service relationship. It is assumed that such motivation waxes and wanes and that active recovery coaching can help the client transcend periods of heightened ambivalence, diminished confidence, and recovery-induced anxiety. One of the earliest examples of such proactive outreach was the work of the East Harlem Protestant Parish among New York City's Puerto Rican heroin addicts in the 1950s. This faith-based program recruited addicts from the streets and enmeshed them within pro-recovery social clubs and a larger religious community within which they were welcomed and respected (White, 1998).

The proactive engagement of the RM model is particularly suited for individuals whose personal/cultural experiences have engendered an exceptionally high physical and emotional tolerance for pain, and for those who have never known anyone in recovery. Proactive engagement is also important for people of color who:

- lack the knowledge, skills, and financial resources required to navigate complex health and human service systems;

- fear bringing shame to their families (losing "face") by breaking prohibitions on disclosing personal problems outside the family and/or kinship network — shame dramatically enhanced for women;
- have had negative experiences within or distrust formal service systems;
- bring special obstacles to accessing services (e.g., language barriers, undocumented status); and
- possess beliefs about illness and health that conflict with the explanatory metaphors of mainstream service systems.

The RM model of engagement is particularly well suited for people of color whose resistance to treatment flows from the inertia of hopelessness. Where AC models are most effective with individuals ready to take action related to their problems, RM models place great emphasis on the pre-action stages of change and the long-term maintenance stages of change (See Prochaska, DiClemente, & Norcross, 1992 and Prochaska, Norcross, & DiClemente, 1994 for a description of the stages of change)[11]. The model assumes that the scales of long-term recovery are tipped, not by the sobriety decision (alcoholics/addicts make many such decisions), but by the interaction of what precedes and follows such decisions.

Of all the obstacles that proactive engagement is designed to address, perhaps the most difficult in both AC and RM models is the issue of language. Key informants from many ethnic communities emphasized the need for more bilingual professionals and service volunteers. This language barrier will have to be overcome if RM models are to fulfill their potential within ethnic communities. The outreach and assertive continuing care functions, in particular, will require a high level of cultural and linguistic fluency. The RM emphasis on building service capacity within communities offers some hope for expanding such competence.

While this assertive model of engaging and supporting individuals through the stages of recovery is well suited to the obstacles and complex needs presented by many people of color, great care will have to be taken with this aspect of the RM model. The values of benevolence, generosity, and service co-exist with the value of noninterference in the affairs of others within communities of color. The implementation of RM models in communities of color will require considerable care to avoid violating this latter value. The key will be to use RM's assertive approach to engagement and post-treatment monitoring and support, but to do so only with the continuing consent of the community, family, and individual client.

Another dimension of the RM model (emerging from its view of multiple pathways of recovery) is its respect for the power and legitimacy of transformative change as a medium of recovery initiation (Miller & C'de Baca, 2001)[12]. Non-ordinary experiences (e.g., dreams, visions, climactic conversions) have long marked a pathway of addiction recovery for people of color, particularly among those who have led religious and cultural revitalization movements (e.g., Handsome Lake, Malcolm X). In contrast to the conversion style of induction, recovery may also be marked by a reaffirmation and deepening of existing religious/spiritual beliefs and practices, as Morjaria and Orford (2002) found in their study of South Asian American men (see also Manik et al., 1997). Where traditional AC models of treatment tend to discount the power and durability of religious experiences and the role of religious institutions as viable sobriety-based support structures, the RM model celebrates the legitimacy of these experiences and support institutions. It is clear that sustained sobriety can be a byproduct of religious and cultural affiliation and a heightened ethnic identity, whether this occurs within the Nation of Islam, the Indian Shaker Church, or a Buddhist or Hindu Temple. Such recoveries involve not just a redefinition of personal identity, but also a redefinition of oneself as an Indian, African American, Latino, or Asian person. For example, Spicer's studies of recovery in Native American communities found that recovery initiation was associated with heightened Indian identity and the incompatibility between drinking and emerging beliefs about how Indian people should conduct their lives (Spicer, 2001). This recognition of the power of culturally mediated transformative change provides a foundation of respect upon which RM-based organizations can collaborate with religious and cultural revitalization movements within communities of color.

INDIGENOUS HEALERS/INSTITUTIONS AND THE RECOVERY MANAGEMENT TEAM

Many individuals maintain sobriety only after they resume or begin regular involvement in traditional spiritual practices.

—Brave Heart & DeBruyn, 1998

The persistence and revival of indigenous Amerindian healing is due not to a lack of modern treatment services, but to a need for culture-congenial and holistic therapeutic approaches.

—Jilek, 1978

The AC service approach is based on the recognition of AOD problems as a biopsychosocial disorder. As a result, AC treatment interventions are delivered by an interdisciplinary team of physicians, nurses, psychologists, social workers, and addiction counselors. In contrast, the RM model recognizes other dimensions of AOD problems (e.g., economic, political, cultural, spiritual, religious) and broadens the recovery management team to include indigenous community institutions and healers. People of color utilize cultural healing therapies as alternatives or adjuncts to mainstream medicine and psychiatry, with the majority not reporting visits to alternative practitioners to their mainstream service providers (Keegan, 1996). Studies of the course of alcohol problems among American Indians have found remission/recovery rates as high as 60%, with few such recoveries attributable to formal alcoholism treatment (See Spicer, 2001 for a review). American Indians have a long history of abstinence-based religious and cultural revitalization movements, indigenous healers as mediums of alcoholism recovery, and the use of Native medicines and ceremonies as adjunctive supports for recovery (White, 2000b; Coyhis & White, 2002). Growing awareness of this history has spurred calls for culture-congenial therapeutic approaches via an integration of Western treatment methods and traditional Native American healing practices (Jilek, 1974; Weibel-Orlando, 1987; and Westermeyer, 1996). There is similar evidence for indigenous recovery frameworks in the Hispanic/ Latino (Thomas, 1967; Singer & Borrero, 1984; Núñez Molina, 2001), Asian (Das, 1987; Yamashiro, & Matsuoka, 1997) and African-American communities (Leong, Wagner, & Tata, 1995). These indigenous recovery frameworks place great emphasis on the healing power of *regalos* — cultural values and ceremonies. Where traditional treatment programs question the viability and durability of these cultural and religious pathways of recovery (in practice if not in theory), the RM model is open to the inclusion of such institutions and their representatives within the recovery management team. In the RM model, the medicine man/woman, cacique (Indian healer), curandero (Mexican folk healer), Espiritista (Puerto Rican spirit healer), minister, priest, shaman, monk, and herbalist may each play a role within the RM team.

A recent evaluation of gender-specific addiction treatment programs in Illinois found that a significant number of recovering and recovered[13] African-American women are using the Black Church as their primary sobriety-based support structure, but most do so only months after initiating recovery and addressing issues of shame related to their addiction (White, Woll, & Webber, 2003)[14]. Similar documentation exists on the use of religious frameworks of addiction recovery in other communities of color (Núñez Molina, 2001; Coyhis & White, forthcoming). This raises an interesting point about the differences between the ways in which individuals initiate recovery and the ways in which they sustain that recovery over time. More specifically, it suggests that some clients of color may use one institution to initiate recovery (e.g., professionally directed treatment, Alcoholics Anonymous, or Narcotics Anonymous), but use culturally indigenous institutions to sustain recovery (e.g., the Black Church). Failure to sustain recovery could thus be viewed, not as a need for more recovery initiation services (the AC treatment model), but as a need to find a cultural pathway of long-term recovery maintenance (the RM model).

The RM model assembles professional and indigenous service teams to meet the unique recovery support needs of each client and family. The rationales for the use of such non-traditional teams are to expand the recovery support services available to individual clients and to decrease the number of people needing professional services by expanding natural recovery supports within the larger community. The inclusion of indigenous healers and recovery support institutions rests on a simple assumption: the natural community is an oasis of human and spiritual resources that can be tapped to resolve personal and family problems (McKnight, 1995). In the RM model, the centerpiece of recovery is not the treatment institution, but the client and his or her relationship to this larger community.

The inclusion of non-traditional roles within the RM service team raises the question of credibility and credentialing of service providers within communities of color. Credibility bestowed from the dominant culture has value within communities of color only when the individual with such credentials is further vetted inside the community. This is typified by the concepts of *respeto, personalismo, dignidad,* and *confianza* within Hispanic/Latino communities — concepts that dictate respect based on personhood rather than financial or occupational status (Soriana, 1995). Credibility in communities of color is more likely to be bestowed upon those with nonjudgmental attitudes, knowledge of the culture, and demonstrated resourcefulness and effectiveness (Sue & Sue, 1999).

Credibility as a healer inside communities of color requires two things: *experiential knowledge* and *experiential expertise* (Borkman, 1976). Experiential knowledge requires wisdom gained about a problem from close up — first-hand versus second-hand knowledge. Experiential knowledge comes from having experienced, lived with, or done battle with addiction and from having participated in one's own or other's recovery. This does not explicitly require that all volunteer or paid support staff be recovered or recovering, but it does require that they have learned about addiction and recovery from close proximity. Experiential expertise requires the ability to use this knowledge to effect change in self or others. This latter credential — granted through the community "wire" or "grapevine" (community story-telling) — bestows credibility that no university can grant. It is bestowed only on those who offer sustained living proof of their expertise as a recovery guide within the life of the community. Such persons may be professionally trained, but their authority comes, not from their preparation, but from their character, relationships, and performance within the community. RM models capitalize on such experiential expertise by recruiting indigenous healers as legitimate members of recovery management teams, e.g., outreach workers, recovery coaches, and culturally grounded therapists/ nurses/physicians.

RM also turns those seeking help into sources of support for others via their involvement in mutual support groups, peer-based service models, and recovery advocacy organizations. Within communities of color, there is a long history of the concept of "wounded healer" (the idea that surviving a life-threatening illness or experience bestows knowledge and an obligation to help others facing this illness or experience), and a tradition of helpers credentialed by "calling" (White, 2000b). By transforming the process of recovery from an interaction between a professional and a patient to reciprocal support among members of a community of recovering and recovered people, RM taps this wounded healer tradition and utilizes what has been christened the "helper-therapy principle" (the therapeutic effects of helping others) (Reissman, 1990, 1965). Converting service recipients into service dispensers exponentially expands indigenous recovery resources within communities of color. Reaching out to the suffering alcoholic/addict has been espoused by leaders of American recovery communities, from the Washingtonian mantra, "You've been saved, now save another" (White, 1998) to what Malcolm X referred to as "fishing for the dead" (Myers, 1993, p. 82). With its emphasis on transforming people who have been part of the problem into part of the solution, RM creates a cadre of people whose living example and recovery advocacy activities can help neutralize the particularly intense stigma that has long been attached to addiction in communities of color.

PEOPLE OF COLOR AND THE CRIMINAL JUSTICE AND CHILD WELFARE SYSTEMS

People of color, particularly African Americans, are over-represented within America's criminal justice and child welfare systems. Constituting only 12.1% of the U.S. population (U.S. Census Bureau, 2000) and 15% of illicit drug consumers (SAMHSA, 1998), African Americans constitute 56.7% of those currently in state prison on drug offenses (Harrison & Beck, 2003). Studies have also shown that race plays an important role in involvement in child protection services. Although rates of drug use during pregnancy are nearly identical for African American and White women, African American women are ten times more likely to be reported to child protection authorities for prenatal drug exposure (Neuspiel, 1996; Chasnoff, Landress, & Barret, 1990). Any intervention into alcohol and other drug problems in communities of color must recognize the dominant role of the criminal justice and child welfare systems as treatment referral sources.

The AC model of intervention is strongly linked to these systems, and that is in itself a problem. People of color with high problem severity and complexity (e.g., multiple problems) continue to be routinely placed in brief interventions that have little chance of success, and then are punished (via incarceration or loss of custody of children) when those failed outcomes occur, on the grounds that "they had their chance." The financially motivated collaboration of the treatment system in this process is altering the perception of treatment institutions from institutions of service and care to institutions of coercion and control. Masked behind euphemisms such as "treatment works" is the story of how addiction treatment programs have become an extension of the criminal justice and child protection systems within communities of color. We would argue that it is not enough to deflect people of color into treatment as an alternative to incarceration or family disintegration. The treatment received must be designed in such a way as to offer a realistic chance of success. Punishing people with high problem severity for failing to achieve sustained abstinence following treatment within an AC model is part of a long history of "blaming the victim" within communities of color.

It remains to be seen whether RM models will offer a more viable option for people of color involved in the criminal justice and child welfare systems, but RM models do have several characteristics that make success more likely. First, the longer duration of service contact in the RM model is more realistic and constitutes more of a real "chance" than treatment based on the AC model. The RM emphasis on engagement and sustained monitoring and support is very congruent with such criminal justice initiatives as intensive probation, drug courts, and sentence circles. It is also congruent with the gender-specific addiction treatment models emerging within the child welfare system (White, Woll, & Webber, 2003). What RM may contribute is the birth of collaborative models that combine the surveillance functions of the criminal justice and child protection systems with sustained mechanism of recovery support and early re-intervention. Such models could span a continuum of intervention points from diversion programs to community re-entry from prison. More effective systems of intervention and support could decrease the number of people entering, and widen the doorways of exit from, the criminal justice and child protection systems. RM models could be built on the peer-based engagement and support models that have been used to reach addicted people of color within the CJ system, e.g., the Nation of Islam, Winner's Circle.

EXPANDED MENU OF SERVICES AND CATALYTIC METAPHORS

Metaphors are culturally-grounded figures of speech that in their subtlety, complexity and power strike deep emotional cords that ignite processes of personal transformation.

—White & Chaney, 1993

...transformations of the self and its relationship to core symbols in a particular cultural system of meaning appear to lie at the heart of how people are restored to wholeness following their problematic involvements with alcohol.

—Spicer, 2001

The AC model of addiction treatment is based on the development of "programs" (a prescribed combination and sequence of therapeutic activities) that clients experience with minimal variation. Program activities and protocols focus on detoxification, problem stabilization, and recovery initiation. RM models, by placing equal or greater emphasis on pre-treatment engagement and post-treatment recovery maintenance, expand the service menu considerably and, in the process, redefine the very identity of treatment institutions.

The RM service menu is based on three premises:

1. People with AOD problems represent multiple clinical subpopulations with diverse needs: the effectiveness of treatment and support services varies considerably across clinical subpopulations and individuals within these subgroups.
2. There are developmental stages of long-term recovery: the same individual may need different treatment and support services at different stages of his or her addiction and recovery careers.
3. There are qualitative differences between AOD problems and the processes used in their resolution within communities of color.

RM replaces the treatment "program" with a large menu of service and support activities that are uniquely combined and supplemented to meet the stage-dependent needs of people in recovery. In this model, the service menu is constructed using frameworks of healing drawn first from the client's own cultural background, e.g., the use of specialized therapies such as the Japanese psychotherapeutic approach known as *Naikan,* in which the patient is sequestered for self-reflection on his or her character and relationships under the guidance of periodic visits from the therapist (*sinsei*) (Das, 1987). RM seeks to initiate and sustain recovery within the framework of cultural values using methods that markedly differ from client to client (See Flores, 1985-86). The shift toward a multicultural menu of values and service activities requires a high degree of individualization and a more sophisticated, comprehensive knowledge of the personal, intracultural, and trans-cultural processes of long-term recovery.

RM proponents are also interested in the kinds of words, ideas, metaphors, and rituals that initiate and strengthen recovery, mark the shift from one stage of recovery to the next, and sustain recovery over a prolonged period of time. This interest is congruent with the belief in the power of words (speeches, sermons, and stories) and healing ceremonies within communities of color. The following assumptions describe the potential role of words, ideas, metaphors, and rituals in the addiction recovery process.

1. Words, ideas, metaphors, and rituals can exert an enslaving or liberating effect on one's relationships with alcohol and other drugs (White & Chaney, 1993; White, 1996).
2. Words, ideas, metaphors, and rituals that serve as a catalyst for change in one person or cultural group may have no such power with other persons or cultural groups. There are specific ethnic/cultural worldviews, and the elements of these worldviews constitute the raw materials from which pathways of resilience to and recovery from AOD problems must be constructed (Taylor, 1992).
3. Catalytic metaphors[15] evolve and recycle within cultures over time. Their use as agents of transformation rests on their contemporary power; they must resonate within the present cultural and personal experience of the individual seeking recovery.
4. The growing phenomenon of biculturalism suggests that individuals may be able to combine or sequence metaphors from two or more cultures to initiate recovery or shift from one stage of recovery to the next.
5. Addiction treatment programs serving heterogeneous populations must provide a diverse menu of organizing words, ideas, metaphors, and rituals to widen the

doorways of entry into recovery and support culturally mediated stages of long-term recovery (White, 1996).

The following observations reflect the ways in which words, ideas, metaphors, and rituals have been used by historically disempowered peoples to initiate and sustain recovery from addiction.

1. During the peak period of contact and colonization, people of color are prohibited from drinking or provided only controlled opportunities for drinking (e.g., Slave Code prohibitions on drinking, Federal prohibition of the sale of alcohol to American Indians) and are targeted via drug prohibition laws (e.g., anti-opium ordinances aimed at Chinese immigrants, anti-cocaine laws aimed at African Americans, anti-peyote laws aimed at American Indians, and anti-marijuana laws aimed at Mexican immigrants) (See Musto, 1973; Helmer, 1975; Morgan, 1983).

2. Patterns of psychoactive drug use and their effects upon people of color are exaggerated or fabricated as part of a racial mythology that justifies colonization and cultural domination (e.g., Native American "firewater myths") (Coyhis & White, forthcoming; Morgan, 1983)

3. People of color, in their early struggles for liberation, use the consumption of alcohol and other drugs to cope with feelings of hopeless and to deal with historical trauma.

4. Political and religious leaders within communities of color subsequently link AOD use to historical oppression, portray alcohol and other drugs as weapons of continued colonization and domination of their communities (Tabor, 1970; Herd, 1985), and portray sobriety as an act of resistance and liberation (Douglas, 1855; Cheagle, 1969).

5. Recovery mutual aid movements arising out of historically disempowered people emphasize metaphors of resistance, emancipation, and power, e.g., "I have a problem that once had me" (Kirkpatrick, 1986), "I will take control of my life" (Williams & Laird, 1992).

6. Heightened consciousness of racial history and identity can be a pathway of entry into recovery, or it can be part of a process of discovery in the later stages of recovery (Green, 1995).

By recognizing multiple pathways and styles of long-term recovery, the RM model embraces and works within these alternative frameworks of recovery. It views tenets of belief about AOD problems and their resolution within their historical context and in terms of their utility for initiating or anchoring recovery. This requires considerable knowledge of indigenous cultures and fluency with prevailing cultural or religious metaphors that can incite or strengthen the process of addiction recovery. The viability of a particular metaphor for understanding AOD problems and ways in which they can be resolved varies widely between cultures and varies widely across individuals (e.g., by degree of acculturation). The question is not: Which explanatory metaphor is true? The question is: Which organizing metaphor, by explaining things that are otherwise inexplicable, serves as a catalyst for personal, family, and community healing? There are many people of color who have found recovery through mainstream treatment and recovery support organizations (e.g., A.A./N.A.), but there are also many people of color who have recovered from addictions who neither portray themselves as having suffered from the disease of alcoholism/addiction nor portray themselves today as alcoholics or addicts in recovery. They have found alternative rationales for sobriety and different metaphors to explain who they once were and who they are today (see Spicer, 2001).

There is no dominant organizing metaphor for recovery within the RM model. With its operational motto, "recovery by any means necessary," the RM model is broad enough to embrace clients who talk about their addictions in terms of:

- disease and recovery,
- habit and choice,
- badness (crime) and reformation,
- sin (idolatry, demon-possessed) and redemption (God-touched),
- cursed (for breaking cultural taboos) and healed,
- excess and harmony (balance),
- shame and honor (face),
- genocide and personal/cultural survival, or
- messed up and worn out ("sick and tired of being sick and tired").

The goal of RM is not to impose an organizing metaphor for recovery, but to work within whatever metaphors individuals and families find most personally and culturally meaningful.

The same broad perspective applies to transformative rituals. Where the dominant AC models of intervention into AOD problems rely on rituals of getting into oneself (e.g., psychotherapy), RM models are open to other cultural frameworks of recovery that involve a process of getting out of oneself and relying on resources and relationships beyond the self. Where the former view recovery as a process of self-exploration, the latter recognize the potential of recovery initiation via processes of self-transcendence — a value much more congruent with the spiritual-focused and community-focused ethos of communities of color.

SUSTAINED MONITORING AND SUPPORT

Chronic diseases require chronic cures.

—Kain, 1828

If addiction is best considered a chronic condition, then we are not providing appropriate treatment for many addicted patients.

—McLellan, 2002

Communities of color have become distrustful of promised quick fixes because so many of those promises have been betrayed. Professionals come and go; programs come and go; agencies come and go. Arguments over whether addiction treatment should consist of five sessions or 25 sessions, five days or 30 days, cognitive or family therapy are all arguments inside the acute care model of admission, treatment, and discharge. The inherent brevity of acute interventions into complex, chronic problems is often experienced as superficial pacification, professional disinterest, and abandonment. People of color, who tend to enter addiction treatment at later stages of problem severity and with a greater number of co-occurring problems (Bell, 2002), are ill-served by service models whose low intensity and short duration offer little opportunity for success. At a practical level, the acute model provides few options: regular readmission for detoxification and respite, demoralization and a cessation of treatment-seeking, or a search for recovery maintenance outside the realm of professionally directed treatment.

Communities of color need stable recovery support institutions that can move beyond brief experiments in recovery initiation toward prolonged recovery maintenance. It is this very need that has contributed to the dramatic growth of A.A., N.A., and recovery-focused ministries in communities of color. For those who need sustained professional support, RM provides a culturally viable model of addiction treatment that replaces crisis intervention with a much longer, but lower-intensity, continuum of pre-treatment, in-treatment, and post-treatment recovery support services.

A RECOVERY MANAGEMENT PARTNERSHIP

*Each patient carries his own doctor inside him. They come to us not knowing
that truth. We are at our best when we give the doctor who resides within each
patient a chance to go to work.*

—Albert Schweitzer, From *Reverence for Life*, 1993

The service relationship within acute care approaches to addiction treatment
is based on an "expert" model of problem intervention. In this model, the service
professional is assumed to have considerable knowledge, resources, and power,
while the service recipient is assumed to suffer from one or more problems that he
or she does not understand and cannot resolve. The role of the expert is to diagnose
the problem, treat the problem, and briefly educate the client regarding his or her
continued self-care responsibilities related to the problem. Failure to resolve the
problem is usually attributed to the lack of "patient compliance" with the expert's
recommendations. The service relationship within the AC model of intervention,
whether in the form of an emergency room visit for a broken bone or brief addiction
treatment, is hierarchical, transient, and commercialized. It reflects what Eisler (1987)
has christened the "dominator model" of interpersonal relationships.

The historical victimization and abandonment of people of color have left
a legacy of mistrust and caution when approaching relationships characterized by
high discrepancies of power, brevity of contact, and paid helpers. Given this legacy,
developing trust in service relationships with people of color requires testing and time,
and time is the one commodity the AC model, by definition, cannot provide.

RM models provide an alterative by providing continuity of contact in a
sustained service relationship, shifting the nature of that relationship from one based
on hierarchy to one based on a recovery management partnership, and incorporating
support relationships that are natural (reciprocal) and non-commercialized. In the
RM partnership, it is assumed that strengths and weaknesses exist on both sides of
the relationship, and that there is no universally effective professional intervention
for severe AOD problems. Where the expert model is based on a teacher-student
relationship, the partnership model assumes that learning will be mutual within the
service relationship. A number of recovery initiation and maintenance strategies are
co-developed and tried within the partnership relationship until the most effective
strategy is found. At any point, if previously successful strategies are no longer
working, experiments are reinitiated to develop new, more stage-appropriate strategies.

This approach rests on the assumption that strategies that work to achieve stability in early recovery may not work in the later stages of recovery. Continuity of contact over time is crucial to the RM model, making the issue of high staff turnover a potential Achilles heel of the RM model.

A second Achilles heel of the RM partnership model is the danger that it could evolve into patterns of prolonged dependency that already exist in the AC model. Cultivating professional dependence and creating "system-sophisticated" clients who know how to "do treatment" and manipulate resources to sustain active addiction is counterproductive and constitutes another form of colonization (using such clients as a cash crop to run the institutional economies of service industries and sustain the careers of service professionals). The goal of RM is a habilitation process that replaces dependency on formal service systems with interdependency within a larger social and cultural community. The essential principle is that professionally directed services are the last, not the first, line of response to AOD problems, and that professionally delivered RM services should provide only what cannot be provided within the larger network of family and indigenous community supports.

Another aspect of the RM service relationship is that the roles of service professionals within this model are multidimensional rather than specialized. In the RM model, the functions of outreach, engagement, assessment, case management, therapy, advocacy, and prevention may all exist over time within the same service role and relationship. This requires a higher level of cross-training than is necessary in the AC model. This broadening of the service role and extension of the duration of the service relationship also forces a rethinking of some of the ethical and relationship boundary guidelines that have governed the delivery of addiction treatment. Such guidelines in the AC model are based on the standards governing professional-client relationships in medicine, psychiatry, psychology, and social work. As they have developed in the modern evolution of addiction counseling, such guidelines have generally prohibited or discouraged disclosure of one's recovery status, emotional self-disclosure, contact with clients in their natural environment, gift giving and receiving with clients, and contact with clients after the period of primary treatment (See White and Popovits, 2002). Such guidelines require rethinking in the transition from AC models to RM models, with the ultimate arbitrator of the level of authority and formality within the RM relationship defined by the cultural context and the comfort level of the individual and family receiving services (See Matsuyoshi, 2001). While RM models retain a clear sense of behaviors in the service relationship that are "never okay," the zone of behaviors that are "sometimes okay and sometimes not okay" is significantly expanded. This requires a higher degree of supervision regarding boundary appropriateness in different cultural contexts and over the stages of a long-term recovery support relationship.

RM models may also force agencies to fundamentally redefine their institutional identities from one of a service-oriented business to that of a member of multiple communities of recovery — membership that brings its own demands for accountability related to competence, consistency, and sustained access to services. Providing continuity of support and defining oneself in terms of personal and institutional membership in local communities of recovery are much more congruent with the natural patterns of helping within communities of color than are the "expert" or "business" models of delivering acute addiction treatment services.

CULTURALLY NUANCED RESEARCH AND EVALUATION

Indian communities recognize all too well that the research process can be intrusive and the results invidious, divisive, and scandalous.

—Beauvais & Trimble, 1992

...attempts to evaluate service programs must have a dual acceptability; that is, they must be acceptable to the rigors of scientific exploration as well as the African-American ethos and worldview.

—Butler, 1992

Both the acute model and the recovery management model aspire to be evidence based, but the former is based primarily on short-term scientific studies of the efficacy (what works under ideal conditions) and effectiveness (what works under real conditions) of a single episode of brief intervention (McLellan, 2002). The first change within the RM approach to research and evaluation is to extend the time frame under which judgments of efficacy and effectiveness are rendered (White, Boyle, & Loveland, 2002). Evidence that short-term effects of intervention (e.g., brief periods of sobriety) predict later therapeutic outcomes (e.g. sustained recovery) (see Weisner, et al., 2003) tells only part of the story. Time-related deterioration of effects, delayed positive effects, and delayed iatrogenic (harmful) effects of service interventions can be identified only via longitudinal studies. It is also possible that multiple interventions into chronic disorders may have cumulative or synergistic effects (from particular service combinations and sequences) not identifiable through the evaluation of a single service episode.

Because RM is based on a long-term health management partnership with individuals, families, and communities, it calls for a heightened level of sensitivity to constituency attitudes toward scientific research. In communities of color, researchers encounter two significant issues: 1) the distrust of culturally dominant research and 2) different ways of knowing.

People of color and communities of color have been wounded in a number of ways by culturally dominant research studies. They have been subjected to grossly unethical research practices (e.g., withholding medical treatment from 399 African American share-croppers in the Tuskegee Syphilis Study). They have been stereotyped via reports characterizing the presence or absence of AOD problems in terms of racially dictated biological vulnerability — from the "firewater" myths of racial vulnerability of Native Americans (Westermeyer, 1974; Leland, 1976) to the myth of racial invulnerability of Asians (O'Hare & Tran, 1998[16]). They have been wounded by the assumption of universal applicability — the misapplication of research findings from studies in which no people of color were included. Communities of color have been injured by bad ("junk") science, such as the now-discredited sensationalist literature on crack cocaine and "crack babies" that turned the criminal justice and child welfare systems into occupying institutions within poor communities of color (See Frank, Augustyn, Knight, et al., 2001). They have been shamed by research designs and interpretations that dramatized the problems within communities of color while ignoring their strengths and resiliencies (Coyhis & White, 2002). Observers from within ethnic communities (Casas, 1992) have also been very critical of how communities of color have been used as a valuable resource to enrich individual careers and institutions in exploitive processes that returned nothing to communities of color.

Given this history, science, scientists, and scientific institutions bear a continued burden of proof regarding their safety, relevance, and benefit to communities of color. Achieving such credibility will require, at a minimum, the inclusion of community of color leaders and members in the design, conduct, interpretation, and dissemination of research and evaluation studies (Hermes, 1998). It will require plotting the long-term pathways of addiction recovery in communities of color. It will require coming to grips with different ways in which communities of color determine what is true and what works in the addiction recovery arena. What is most significant, it will shift ultimate ownership of research from academic and funding institutions to the community being studied.

Scientific knowledge assumes that truth can be discovered through professional observation and the rational analysis of findings from controlled experiments. It is predicated upon distance and objectivity (knowledge from outside) and is judged to exist only when it has been documented in writing and subjected to professional peer review. There are two other ways of knowing within communities of color, and these exist more in oral tradition than in written words. The first, *historical/cultural truth*, asks, "What has been our past experience on this issue?" Racial memory is an important source of knowledge in communities of color — a source that seems alien to the highly individualist values and "now" orientation of the dominant American culture. Within communities of color, community elders rather than scientists are the ultimate authorities.

The second way of knowing, *experiential knowledge*, is based on the contemporary experiences of individuals, kinship networks, and fellow community members. This way of knowing tends to be concrete, pragmatic, holistic, and commonsensical (Borkman, 1976). One of the authors (Sanders) once attended a seminar in which a renowned researcher on problem gambling declared based on his research that Blacks and Latinos did not have significant problems with gambling. This conclusion did not match his historical/cultural truth as an African American, or the experiential knowledge drawn from his extended family and neighborhood (within which underground and state-sponsored lotteries were a prominent feature). When Sanders asked about the nature of the expert's research, he learned that it was based on a membership survey of Gamblers Anonymous conducted at predominately suburban meeting sites. When Sanders did his own research using focus groups with African Americans and Latinos in urban areas, he discovered clear patterns of problem gambling within these communities.

Word-of-mouth knowledge, captured in the collective stories of a community or a people, constitutes a key source of truth in communities of color. Communities of color do not reject science as much as require that its findings be filtered through the sieve of personal and community experience. In contrast to scientific knowledge, this way of knowing assumes that truth can be discovered only through proximity and experience (knowledge from inside). The authors have witnessed mainstream scientists speaking at "town meetings" in African American communities. When these scientists decry the lack of evidence on the effectiveness of indigenous frameworks of recovery (e.g., faith-based and other cultural mediums of recovery), they are somewhat flummoxed to see members of the audience stand to declare that they or their family members are the "living proof" of such effectiveness. David Whiters of Recovery

Consultants of Atlanta, Inc. notes, "I have watched many among the African American community begin their recovery in traditional recovery programs, only to find sustained recovery in the Black Church" (Personal Communication, December, 2003). Such long-term observations over spans of time that far exceed the follow-up periods in most research studies constitute their own form of collective truth. Living stories (experiential authority) have more power and cultural credibility than statistics (professional/scientific authority) within many communities of color. Living stories are best viewed as a unique and legitimate type of evidence rather than "myths" or "folklore" (Hermes, 1998). This does not mean that the usual methods of scientific analysis are abandoned, but that voices of the community are allowed to reach directly those who hear and read about the community through the medium of scientific research.

RM models will be required to pass the litmus test of multiple ways of knowing if they are to achieve credibility within and outside communities of color. The development of evidence-based services is a fundamental tenet of RM, but in communities of color the nature of that evidence will have to be broadened via qualitative studies that capture the historical and contemporary experience within communities of color. RM models in communities of color will also have to shift from an exclusively academic to a more activist orientation (studying questions of importance to the community, focusing on knowledge that can facilitate positive personal, family, and community change), enter into a research partnership with the community (e.g., control over design, conduct, interpretation, and dissemination), and respect the community's ownership of its own knowledge. We also anticipate that research in communities of color will shift from summative evaluation (measuring the effects of an intervention only after it is concluded) to formative evaluation (measuring and communicating the effects of an intervention at multiple points during and after its delivery, so that it can be refined and improved).

A RECOVERY MANAGEMENT AGENDA

This paper has contrasted acute care (AC) and recovery management (RM) models of intervention into serious AOD problems. It is suggested that RM models offer advantages to communities of color in eight specific areas:

- an ecological perspective on the etiology of AOD problems;
- a broadened target of intervention (including families, kinship networks, and communities);
- a proactive, hope-based model of service engagement;

- the inclusion of indigenous healers and institutions;
- an expanded menu of culturally grounded recovery support services and catalytic metaphors;
- an extended time-frame of recovery support;
- a partnership-based service relationship; and
- a culturally nuanced approach to research and evaluation.

The reader may ask, "Where are these models of recovery management?" The answer is that there may not be any treatment organizations that have fully developed all of the elements of RM described in this paper. RM exists as an emerging model whose service elements are currently being piloted and evaluated. The RM model exists within progressive treatment programs that are experimenting with new approaches to pre-treatment engagement and post-treatment continuing care. The model exists within the growing number of experiments with peer-based recovery support services. It exists within the growing network of peer-managed recovery homes in the United States. And, perhaps most significantly, its potential is demonstrated in the growing number of recovery-focused religious and cultural revitalization movements within American communities of color. That potential exists in a vibrant Wellbriety Movement in Indian Country. It exists within Glide Memorial Church, where a majority of parishioners are in recovery. It exists in the Nation of Islam's outreach to addicted African Americans in prison. It exists in the hundreds of thousands of people of color who each day use Twelve-Step programs and other recovery mutual aid societies to quietly achieve another day of sobriety and wellness. The challenge is to build connecting tissue between treatment and recovery by building bridges between these indigenous recovery movements and addiction treatment institutions.

RM holds great promise in communities of color, but fulfillment of that promise hinges on:

1. involving clients, families, and service professionals from within communities of color in a process of shifting existing interventions from AC models to locally designed, operated, and evaluated RM models;
2. developing recovery management teams and advocacy coalitions via the integration of AOD service providers and indigenous institutions;
3. confronting forces in the community that promote excessive AOD use;
4. enhancing "community recovery capital" (Granfield & Cloud, 1999);

5. increasing the presence and visibility of indigenous sobriety-based support structures;

6. providing recovery education within communities of color; and

7. using recovery role models that illustrate the viability and variety of recovery pathways within communities of color.

Achieving that vision will require that the field of addiction treatment fundamentally redefine the sources of and solutions to AOD problems and, in the process, redefine itself.

The authors conclude this paper as we started it, not as authorities, but as students. Any errors of perception or omission in these pages stand as testimony that this learning is, and will forever remain, incomplete. We submit this paper as a work-in-progress to the communities that helped spawn it and welcome continued guidance as we continue the task of making this alternative vision a reality in communities across America.

REFERENCES AND RECOMMENDED READING

Abbott, P.J. (1998).Traditional and western healing practices for alcoholism in American Indians and Alaskan Natives. *Substance Use and Misuse*, 33(13), 2605-2646.

Beauvais, F. and Trimble, J.E. (1992). The Role of the Researcher in Evaluating American Indian Alcohol and Other Drug Abuse Prevention Programs. In: Orlandi, M.A., eds. *Cultural Competence for Evaluators: A Guide for Alcohol and Other Drug Abuse Prevention Practitioners Working with Ethnic/Racial Communities*, pp. 23-54, Rockville, MD: Office of Substance Abuse Prevention.

Bell, P. (1992). *Cultural Pain and African Americans: Unspoken Issues in Early Recovery*. Center City, MN: Hazelden Educational Materials.

Bell. P. (2002). *Chemical Dependency and the African American*. Center City, MN: Hazelden.

Borkman, T. (1976). Experiential knowledge: A new concept for the analysis of self-help groups. *Social Service Review*, 50, 445-456.

Brave Heart, M.Y. & DeBruyn, L.M. (1998). The American Indian Holocaust: Healing historical unresolved grief. *American Indian and Alaska Native Mental Health Research Journal*, 8(2), 60-82.

Brave Heart, M.Y. (2003). The historical trauma response among natives and its relationship with substance abuse: A Lakota illustration. *Journal of Psychoactive Drugs*, 35(1), 7-13.

Brown, S. (1994). What is the family recovery process? *The Addiction Letter,* 10(10), 1, 4.

Brown, S. and Lewis, V. (2002). *The Alcoholic Family in Recovery: A Developmental Model.* New York: Guilford Press.

Butler, J. (1992). Of kindred minds: The ties that bind. In: Orlandi, M.A., Ed. *Cultural Competence for Evaluators: A Guide for Alcohol and Other Drug Abuse Prevention Practitioners Working with Ethnic/Racial Communities,* pp. 23-54, Rockville, MD: Office of Substance Abuse Prevention.

Casas, J.M. (1992) A Culturally Sensitive Model for Evaluating Alcohol and Other Drug Abuse Prevention Programs: A Hispanic Perspective. In: Orlandi, M.A., Ed. *Cultural Competence for Evaluators: A Guide for Alcohol and Other Drug Abuse Prevention Practitioners Working with Ethnic/Racial Communities,* pp. 75-116, Rockville, MD: Office of Substance Abuse Prevention.

Chasnoff, I.J., Landress, H.J., and Barrett, M.E. (1990). The prevalence of illicit-drug or alcohol use during pregnancy and discrepancies in mandatory reporting in Pinellas County, Florida. *New England Journal of Medicine,* 322:1202-1206.

Cheagle, R. (1969). *The colored temperance movement* (Unpublished thesis). Washington, DC: Howard University, 1969.

Chelsea, P and Chelsea, A. (1985), *Honour of All: The People of Alkali Lake.* (Video) British Columbia, Canada: The Alkali Lake Tribal Council.

Christmon, K. (1995). Historical overview of alcohol in the African American community. *Journal of Black Studies,* 25(3), 318-330.

Compton, W.M., Glantz, M. & Delaney, P. (2003). Addiction as a chronic illness— putting the concept into action. *Evaluation and Program Planning* 26, 353-354.

Coyhis, D. (1999). *The Wellbriety Journey: Nine Talks by Don Coyhis.* Colorado Springs, CO: White Bison, Inc.

Coyhis, D. and White, W. (2003) Alcohol problems in Native America: Changing paradigms and clinical practices. *Alcoholism Treatment Quarterly,* 3/4, 157-165.

Coyhis, D. and White, W. (forthcoming). *Alcohol Problems in Native America: The Untold Story of Resistance, Resilience and Recovery.* Colorado Springs, CO: White Bison, Inc.

Das, A. K. (1987). "Indigenous models of therapy in traditional Asian societies." *Journal of Multicultural Counseling & Development.* 15(1), 25-37.

Dennis, M. L., Scott, C. K., & Funk R. (2003). An experimental evaluation of recovery management checkups (RMC) for people with chronic substance use disorders. *Evaluation and Program Planning,* 26, 339–352

Douglass, F. (1855). *My Bondage and My Freedom.* New York, NY: Miller, Orton, & Mulligan.

Edwards, G., Davis, P., & Savva, S. (2003). Scanning the addiction horizons, 2003: Report on a consultation. *Addiction*, 98(11), 1471-1481.

Eisler, R. (1987). The Chalice and the Blade: Our History, Our Future. Cambridge, MA: Harper and Row.

Flores, P.J. (1985). Alcoholism treatment and the relationship of Native American cultural values to recovery. *International Journal of Addiction*, 20(11-12), 1707-26.

Frank, D.A., Augustyn, M., Knight, W.G., et al, (2001). Growth development and behavior in early childhood following prenatal cocaine exposure: A systematic review. *Journal of the American Medical Association*, 285, 1613-1625.

Godley, M., Godley, S., Dennis, M., Funk, R., & Passetti, L. (2002). Preliminary outcomes from the assertive continuing care experiment for adolescents discharged from residential treatment. *Journal of Substance Abuse Treatment*, 23, 21-32.

Granfield, R., & Cloud, W. (1999). *Coming Clean: Overcoming Addiction without Treatment.* New York: New York University Press.

Green, W. (1995). *Dysfunctional by Design: The Rebirth of Cultural Survivors.* Evanston, IL: Chicago Spectrum Press.

Harrison, P.M. and Beck, A.J. (2002). *Prisoners in 2002.* US Dept. of Justice, Bureau of Justice Statistics. Washington D.C.: US Dept. of Justice, July 2003), Table 15, p., 10.

Helmer, J. (1975). *Drugs and Minority Oppression.* New York: Seabury Press.

Herd, D. (1985). We cannot stagger to freedom: A history of Blacks and alcohol in American politics. In L. Brill and C. Winick, *The Yearbook of Substance Use and Abuse: Volume III.* New York, NY: Human Sciences Press, Inc.

Hermes, M. (1998). Research methods as a situated response: Towards a First Nations' methodology. *Qualitative Studies in Education*, 11(1), 155-168.

Hoffman, F. (1994). Cultural adaptations of Alcoholics Anonymous to serve Hispanic populations. *International Journal of the Addictions*, 29(4), 445-460.

Hser, Y-I, Anglin, M.D., Grella, C., Longshore, D., and Pendergast, M. (1997). Drug treatment careers: A conceptual framework and existing research findings. *Journal of Substance Abuse Treatment*, 14(6), 543-558.

Jilek, W.G. (1974) Indian healing power: Indigenous therapeutic practices in the Pacific Northwest. *Psychiatric Annals* 4(11), 13-21.

Jilek, W.G. (1978) Native renaissance: The survival of indigenous therapeutic ceremonials among North American Indians. *Transcultural Psychiatric Research* 15, 117-147

Kane, J.H. (1828). On intemperance considered as a disease and susceptible of cure. *American Journal of Medical Sciences*, 2(7), 291-295.

Kaplan, L. (1997). A disease management model for addiction treatment. *Behavioral Health Management*, 17(4), 14-15.

Keegan, L. (1996). Use of alternative therapies among Mexican American in the Texas Rio Grande Valley. *Journal of Holistic Nursing*, 14(4), 277-94.

Kirkpatrick, J. (1986). *Goodbye Hangovers, Hello Life* NY: Ballantine Books.

Leland, J. (1976). *Firewater Myths: North American Indian Drinking and Alcohol Addiction*. New Brunswick, New Jersey: Rutgers Center of Alcohol Studies Monograph No. 11.

Leong, F.T.L., Wagner, N.S., & Tata, S.P. (1995). Racial and ethnic variations in help-seeking attitudes. In J.G. Ponterotto, J.M. Casas, L.A. Suzuki, & C.M. Alexander (Eds.), *Handbook of multicultural counseling* (pp. 415-438). Thousand Oaks, CA: Sage.

Lurie, N. (1974). The world's oldest on-going protest demonstration: North American Indian drinking patterns. In: Hundley, N., Ed., *The American Indian*. Santa Barbara, California: CLIO Books, pp.55-76.

Manik, G.S., Cameron, D., Bird, R.H., and Sinorwala, A. (1997). *Resolution of Problem Drinking without Formal Treatment: Comparing Ethnic Minority and Indigenous Caucasian Populations*. Department of Psychiatry: University of Leicester.

Manson, S.M. (1996). The wounded spirit: a cultural formulation of post-traumatic stress disorder. *Culture, Medicine & Psychiatry*, 20(4), 489-98.

Matsuyoshi, J. (2001). Substance abuse interventions for Japanese and Japanese American clients. In: S.L.A. Straussner, Ed., *Ethnocultural Factors in Substance Abuse Treatment*, New York, NY: The Guilford Press, (pp. 393-417).

McKnight, J. (1995). *The Careless Society: Community and its Counterfeits*. New York: Basic Books.

McLellan, A.T., Lewis, D.C., O'Brien, C.P, and Kleber, H.D. (2000). Drug dependence, a chronic medical illness: Implications for treatment, insurance, and outcomes evaluation. *Journal of the American Medical Association* 284(13), 1689-1695.

McLellan, T. (2002). Have we evaluated addiction treatment correctly? Implications from a chronic care perspective. *Addiction*, 97, 249-252.

Merrill, S. & Borrero, M.G. (1984). Indigenous treatment for alcoholism: the case of Puerto Rican Spiritism, *Medical Anthropology*, 8(4), 246-273.

Miller, W. R., & C'de Baca, J. (2001). *Quantum change*. New York: Guilford.

Moore, B.A., & Budney, A.J. (2003). Relapse in outpatient treatment for marijuana dependence. *Journal of Substance Abuse Treatment* 25, 85-89.

Morgan, P. (1983) Alcohol, disinhibition, and domination: A conceptual analysis. In *Alcohol and Disinhibition: Nature and Meaning of the Link*, Ed. by Room and Collins, pp. 405-436, Washington D.C.: U.S. Government Printing Office.

Morjaria, A. & Orford, J. (2002). Role of religion and spirituality in recovery from drink problems: A qualitative study of Alcoholics Anonymous members and South Asian men. *Addiction Research and Theory*, 10(3), 225-256.

Musto, D. (1973). *The American Disease: Origins of Narcotic Control*. New Haven: Yale University Press.

Myers, W. D. (1993). *Malcolm X: By Any Means Necessary*. New York: Scholastic.

Neuspiel, D.R. (1996). Racism and perinatal addiction. *Ethnicity and Disease* 6:47-55.

Núñez Molina, M, (2001) Espiritismo: Community healing among Puerto Ricans: Espiritismo as a therapy for the soul. In M. Fernández Olmos (Ed.), Healing Cultures, New York: St. Martin Press.

Office of Applied Studies (OAS). (2000). *National Household Survey on Drug Abuse: Main Findings* 1998. Rockville, MD, Substance Abuse and Mental Health Services Administration.

Office of Applied Studies (OAS). (2001). *Treatment Episode Data Set (TEDS) 1994-1999: National Admissions to Substance Abuse Treatment Services*. DASIS Series S14, DHHS Publication No. (SMA)01-3550. Rockville, Maryland, 2001: U.S. Department of Health and Human Services. Substance Abuse and Mental Health Services Administration. (Table 4.16.01)

O'Brien, C. and McLellan, T. (1996). Myths about the treatment of addiction. *Lancet*, 347, 237-240.

O'Hare, T.; Tran, T.V. (1998). Substance abuse among Southeast Asians in the U.S.: Implications for practice and research. *Social Work in Health Care*, 26(3), 69-80.

Prochaska, J., DiClimente, C. and Norcross, J. (1992). In search of how people change. *American Psychologist* 47, 1102-1114.

Prochaska, J., Norcross, J. and DiClemente, C. (1994). *Changing for Good*. New York: Avon Books.

The Red Road to Wellbriety (2002). Colorado Springs, CO: White Bison, Inc.

Rieff, P. (1987). *The Triumph of the Therapeutic*. Chicago: University of Chicago Press.

Riessman, F. (1965). The "helper-therapy" principle. *Social Work*, 10, 24-32.

Riessman, F. (1990). Restructuring help: A human services paradigm for the 1990s. *American Journal of Community Psychology*, 18, 221-230.

SAMHSA (1998) *National Household Survey on Drug Abuse: Summary Report 1998*. Rockville, MD: National Institute on Drug Abuse.

Sanders, M. (1993). *Treating the African American Male Substance Abuser*. Chicago: Winds of Change Publishing Company.

Sanders, M. (2002). The response of African American communities to addiction: An opportunity for treatment providers. *Alcoholism Treatment Quarterly*, 20(3/4), 167-174.

Simpson, D.D., Joe, G.W., and Lehman, W.E. (1986). *Addiction Careers: Summary of Studies Based on the DARP 12-year Follow-up*. National Institute on Drug Abuse. Treatment Research Report (ADM 86-1420).

Singer, M and Borrero, M.G. (1984). Indigenous treatment for alcoholism: the case of Puerto Rican spiritualism. *Medical Anthropology: Cross-Cultural Studies in Health and Illness*. 8, 246-273.

Soriano, M. (1995).Latinos in rehabilitation: Implications for culturally-appropriate counseling. *NARPPS Journal*, 19(2), 67-72.

Spicer P. (2001). Culture and the restoration of self among former American Indian drinkers. *Social Science & Medicine*, 53(2),227-40.

Sue, DW & Sue, D. (1999). Counseling the Culturally Different: Theory and Practice. New York: John Wiley and Sons.

Schweitzer, A. (1993). (Compiled by Harold Robles) *Reverence for Life: The Words of Albert Schweitzer* New York: HarperCollins Publishers.

Tabor, M. (1970) Capitalism plus Dope Equals Genocide. Black Panther Party, U.S.A.

Taylor, T.B. (1992). Imago Dei: A discussion of an Afrocentric spiritual model of prevention. *In Spirituality and Prevention*, pp. 49-57, Springfield, IL: Prevention Resource Center.

Taylor, V. (1987). The triumph of the Alkali Lake Indian band. *Alcohol Health and Research World* Fall, 57.

Thomas, P. (1967). *Down These Mean Streets*. New York: Alfred-A. Knopf.

U.S. Census Bureau, Dept. of Commerce, Census 2000. http://www.census.gov/population/cen2000/phc-tl/tab01.txt.

Weibel-Orlando, J. (1987) Culture-specific treatment modalities: Assessing client-to-treatment fit in Indian alcoholism programs. In: Cox, W., Ed., *Treatment and Prevention of Alcohol Problems: A Resource Manual*. Orlando: Academic Press.

Weisner, C., Ray, G.T., Mertens, J.R., Satre, D.D., and Moore, C. (2003). Short-term alcohol and drug treatment outcomes predict long-term outcome. *Drug and Alcohol Dependence* 71, 281-294.

Westermeyer, J. (1974). "The drunken Indian:" Myths and realities. *Psychiatric Annals*, 4(11):29-36.

Westermeyer, J. (1996). Alcoholism among New World Peoples: A critique of history, methods, and findings. *American Journal on Addictions* 5(2),110-123.

White, W. (1996). *Pathways from the Culture of Addiction to the Culture of Recovery*. Center City, MN: Hazelden.

White, W. (1998) *Slaying the Dragon: The History of Addiction Treatment and Recovery in America*. Bloomington, IL: Chestnut Health Systems.

White, W., Boyle, M., & Loveland, D. (2002). Alcoholism/addiction as a chronic disease: From rhetoric to clinical reality. *Alcoholism Treatment Quarterly*, 20, 3 / 4, 107-130.

White, W., Boyle, M. And Loveland, D. (2003) Recovery management: Transcending the limitations of addiction treatment. *Behavioral Health Management* 23(3):38-44. (http://www.behavioral.net/2003_05-06/featurearticle.htm).

White, W., Boyle, M, Loveland, D, and Corrigan, P. (2003). What is Behavioral Health Recovery Management? A Brief Primer. http://www.bhrm.org.

White, W. and Chaney, R. (1993) *Metaphors of Transformation: Feminine and Masculine*. Bloomington, IL: Chestnut Health Systems.

White, W. (2000a) Addiction as a disease: The birth of a concept. *The Counselor* 1(1):46-51, 73.

White, W. (2000b) The history of recovered people as wounded healers: I. From Native America to the rise of the modern alcoholism movement. *Alcoholism Treatment Quarterly.* 18(1), 1-23.

White, W. and Popovits, R. (2002). *Critical Incidents: Ethical Issues in the Prevention and Treatment of Addiction.* Bloomington, IL: Chestnut Health Systems.

White, W., Woll, P and Webber, R. (2003) *Project SAFE: Best Practices Resource Manual.* Chicago, IL: Illinois Department of Human Service, Office of Alcoholism and Substance Abuse.

Williams, C. with Laird, R. (1992). *No Hiding Place: Empowerment and Recovery for Troubled Communities.* New York, NY: Harper San Francisco.

Womak, M.L. (1996). The Indianization of Alcoholics Anonymous: An examination of Native American recovery movements. Master's thesis, Department of American Indian Studies, University of Arizona.

Yamashiro, G., & Matsuoka, J.K. (1997). Help-seeking among Asian and Pacific Americans: A multiperspective analysis. *Social Work*, 42(2), 176-186.

William L. White

Acknowledgements: Work on this paper was supported by the Behavioral Health Recovery Management project (*www.bhrm.org*), funded by the Illinois Department of Human Services' Office of Alcoholism and Substance Abuse (OASA). The views expressed here are the authors' and do not necessarily reflect the policies of OASA. The authors would like to thank the many individuals who commented on early drafts of this paper. The suggestions of the following were particularly helpful: Michael Boyle, Don Coyhis, Maya Hennessey, Marco Jacome, Linda Kurtz, Tom Murphy, Nancy O'Brien, Jose Ortiz, Joe Powell, Joyce Rawdhetubhai, Richard Simonelli, Arturo Valdez, and David Whiters.

ABOUT THE GREAT LAKES ADDICTION TECHNOLOGY TRANSFER CENTER

The Great Lakes Addiction Technology Transfer Center (ATTC) is part of a national network that includes 14 regional ATTC's and a National Office. Funded by the Substance Abuse and Mental Health Services Administration, Center for Substance Abuse Treatment (SAMHSA/CSAT), the ATTCs have been charged with the mission of unifying science, services, and education to transform lives. Established in 1998, the Great Lakes ATTC is part of the Jane Addams College of Social Work, University of Illinois at Chicago. The Great Lakes ATTC uses educational products, training, technical assistance, information dissemination, collaboration, systems-change initiatives, and other technology transfer interventions to help prepare the addiction treatment field and allied health fields for the most effective evidence-based practice. The Great Lakes region includes Illinois, Indiana, Michigan, Ohio, and Wisconsin.

FOOTNOTES

[1]   The initial Rand Report included the finding: "...it appears that some alcoholics do return to normal drinking with no greater likelihood of relapse than alcoholics who choose abstention..." (Quoted in White, 1998). Controversies surrounding this report led to a second report that softened the initial report's findings.

[2]   Drs. Mark and Linda Sobell published a series of scientific reports documenting that some alcoholics achieve controlled drinking (Sobell and Sobell, 1973, 1976, 1978). These reports were followed by a re-evaluation by Pendery, Maltzman, and West (1982) that challenged the Sobell's findings and their professional integrity. The Sobell weathered blistering personal and professional attacks in spite of being later cleared of wrongdoing by two separate scientific panels (Dickens, Doob, Warwick, & Winegard, 1982; Trachtenberg, 1984)

[3]   The reference to Damascus refers to the Biblical account of the transformation of Saul of Tarsus, the orthodox Jew and persecutor of Christians, into St. Paul, the Christian missionary, on the road from Jerusalem to Damascus.

[4]   The thirteenth step is a euphemism for romantic involvement between AA members and, more specifically, the sexual overture by an older AA member to a newly sobered AA member.

[5]   While we have limited our discussion to communities of color, many reviewers (including Hennessey and Simonelli) of early drafts of this paper were struck by how applicable the ideas and strategies set forth in this paper are to women of all ethnic backgrounds.

[6]   All future references to American Indians or Native Peoples are intended to include Alaskan Natives.

[7]   Cultural competence has been defined as "a set of congruent behaviors, attitudes, and policies that come together in a system, agency or among professionals and enable that system, agency or those professions to work effectively in cross-cultural situations." Cross, T., Bazron, B., Dennis, K., & Isaacs, M., (1989). Towards A Culturally Competent System of Care Volume I. Washington, DC: Georgetown University Child Development Center, CASSP Technical Assistance Center.

[8]   Maria Yellow Horse Brave Heart (2003) has defined historical trauma as "cumulative emotional and psychological wounding over the lifespan and generations, emanating from massive group trauma experiences."

[9]   Rehabilitation assumes the existence of and need for replenishment of recovery capital; habilitation assumes the lack of pre-existing recovery capital and the need to dramatically reconstruct personal identity, interpersonal relationships, and a sobriety-based lifestyle.

[10]   Nation-building as used here refers to the process of linking the disempowered community into a larger consciousness and identity and a process of healing that seeks to heal historically

      disempowered communities AND the dominant culture of which they are such integral parts. One of our reviewers (Simonelli) called this "the next frontier of healing."

11   Research on developmental stages of change is in its infancy, and the emerging models tend to portray recovery for individuals and families in very linear terms. We suspect, and thank Tom Murphy for reminding us, that these processes are much more dynamic than what is conveyed in a linear, four-to-five-step model. Recovery, particularly for historically disempowered people, may be much more comparable to the subtle patterns and surprise-revealing pathways of a Japanese garden than that of a ladder.

12   Miller and C'de Baca describe transformative change as dramatic alterations of personal identity and character that are "vivid, surprising, benevolent and enduring." (p.4).

13   See White, 2002 for a discussion of the distinction between recovered and recovering.

14   The source of that shame transcends self-perceived sins of omission and commission and reaches to the very core of their identities as women and as African-American women.

15   Catalytic metaphors are concepts that spark breakthroughs in perception of self and the world at such a profound level that they incite beliefs, behavior, identity, and relationships.

16   The so-called "Asian flushing response" to alcohol among some Asians does not constitute a universal protective factor against alcoholism and alcohol-related problems in Asians. There is growing evidence that cultural, not biological, factors shape the prevalence and patterns of alcohol problems across highly diverse Asian populations.

Great Lakes (HHS Region 5)

ATTC Addiction Technology Transfer Center Network
Funded by Substance Abuse and Mental Health Services Administration

Linking Addiction Treatment and Communities of Recovery: A Primer for Addiction Counselors and Recovery Coaches

WILLIAM L. WHITE, MA
AND ERNEST KURTZ, PHD

Linking Addiction Treatment and Communities of Recovery: A Primer for Addiction Counselors and Recovery Coaches

INTRODUCTION

A long-tenured addictions counselor sheepishly shared that he was leaving the field—that it was getting harder and harder for him to feel good about what he was doing. He elaborated as follows, "Something got lost on our way to becoming professionals—maybe our heart. I feel like I'm working in a system today that cares more about a progress note signed by the right color of ink than whether my clients are really making progress toward recovery. I feel like too many treatment organizations have become people and paper processing systems rather than places where people transform their lives. Too much of our time is spent fighting for another day or a couple of extra sessions for our clients. I'm drowning in paper. We're forgetting what this whole thing is about. It's not about days or sessions or about this form or that form, and it's not about dollars; it's about RECOVERY!"[7]

At a recent gathering of Native American leaders, speaker after speaker referenced the disconnection between the world of addiction treatment and the cultural life within Native communities. In their culture, there is no separation between the individual, the family and the tribe. All have suffered wounds from alcohol and other drugs, and all need recovery processes that reflect an understanding of their historical trauma and current circumstances. The speakers advocated healing the community so that the community could in turn serve as a healing sanctuary for individuals and families.

With great sadness, the counselor reflects, "The kids who come here do so well while they are in treatment, but so many of them relapse in the days and weeks

---

[7] Many reviewers responded to this first paragraph just as audiences do around the country when we present this material. As one reviewer noted, "The treatment system across the nation is being strangled in its own red tape." Another reviewer saw what has occurred within addiction treatment within the larger industrialization and commercialization of health care and suggested the need for broad patient-centered renewal processes. We agree.

following their discharge. We bring them back to treatment and they seem to do well again but often repeat the relapse pattern when they go back home. How can they do so well in treatment and so poorly in their natural environments?"

An A.A. old-timer laments the lost service ethic among local groups in his community and recounts times when Twelve Step calls were something more than telling someone to call the local detox center. He feels that the service ethic weakened in tandem with the expansion of addiction treatment.

The growing interest in recovery research, the advent of recovery coaches and recovery support centers and the expanded funding for peer-based recovery support services all reflect efforts to recapture the field's lost recovery focus and reconnect the treatment experience to recovery and treatment institutions to the larger communities in which they are nested. There are increasing calls to shift addiction treatment from ever-briefer episodes of acute stabilization to a more global process of sustained recovery management (McLellan, Lewis, O'Brien, & Kleber, 2000). This would extend the role of the addiction counselor beyond the earliest stages of recovery initiation to the more complex processes of recovery stabilization and maintenance within the natural environment of each client and family. A critical aspect of that process involves connecting recovering individuals and families to local recovery support groups and communities of recovery as well as nurturing the development of such supports where they do not yet exist (White, Boyle & Loveland, 2002).

At the same time, many communities of recovery are experiencing a revival in service work as new recovery advocacy groups, in the language of the Connecticut Community of Addiction Recovery, "organize the recovery community's ability to care." Such organizations are acting on the belief that the recovery community has a responsibility to reach out to treatment organizations as well as to individuals and families who are entering and leaving treatment. These recovery advocacy groups are discovering a growing vanguard of people in long-term recovery who are responding with their time, their talents, their financial resources, and, most importantly, their stories to help those whose current suffering was once their own.

This monograph explores how to best facilitate this connection between the worlds of addiction treatment and addiction recovery. It is divided into six topical discussions:

1) The historical forces that are sparking a re-evaluation of the design of addiction treatment in the United States,

2) A review of the scientific evidence supporting the shift from an exclusively acute care (AC) model of treatment to a model of sustained recovery management (RM),

3) The growth, current status and growing diversity of American communities of recovery,

4) Strategies for building relationships between treatment organizations and local communities of recovery,

5) Procedures that can be used to assertively and effectively link clients to recovery support groups, and

6) Integrating this linkage process within a larger menu of post-treatment recovery support services.

This monograph is a follow-up to our recently released monograph, *The Varieties of Recovery Experience* (posted at http//:www.glattc.org). Our work on these recovery-themed papers began in 1998 with the establishment of the Behavioral Health Recovery Management Project funded by the Illinois Department of Alcoholism and Substance Abuse. Subsequent support has been provided by the Great Lakes Addiction Technology Transfer Center and (for this latest monograph) the Institute for Research, Education and Training in Addictions (IRETA). We extend a special thanks to Dr. Michael Flaherty and Charlie Bishop Jr. for their guidance on the development of the content of this essay and for their helpful reviews of early drafts. We would also like to thank the following individuals for their helpful feedback and suggestions: Jim Balmer, Ben Bass, Maryanne Frangules, Bev Haberle, Earl Harrison, Maya Hennessey, Martin Nicolaus, Bob Savage, Jason Schwartz, Richard Simonelli, Pat Taylor, Phillip Valentine, and Pam Woll.

A BRIEF NOTE ON LANGUAGE

The groups in which people regularly meet for mutual support in their recovery from alcohol and other drug problems have gone by many designations (*self-help, mutual aid, peer support* and *recovery support*). In the following pages, the terms *recovery mutual aid groups* and *recovery support groups* will be used interchangeably to refer to these groups. The larger networks of people and activities in which support group meetings are imbedded are referred to as *communities of recovery*. The term *recovery community* is used to convey the whole of these increasingly diverse communities of recovery. The phrase *recovery support services* refers specifically to non-clinical (not requiring training in diagnosis and treatment) services that aid recovery initiation and maintenance, e.g., activities such as monitoring (check-ups), modeling, sharing, encouraging, coaching/advising, linking, advocating and organizing. *Addiction,* as used in the following pages, is an umbrella term for substance use disorders that are characterized by severity and chronicity. Our choice to use it reflects our belief that severity and chronicity are the best predictors of those who will most need affiliation with communities of recovery to initiate and sustain the recovery process.

A SPECIAL NOTE TO ADMINISTRATORS AND SUPERVISORS

This monograph is written primarily for those working on the front lines of addiction treatment and recovery, particularly the addiction counselors and recovery coaches who bear responsibility for linking clients to local communities of recovery. We would be remiss, however, if we did not acknowledge the crucial roles administrators and clinical supervisors play in shaping the milieu within which such linkage processes can occur. We hope that as you read these pages you will reflect on what changes in treatment philosophy and service protocol would facilitate this linkage process. We have written earlier papers addressing this question and it is our intent to follow this paper with one focusing specifically on clinical supervision within recovery-oriented systems of care. We invite you to email us in care of the first author (<u>bwhite@chestnut.</u> <u>org</u>) to request copies of those articles or to share your questions, thoughts and suggestions related to what should be addressed within that next paper.

We do want to respond briefly to the question: Who will pay for recovery coaches and for assertive approaches to post-treatment continuing care and recovery support services? We anticipate that financial support for such roles and the reimbursement of post-treatment recovery support services will be a part of the restructuring of addiction treatment from an acute care model to a model of sustained recovery management. Such roles and services are already being financially subsidized through the Center for Substance Abuse Treatment's Recovery Community Support Program and Access to Recovery Program, several state systems (e.g., CT, AZ) and by some managed behavioral health care systems. We anticipate a day soon when it would be unthinkable to provide services designed to initiate addiction recovery without also providing the support services that play such a crucial role in maintaining recovery.

HISTORICAL BACKGROUND: TOWARD A RECOVERY PARADIGM

From Problem Conceptualization to Treatment Strategies: Cultures across the world have embraced widely divergent views of the origin of alcohol and other drug (AOD) problems. AOD problems and their resolution have been defined in religious terms (sin and redemption), spiritual terms (hunger for meaning and personal transformation), criminal terms (amorality/immorality and reformation), medical/ disease terms (sickness and recovery), psychological terms (flawed thinking/coping and maturation), and socio-cultural terms (historical trauma/oppression and liberation/ cultural renewal). These highly divergent approaches and their historical roots have been a subject of considerable debate (see Miller & Kurtz, 1994; Kurtz, 2002).

The question of which model is "true" or "works" is not a trivial one. The model choice dictates cultural/professional ownership of AOD problems—whether these problems belong to priests, judges, physicians, psychologists, addiction counselors or community activists. The chosen model dictates particular intervention philosophies and settings (whether the alcoholic is punished in a jail cell or counseled in a treatment center) and offers organizing metaphors for individuals and families impacted by AOD problems. All of the noted models begin with an understanding of the primary cause of AOD problems and then derive resolution strategies congruent with that understanding. This paper, in contrast, asks, "What if addiction treatment, addiction counseling and related recovery support services were designed, not on a particular view of the etiology of addiction, but on the lessons drawn from millions of people who have achieved long-term addiction recovery?"

Treatment, Recovery, Community: Modern addiction treatment came of age in the 1960s and 1970s as a community-based phenomenon. Programs of that era were birthed out of grassroots community advocacy efforts and held accountable to their founding visions through:

- representation of recovered and recovering people and their families on agency boards and advisory committees,
- recruitment of staff from local communities of recovery,
- vibrant recovery volunteer programs, and
- regular meetings between the treatment agency and the service committees of local recovery support fellowships.

Treatment agencies of this era, because of their reliance on local funding, were also accountable to local governments and allied service agencies. Through the processes of professionalization, industrialization and commercialization in the 1980s, most treatment programs ceased being community-based agencies and redefined themselves as businesses. In the process, they became less reliant on local funding, less accountable to local communities and less connected to local communities of recovery. Today, treatment institutions are vulnerable to the charge that they are disconnected from their founding roots—that treatment has become detached from the larger and more enduring process of recovery and disconnected from the physical and cultural contexts in which that recovery succeeds or fails (White, 2001a; White & Hagen, 2005).

The Varieties of Recovery Experience: Another category of influence on the process of linking people to communities of recovery is the growth and diversification of recovery support societies in the United States and around the world (Humphreys, 2004). The growth, geographical dispersion and longevity of Alcoholics Anonymous (A.A.) has positioned A.A. as the most visible recovery mutual aid fellowship in the United States. That said, there is a growing diversification of styles of Twelve Step recovery experience and a proliferation of explicitly religious and secular alternatives to Twelve Step programs. This growth and diversification of recovery support groups as well as the growing recognition of different styles of recovery initiation and maintenance require a greater level of knowledge and skill for those linking individuals to post-treatment recovery support services (White & Kurtz, 2005). It also requires understanding the difference between linking a client to recovery support meetings and linking a client to the larger community of recovery within which such meetings are imbedded (Balmer, personal communication, 2006).

Emerging Movements: There are two emerging movements that, by their success or failure, will shape the future of addiction treatment and recovery in America. The first is a treatment renewal movement. Led by front line service providers from across the country, the goals of this movement include reconnecting treatment to the process of long-term recovery and rebuilding relationships between treatment organizations, local communities and local recovery support groups (White, 2002). A second movement, the new recovery advocacy movement, rose in reaction to the restigmatization, demedicalization and recriminalization/penalization of AOD problems in the 1980s and 1990s. This movement has been led organizationally by a coalition of the Faces and Voices of Recovery, the National Council on Alcoholism and Drug Dependence, the Johnson Institute, the Legal Action Center, and (until recently) the Center for Substance Abuse Treatment's Recovery Community Support Program.[8] The goals of this movement include reaffirming the reality of long-term addiction recovery, celebrating the legitimacy of multiple pathways of recovery, enhancing the variety, availability, and quality of local/regional treatment and recovery support services and transforming existing treatment businesses into "recovery-oriented systems of care" (White, 2000; White & Taylor, in press).

Toward a Recovery Paradigm: Something is shifting in the behavioral health arena. Pathology and intervention paradigms are yielding to an emerging recovery paradigm in both the addictions and mental health fields (White, 2004a, 2005; White, Boyle, Loveland, 2004; Anthony, Gagne, & White, in press). The earliest calls for this reconnection of treatment and recovery came from tenured addictions professionals (See Zweben, 1986; Morgan, 1995, a,b; Else, 1999), a new generation of recovery advocates (e.g., Don Coyhis, Bev Haberle, Bob Savage, Philip Valentine), leading research scientists (McLellan, Lewis, O'Brien & Kleber, 2000), and state and federal policy makers (See http://www.dmhas.state.ct.us/recovery.htm and http://alt.samhsa. gov/news/NewsReleases/040303fs_atr_facts.htm).

Implications for the Addictions Counselor and Recovery Coach: For those involved in the face-to-face work of providing addiction counseling and recovery support services, this shift toward a recovery paradigm is pushing a(n):

- greater focus on what happens BEFORE and AFTER primary treatment,

---

[8] In 2002, the Center for Substance Abuse Treatment shifted the philosophy of its Recovery Community Support Program (RCSP) grants from a focus on recovery advocacy to a focus on peer-based recovery support services.

- transition from professional-directed treatment plans to client-developed recovery plans (Borkman, 1997)(See Sidebar),
- greater emphasis on the physical, social and cultural environment in which recovery succeeds or fails (e.g., shift from clinic-based aftercare to community-based continuing care)(Donovan, 1998),
- integration of professional treatment and indigenous recovery support groups (White & Sanders, 2004),
- increased use of peer-based recovery coaches (guides, mentors, assistants, support specialists) (White, 2004b), and an
- integration of paid recovery coaches and recovery support volunteers within interdisciplinary treatment teams.

How Recovery Plans (RP) Differ From Treatment Plans (TP)

1. The RP is developed, implemented, evaluated and refined by the client, not the treatment professional.
2. The RP is based on a partnership/consultation relationship between professional and client rather than an expert-patient relationship.
3. The RP is broader in scope, encompassing such domains as physical health, education, employment, finances, legal, family, social life, intimate relationships, and spirituality, in addition to the resolution of AOD problems.
4. The RP consists of a master plan of long-term recovery goals and a weekly action plan of steps that will mark progress toward those goals.
5. The RP emphasizes drawing strength and strategies from the collective experience of others in recovery.

Source: Borkman, T. (1997) Is recovery planning any different from treatment planning? *Journal of Substance Abuse Treatment* 15(1), 37-42.

This shift to a recovery paradigm is not without its sources of resistance and potential pitfalls. The obstacles that slow this shift are:

- conceptual (difficulty shifting from problem-focused to solution-focused thinking; difficulty thinking outside the acute care intervention model),

- personal/professional (a perceived loss of professional pride/status/power by addiction professionals, hesitancy to acknowledge the experiential wisdom of the recovery community, and reluctance to accept indigenous healers as peers) (Schwartz and Bass, personal communications, 2006),
- financial (the lack of financing models for post-treatment support services),
- technical (lack of evidence-based recovery support service protocol),
- ethical (the absence of ethical codes to guide the delivery of peer-based recovery support services), and
- institutional (weak infrastructures of addiction treatment organizations, particularly the exceptionally high turnover of service roles in the addiction treatment field).

While these obstacles are significant, the greatest obstacle may well turn out to be the tendency for treatment professionals to declare that they are already "recovery-oriented" or to mask treatment as usual behind a new recovery-focused rhetoric.

Working through these obstacles are recovery advocates and visionary professionals who "get it" and are willing to be part of this recovery advocacy and recovery support movement. Some of you reading these words may not fully realize it, but you were born for this moment in time. Your personal and professional experiences to date have prepared you to play a leadership role within this window of opportunity within the history of addiction treatment and recovery in America. It is the hope of the authors that you and others will use our discussions here to develop a personal vision of the role that you could play in widening the doorways of entry into addiction recovery and in enhancing the quality of life of people in recovery.

SCIENTIFIC BACKGROUND : POST-TREATMENT OUTCOMES, ROLE OF CONTINUING CARE, ROLE OF RECOVERY MUTUAL AID PARTICIPATION, IMPORTANCE OF POST-TREATMENT CHECK-UPS AND SUPPORT

If addiction is best considered a chronic condition, then we are not providing appropriate treatment for many addicted patients. Dr. Tom McLellan, 2002

The shift to a recovery paradigm is propelling the call for non-clinical alternatives to treatment, early identification and recovery engagement services, in-treatment recovery support services to increase successful treatment completion (now only about 50% of those admitted)(SAMHSA, 2002), and post-treatment monitoring and recovery support services. This paper focuses on the latter of these changes. To bolster our argument for post-treatment recovery support services, we offer the following propositions.[9]

The need for post-treatment check-ups and recovery support services intensifies as problem severity increases and recovery capital decreases. (*Recovery capital* is the quantity and quality of internal and external resources that one can bring to bear on the initiation and maintenance of recovery)(Granfield & Cloud, 1999). Not everyone with an AOD problem needs professional treatment or prolonged post-treatment continuing care. Many individuals with AOD problems resolve these problems without professional assistance, without involvement in recovery support

---

[9] This is not to say that linkage to recovery communities is something that should occur after treatment, but we do emphasize the role of such linkages on post-treatment recovery outcomes. We agree with several reviewers suggesting that this linkage could occur at the earliest point of service contact, including people who are on a waiting list for admission to treatment.

groups, or through brief professional intervention. Those who require a larger dose, intensity and duration of professional and peer support services to resolve these problems are characterized by greater personal vulnerability (e.g., family history, age of onset, developmental victimization), greater problem severity, greater problem complexity (e.g., presence of co-occurring medical/psychiatric illness), and fewer family and social supports for long-term recovery (White, 2005). The increased representation of clients entering treatment with multiple personal/family/environmental problems (and complex histories of intergenerational transmission of those problems) calls for a longer period of service provision (but not necessarily longer lengths of stay in acute levels of treatment) and an expanded menu of clinical and non-clinical recovery support services.

Addiction treatment outcomes are compromised by the lack of sustained recovery support services. Reports of treatment effectiveness note robust effects. Treatment follow-up studies report an average full remission rate of one third and significant reductions in AOD use/AOD-related problems for most clients (Miller, et al, 2001). Hundreds of thousands of people have entered recovery through the pathway of professional treatment, but claiming that "treatment works" as a result of these findings masks the fact that the majority of people completing addiction treatment resume AOD use in the year following treatment (Wilbourne & Miller, 2003), with over half of all post-treatment lapses and relapses occurring within 30 days of discharge (80% within 90 days of discharge)(Hubbard, Flynn, Craddock & Fletcher, 2001).

Professionally-directed, post-discharge continuing care can enhance recovery outcomes, but only 1 in 5 clients actually receives such care (Ito & Donovan, 1986; Johnson & Herringer, 1993; Godley, Godley, & Dennis, 2001; Dennis, Scott, & Funk, 2003; McKay, 2001). Strategies proven to increase continuing care participation (e.g., the use of a brief orientation session on continuing care, behavioral contracting, telephone prompts)(Lash, 1998; Donovan, 1998) are not mainstream practices in addiction treatment. Nothing conveys more clearly the acute care model of addiction treatment in the United States than the "afterthought" status and virtually non-existent budgets supporting continuing care following "primary treatment." The self-contained, brief episodes of *assess, diagnose, treat, discharge, terminate the service relationship* that typify most addiction treatment would be unthinkable in the treatment of any other chronic medical condition. Addiction professionals do not do assertive post-treatment monitoring and early re-intervention, but there is substantial anecdotal evidence that drug dealers and addicted peers do.

Participating in peer-based recovery support groups following treatment enhances long-term recovery outcomes, but without ancillary support, there is high attrition in such participation among those discharged from treatment (Mäkelä, Arminen, Bloomfield, Eisenbach-Stangl, Bergmark, Kurube, et al., 1996). Overall dropout rates in A.A. range between 35-68%, with most of this attrition occurring in the first weeks and months of contact with A.A. (Emrick, 1989). The two most recent and largest studies of attrition in A.A. participation during the year following discharge from treatment reported 41% and 40% dropout rates (Tonigan, Miller, Chavez, Porter, Worth, Westphal, Carroll, Repa, Martin & Tracy, 2002; Kelly and Moos, 2003). Active linkage (education about the potential value of peer support; facilitating direct connection to a person or specific group) can increase affiliation with a recovery mutual aid society (Weiss, et al 2000), but studies reveal most referrals from treatment professionals to mutual aid organizations are of the passive variety (verbal suggestion only) (Humphreys, et al 2004).

At present, the resolution of severe substance use disorders can span years (sometimes decades) and multiple treatment episodes before stable recovery maintenance is achieved (Anglin, Hser, & Grella, 1997; Dennis, Scott, & Hristova, 2002). AOD drug dependencies resemble chronic disorders (e.g., type 2 diabetes mellitus, hypertension and asthma) in their etiological complexity, variable pattern of onset, prolonged course (with waxing and waning of symptom severity), treatment (sustained management rather than cure), and clinical outcomes (O'Brien & McLellan, 1996; McLellan, et al, 2000). To characterize addiction as a chronic disorder is not to suggest that recovery is not possible. There are millions of people in stable, long-term recovery from addiction (Humphreys, 2004; Dawson, et al, 2005), but the processes of recovery are more complex than what is portrayed to the public and to individuals and families entering treatment.

For many individuals, recovery sustainability is not achieved in the short span of time treatment agencies are currently involved in their lives. When addiction treatment agencies discharge clients following a brief episode of services, they convey the illusion that continued recovery is self-sustainable without further professional support. However, research data reveals that durability of recovery from alcoholism (the point at which risk of future lifetime relapse drops below 15%) is not reached until after 4-5 years of sustained remission (De Soto, O'Donnel, & De Soto, 1989; Jin, Rourke, Patterson, Taylor, & Grant, 1998). This recovery durability point is even longer for recovery from narcotic addiction (Simpson & Marsh, 1986; Hser, Hoffman, Grella, & Anglin, 2001). Such findings beg for models of sustained post-treatment check-ups and support comparable to the assertive post-treatment monitoring used in other chronic disorders, e.g., diabetes, heart disease, cancer. While the effects of acute treatment erode with time, the influence of the post-treatment environment increases. That is the environment we must niche within and remain within if we are truly interested in long-term recovery.

Addiction treatment has become the revolving door it was intended to replace. Addiction treatment was birthed in part to eliminate the "revolving door" through which alcoholics and addicts cycled through the criminal justice system and public hospitals. Addiction treatment programs have now become that revolving door. Today, 64% of persons entering publicly-funded treatment in the United States have already had one or more prior treatments (22% with 3-4 prior treatments; 19% with 5 or more prior treatments)(OAS, 2005). Between 25-35% of clients who complete addiction treatment will be re-admitted to treatment within one year, and 50% will be readmitted within 2-5 years (Hubbard, Marsden, Rachal, Harwood, Cavanaugh, & Ginzburg, 1989; Simpson, Joe, & Broome, 2002).

There may be cumulative and synergistic effects resulting from multiple treatment episodes. Long-term studies of clients treated for *substance dependence* in publicly funded programs reveal that the majority of those who achieve stable recovery do so after 3 to 4 episodes of treatment over multiple years (Anglin, Hser, & Grella, 1997; Dennis et al., 2005; Grella & Joshi, 1999; Hser, Anglin, Grella, Longshore, & Prendergast, 1997; Hser, Grella, Chou, & Anglin, 1998). This raises the potential for linking and integrating multiple episodes to enhance their power to facilitate recovery initiation and maintenance. According to studies of clients who relapse following discharge from primary treatment, the best predictor of recovery at five years following discharge is readmission to treatment (Mertens, Weisner & Ray, 2005). We need to find ways to strategically link these episodes of care to shorten addiction careers.

There is a growing body of evidence that enmeshing clients with high problem severity and low recovery capital within sober living communities can dramatically enhance long-term recovery outcomes (Jason, Davis, Ferrari & Bishop, 2001). A just-completed study compared the post-treatment recovery of individuals discharged from addiction treatment who were randomly assigned to either an Oxford House (one of the 1,200 Oxford Houses in the U.S.) or to traditional post-treatment "aftercare" (access to outpatient continuing care groups). The Oxford House members had less than half the rate of substance use, twice the monthly income, and a third of the incarceration rate of those assigned to traditional aftercare (Jason, Olson, Farrari & Lo Sasso, in press).

This confirms earlier research on the importance of social support in the recovery process (Jason, Davis, Ferrari & Bishop, 2001; Humphreys, Mankowski, Moos & Finney, 1999) and suggests the need for greater linkage between addiction treatment institutions and this growing network of sober housing resources and sober social communities.

    <u>Conclusions: 1. *Most people discharged from addiction treatment are precariously balanced between recovery and re-addiction in the weeks, months and even years following treatment. 2. Post-treatment check-ups and support and assertive linkage to communities of recovery and other recovery support services can significantly enhance long-term recovery outcomes.*</u> The findings of two recent Chicago studies stand as confirmation of these conclusions. Scott, Foss and Dennis conducted quarterly monitoring interviews of 1,326 clients over three years following an index episode of addiction treatment. Each client was categorized each quarter as 1) in the community using, 2) incarcerated, 3) in treatment, or 4) in the community not using. More than 80% of the clients changed status one or more times over the course of the three years (Scott, Foss & Dennis, 2005). In the second study, Dennis, Scott and Funk (2003) randomly assigned 448 individuals discharged from Chicago addiction treatment facilities to either a recovery management checkup (RMC) group (who received quarterly assessments, motivational interviewing, and, if needed, re-linkage to treatment services) or a control condition (quarterly status assessment only). The study found that those clients assigned to the RMC condition were more likely than those in the control group to return to treatment, to return to treatment sooner, and to spend more subsequent days in treatment. Most significantly, RMC participants experienced significantly fewer total quarters in need of treatment and were less likely to need treatment at 2 years follow-up.

    The fragileness of post-treatment adjustment and evidence that multiple treatment episodes can precede stable recovery raise the possibility that addiction and treatment careers could be shortened and recovery careers extended if post-treatment check-ups and support were provided for substance use disorders in the manner they are being provided for other chronic conditions. In the long run, check-ups and support could:

- decrease the total number of acute treatment episodes required to achieve long-term recovery,
- speed admission when such treatment is needed,
- enhance the dose of treatment and support services received, and

- hasten recovery stabilization and maintenance.

The studies of Dennis, Scott and colleagues (2003) and McKay's (2005) recent review of research on extended interventions confirm the potential importance of post-treatment monitoring (via recovery check-ups and active linkage to recovery supports). There is also evidence that such effects can be achieved using low-cost delivery formats (e.g., telephone-based check-ups and support) (McKay, 2005). The Connecticut Community of Addiction Recovery is currently being funded through the Connecticut Department of Mental Health and Addiction Services to pilot a telephone-based recovery support project for individuals who have been discharged from addiction treatment (Boffman, Fisher, Gilbert & Valentine, in press).

AMERICAN COMMUNITIES OF RECOVERY: A BRIEF INTRODUCTION

A Long and Rich History: American recovery mutual aid societies predating A.A. include abstinence-based Native American religious and cultural revitalization movements (from the early 1730s), recovery circles of the Delaware Prophets, Handsome Lake Movements, Shawnee and Kickapoo Prophet movements, Indian Shaker Church, Native American Church and today's Wellbriety Movement, the Washingtonians (1840s), the Fraternal Temperance Societies (1850-1900), the Ribbon Reform Clubs (1870s), institutional support groups such as the Keeley Leagues and the Godwin Association (1870s-1890s), and such faith-based groups as the Drunkard's Club, the United Order of Ex-Boozers and the Jacoby Club (early 20th century) (White, 2001b). The history of A.A. has been marked by progressive growth in membership and groups, a diversification of A.A. member characteristics (by age, gender, ethnicity, sexual orientation, occupational background, etc.), and a growing diversity of styles of recovery within A.A. Adaptations of A.A.'s Twelve Steps began with Alcoholics Victorious (1948) and Narcotics Anonymous (1947, 1953), with alternatives to Twelve Step recovery programs growing rapidly in the last quarter of the twentieth century. .

Today, there are explicitly religious, spiritual (but not religious), and secular frameworks of addiction recovery in the U.S. Recovery support groups that emphasize the role of spirituality in recovery are represented by mainstream Twelve Step groups. Faith-based recovery support structures include Alcoholics Victorious, Teen Challenge, Alcoholics for Christ, Overcomers Outreach, Liontamers Anonymous, Mountain Movers, High Ground, Free N' One, Victorious Lady, Celebrate Recovery, Millati Islami and many local recovery ministries. Secular frameworks of recovery include Women for Sobriety (WFS), Secular Organization for Sobriety-Save Our Selves (SOS), Rational Recovery (RR), Men for Sobriety (MFS), Moderation Management (MM), SMART Recovery®, and LifeRing Secular Recovery (LSR) (White & Kurtz, 2005).

The major addiction recovery support groups are profiled in the Mutual Support Resources Guide that is posted at the Faces & Voices of Recovery Website (http://facesandvoicesofrecovery.org/resources/support_home.php) and updated monthly by its developers, Drs. Ernie and Linda Kurtz. The Faces and Voices Guide catalogues group and Internet-based mutual recovery support resources. A summary chart of American addiction recovery mutual aid groups is displayed in table 1 in the Appendices, profiling each organization's founding date, membership size, philosophical orientation (secular, spiritual, religious), primary support format (face-to-face meetings or Internet-based support), and any special group focus. This table can serve as a tool in matching individuals to particular groups, but the most detailed info and web links to these groups can be found at the Faces and Voices Website.

Varieties and Commonalities: Studies of recovery support structures reveal a diversity of catalytic metaphors that individuals use to understand and alter patterns of AOD use/problems. Metaphors are terms or phrases (crystallizations of ideas) that through analogy have the power to label and elucidate complex experience. Metaphors create breakthroughs in perception that enhance understanding of oneself and the self-world relationship. Catalytic metaphors are words/ideas that are so penetrating that they drive profound changes in personal behavior, personal identity and interpersonal relationships. There is, for example, a long history of the use of medical metaphors to understand addiction, e.g., *disease, illness, allergy.* Such constructs are "true" for many persons in the sense that they validate and make sense of otherwise incomprehensible and sanity-challenging experiences. They are metaphorically true to the extent that they provide a cognitive cornerstone through which some individuals can organize their movement from addiction to recovery via the processes of story reconstruction and storytelling (White, 1996).

The proposition that there are many pathways and styles of recovery rests on the existence of a wide range of words, ideas, metaphors and experiences that can serve as a catalyst for recovery initiation and maintenance. There are, for example, recovery programs that place the transcendence of self at the center of the recovery experience (e.g., A.A.'s powerlessness, acceptance, surrender; being "born again" in Christian recovery frameworks). But there are alternative frameworks that emphasize assertion of self (e.g., Women for Sobriety's "I have a drinking problem but it no longer has me. I am the master of it and I am the master of myself.") (Kirkpatrick, 1986, p. 166.) The variability of these frameworks is also seen when contrasting empowerment psychotherapies with models of alcoholism treatment that have tended to extol the importance of surrender and humility in the recovery process (Tiebout, 1949). Where most recovery frameworks focus on individual experience, frameworks arising within historically disempowered communities often use catalytic metaphors that focus on collective experience (historical trauma, genocide, cultural survival/renewal) as frameworks to understand the etiology of AOD problems and provide a rationale for rejection of alcohol and other drugs (e.g., The Red Road) (Coyhis, 2000).

Core ideas, organizational structures, meeting formats, communication styles, and daily recovery rituals differ considerably across the growing spectrum of American recovery mutual aid groups, but these groups also share many common characteristics. All recovery support groups:

- contain members who have transformed their lives using the group's key ideas and methods,
- provide an esteem-salvaging answer to the question, "Why me?" (How did I come to develop a problem in my relationship with alcohol and/or other drugs?),
- provide a rationale for dramatically altering one's pattern of AOD consumption,
- provide daily prescriptions for recovery maintenance, and
- enmesh each individual in a sanctuary of shared "experience, strength and hope."

A point crucial to this paper is that all recovery support groups have individuals who fully respond to their respective programs of recovery, individuals who partially respond, and individuals who do not respond at all (Morgenstern, Kahler, Frey & Labouvie, 1996). There are also individuals who initiate and sustain recovery within a particular mutual aid group, individuals who simultaneously attend different mutual aid groups (attending WFS and A.A. meetings concurrently), individuals who initiate recovery in one group and then shift affiliation to another group (e.g., movement from N.A. to A.A.), and individuals who initiate recovery in a group like A.A., then disengage from active participation in A.A., but successfully sustain long-term recovery (See White and Kurtz, 2005). There are individuals with severe AOD problems who experience natural recovery—the initiation and maintenance of recovery without professional treatment or involvement in a recovery mutual aid group (Tuchfeld, 1981; Biernacki, 1986, Granfield & Cloud, 1999).

So what do we make of all this? Given this diversity in styles of recovery initiation and maintenance, the best strategy is for each treatment program and addictions professional to develop a broad menu of recovery-focused ideas, activities, and mutual aid structures that can be offered to clients. Our job is not to coerce or convince clients that one particular framework of recovery is the best. Rather, it is to offer each client exposure to the successful pathways of recovery that others have used and to help each client find a framework and style of recovery that achieves a personal fit.

So what are the facts about recovery mutual aid groups in America? The following historically and scientifically grounded propositions constitute a good starting point.

1. Americans with severe alcohol and other drug problems have banded together for mutual support in recovery for more than 250 years (White, 1998, 2001b).

2. A.A., due to its large membership, wide geographical dispersion, wide adaptation to other problems, and organizational longevity has established itself as the standard by which other recovery mutual aid groups are evaluated (Room, 1989; Kurtz & White, 2003).

3. Participation in recovery mutual aid groups following addiction treatment enhances long-term recovery outcomes (Emrick, Tonigan, Montgomery & Little, 1993, Fiorentine, 1999; Humphreys, et al, 2004).

4. In spite of allegations to the contrary, recent studies confirm A.A. affiliation and recovery rates for women, people of color, young people, and people with co-occurring psychiatric disorders (including those on medication) are comparable to those reported for general A.A. membership (Humphreys, Mavis, & Stoffelmayr, 1994; See White & Kurtz, 2005 for a review).

5. There are alternatives to A.A. and Twelve Step programs that offer different goals (e.g., moderation-based groups), philosophies (e.g., explicitly religious and secular groups), and recovery initiation and maintenance strategies (Humphreys, 2004; White & Kurtz, 2005).

6. Most of what we know from the standpoint of science about recovery support groups is based on studies of A.A., although studies of other recovery support groups have increased in the past 25 years (Humphreys, 2004).

7. Studies of recovery mutual aid groups reveal evidence of a dose effect (recovery stability increases with number of meetings attended) (Humphreys, Moos & Cohen, 1997; Chappel, 1993) and an intensity effect (recovery stability increases with broader pattern of participation (e.g., applying concepts to daily problem solving, reading recovery literature, sober socializing, service work) (Montgomery, Miller & Tonigan, 1995; Humphreys, Moos & Cohen, 1997).

8. Completion of addiction treatment AND participation with recovery mutual aid groups is more predictive of long-term recovery than either alone (Fiorentine & Hillhouse, 2000).

9. All recovery mutual aid groups experience individuals who fully respond, individuals who partially respond, and individuals who do not respond at all to their program (Morgenstern, Kahler, Frey, & Labouvie, 1996).

10. Individuals may initiate recovery through one framework and then shift to another framework to maintain that recovery (e.g., African American women shifting from A.A./N.A. for recovery initiation to use of the church as their primary source of support for recovery maintenance) (White, Woll, & Webber, 2003).

To embrace these propositions, treatment agencies and treatment professionals will need to broaden their tenets to embrace a philosophy of choice, strengthen their relationships with diverse communities of recovery and enhance and individualize their strategies for linking clients to particular communities of recovery (Woll, personal communication, 2006).

Unanswered Questions: Many questions about recovery mutual aid groups remain unanswered. Additional research is needed to enhance our ability to effectively match particular individuals to particular recovery support groups. A short sampling of critical unanswered (even unasked) questions include the following:

1. Are the findings from studies of A.A. applicable to other Twelve Step groups (e.g., N.A./C.A.) and to alternative recovery support structures?

2. What are the patterns of long-term affiliation (or disaffiliation) with A.A., and how are these patterns similar or different for other recovery support groups?

3. Does exposure to a moderation-based support group shorten addiction careers for some individuals by accelerating their commitment to sobriety following failed efforts to maintain moderation guidelines?

4. Which clinical practices in addiction treatment lead to the highest rates of affiliation with recovery support groups following treatment?

5. What are the recovery support needs of people in long-term addiction recovery and how do those needs differ from those in early recovery?

6. What factors contribute to relapse after 5-20+ years of continuous recovery?

7. Does participation in the recovery community outside of mutual support meetings play a role in the stability and quality of long-term recovery?

<u>Mutual Aid Critics</u>: Criticism of recovery mutual aid groups has generally focused on A.A. There is almost a cottage industry of A.A. and Twelve Step critics who contend that 1) A.A. is not successful or is successful with only certain types of alcoholics, 2) A.A.'s religious language keeps many alcoholics from seeking recovery, 3) People become too dependent on A.A. (charges that A.A. is a cult that creates "Twelve Step Zombies"), 4) A.A.'s reliance on a Higher Power undermines personal responsibility and development of internal strengths, 5) A.A. ignores environmental factors that contribute to alcohol problems, and 6) A.A.'s political influence has retarded the scientific advancement of the alcoholism treatment field and contributed to clinical rigidity (reviewed in White, 1998).

Perhaps more troublesome is the allegation in print (e.g., Gilliam, 1999; Fransway, 2000) and on the Internet (e.g., www.aadeprogramming.com or http://health.groups.yahoo.com/group/12-step-free/) that individuals have been harmed by affiliation with A.A. and related recovery support groups. These critiques raise important and currently unanswered (from the standpoint of science) questions such as: are all or particular mutual aid groups contraindicated for certain individuals who could be injured by their experiences within a mutual aid group? If so, what are the recognizable characteristics of such groups, the characteristics of the individuals most vulnerable to injury, and the nature of the injuries they could experience? Until such questions can be fully answered, we recommend promoting a choice philosophy and monitoring each client's ongoing responses to recovery support group participation.

<u>The Choice Philosophy</u>: A choice philosophy is based on the recognition of multiple pathways and styles of long-term recovery and the recognition of the right of each person to select a pathway and style of recovery that represents their personal and aspirational values. Steps that addiction treatment programs can take to actualize a philosophy of choice are outlined below.

Actualizing the Choice Philosophy

- Professional counselors, recovery coaches and volunteers represent the diversity of pathways and styles of recovery.
- Professional counselors and recovery coaches are knowledgeable about the full spectrum of religious, spiritual and secular recovery support groups and can fluently express the catalytic ideas used within each of these frameworks.
- Professional counselors and recovery coaches are aware of patterns of co-attendance (concurrent or sequential participation in two or more recovery support structures, e.g., co-attendance at WFS and A.A. meetings, N.A. participation with later transitioning to A.A. as one's primary recovery support structure).
- Individuals and their families are educated about the variety of recovery experiences and the legitimacy of multiple pathways and styles of recovery.
- Informational materials, lectures and structured exercises that people receive represent the scope of recovery support options, e.g., posting all local recovery support meeting schedules on the treatment agency website and facility bulletin boards, giving each client a wallet card with the central contact numbers of local recovery support groups, profiling local recovery support groups in agency/alumni newsletters.
- Individual choice is respected; individuals receiving services are not demeaned or disrespected for the recovery support strategies they choose; clinical strategies involve motivational interviewing principles and techniques rather than coercion and confrontation.
- Professional counselors and recovery coaches are encouraged to self-identify and bring to supervision negative feelings they may have about a particular pathway of recovery chosen by a client.

Choice and the Stages of Recovery: To implement a choice philosophy, addictions counselors and recovery coaches must reconcile the philosophical and therapeutic value of choice with the growing evidence of how neurological impairments can impair the choice-making abilities of individuals in active addiction and early recovery (Dackis & O'Brien, 2005). The challenge for the addictions counselor or recovery coach is distinguishing authentic choice from what A.A. calls "stinkin' thinkin'", what Rational Recovery calls the addictive voice or "Beast," what Secular Organization for Sobriety refers to as the "lizard brain," what LifeRing Secular Recovery calls the "addict self" (versus the "sober self"), and what Christian recovery groups refer to as the "voice of the Devil?" Given the dichotomy between the sober self and the addicted self, the question becomes, "who's really choosing: Dr. Jekyll or Mr. Hyde?" Some would frame this as separating what each client wants/needs from what his or her disease wants/needs.

One way to partially reconcile this dilemma is to view recovery as a progressive rehabilitation of the will—the power to reclaim personal choice (Smith, 2005). At a practical level, this means that the first day of detox may not be the best time to rely exclusively on client choice. Without rehabilitation of the power to choose and an encouragement of choice, we get, not sustainable recovery, but superficial treatment compliance. To effectively apply a philosophy of choice will require discretion and skill where immaturity, acute psychiatric symptoms, drug impairment and impaired ability to read social cues severely limit choice generation, choice analysis and capacity to stick with any personal resolution. In such cases, we must carefully plot a path between complete autonomy (total choice and clinical abandonment) and paternalism (no choice). Scientific confirmation of this stance is found in a study in which people with severe alcohol problems, recognizing their impaired decision-making capacities, preferred therapist-set goals in treatment; whereas those with less severe problems preferred self-set goals (Sobell, Sobell, Bogardis, Leo & Skinner, 1992).

Creating Informed Consumers: A philosophy of choice is viable only with persons who have the neurological capacity for decision-making, who believe they have the right to make their own choices and who are aware of and can evaluate available service and support options. Creating informed, assertive consumers of addiction treatment and recovery support services can be enhanced by: 1) affirming the service consumer's right to choose, 2) distributing and reviewing consumer guides on treatment and recovery support services published by recovery advocacy organizations, 3) teaching service consumers how to recognize quality services, 4) encouraging consumers to visit service options before making a decision (versus taking whatever is offered them), and 5) defining the criteria by which the client and service specialist will know if participation in a particular group is working or not working (Bev Haberle, personal communication). Similar considerations need to be extended to educate the family members of those needing or seeking recovery.

Choice and Limited Resource Alternatives: Another obstacle to implementing a choice philosophy is the limited recovery support options available today within

William L. White

many communities. Altering that situation requires moving from a clinical perspective to a recovery community development perspective. Recovery options are expanding, clients are using these options (either alone or in patterns of co-involvement with one or more support groups), and progressive treatment organizations are playing a role in nurturing the development of expanding recovery support resources. We will describe shortly how this can be achieved.

BUILDING RELATIONSHIPS BETWEEN TREATMENT ORGANIZATIONS AND LOCAL COMMUNITIES OF RECOVERY

An emphasis on changing social networks to be conducive to recovery could heighten clinical effectiveness and prevention efforts within communities.

-Constance Weisner, Helen Matzger & Lee Ann Kaskutas, 2005

More work is needed to strengthen the ability of addiction treatment...to link patients to self-help programs and support their on-going participation in them.

James McKay, 2005

...interventions should focus on enhancing continuation in AA and on identifying other mutual aid groups that may provide similar benefits. –Rudolf & Bernice Moos, 2005

Relationships between treatment organizations, recovery mutual support groups and recovery community organizations have changed dramatically over the past 40 years. As noted earlier, the pattern of collaboration that once existed between treatment agencies and local mutual aid groups dissipated in the professionalization of addiction counseling and the industrialization of addiction treatment. The evidence presented earlier in this paper suggests the need to re-link addiction treatment to indigenous communities of recovery.

Linkage Philosophy: There are three critical points in shaping a philosophy of linkage between treatment agencies/professionals and recovery mutual aid groups and recovery community organizations. The first is that professional treatment can be viewed as an adjunct to recovery mutual aid groups, rather than seeing such groups as an adjunct to treatment. Secondly, recovery mutual aid groups can serve as an alternative to professional treatment (Humphreys & Moos, 2001; White & Kurtz, 2005). Let us state again recent findings that participation in professional treatment and recovery support groups generates better long-term recovery outcomes than participating in either professional treatment or recovery support groups alone (Fiorentine & Hillhouse, 2000). These findings are based on clinical studies of individuals who present to treatment with severe AOD problems and limited recovery support networks. There are, however, situations where recovery mutual aid groups stand as an appropriate initial choice over admission to professionally-directed addiction treatment. This occurs when individuals present with lower problem severity and high recovery capital (internal and external recovery support assets). In this case, an individual could be referred to a recovery support group and their responses monitored to see if he or she can initiate and sustain recovery without the need for professional treatment. This alternative can potentially avoid the expense of treatment and the stigma and discrimination that can accompany diagnosis and treatment of a substance use disorder. Within this philosophical stance, addiction treatment is not the first line of response for AOD problems, but a safety net for those individuals who cannot resolve AOD problems through nonprofessional family and community supports.

A second point in this linkage philosophy is the need to respect the principles and guidelines recovery support groups have established to govern their relationships with outside organizations. Efforts must be made by the treatment agency to understand and abide by such principles as they differ from group to group. Twelve Step groups rely on codified traditions that govern their group life and their external relationships. A.A.'s Twelve Traditions, for example, would suggest that addiction treatment agencies not:

- refer individuals to closed A.A. meetings who do not meet A.A.'s requirement for membership as set forth in Tradition Three ("The only requirement for A.A. membership is a desire to stop drinking.")
- involve A.A. service committees in matters unrelated to carrying a message of hope to alcoholics (Tradition Five: "Each group has but one primary purpose— to carry the message to the alcoholic who still suffers.")
- use the A.A. name in any promotional material that would inadvertently convey A.A.'s endorsement of the treatment agency or that A.A. was affiliated with or a part of the treatment agency (Tradition Six: "An A.A. group ought never endorse, finance, or lend the A.A. name to any related facility or outside

enterprise, lest problems of money, property, and prestige divert us from our primary purpose.")

- offer financial contributions to A.A. (Tradition Seven: "Every A.A. group ought to be fully self-supporting, declining outside contributions.")
- entitle roles (e.g., "A.A. Counselor") with names that convey the professionalization of the A.A.'s service to still-suffering alcoholics (Tradition Eight: "Alcoholics Anonymous should remain forever non-professional, but our service centers may employ special workers.")
- solicit A.A.'s opinion on any outside issue or otherwise draw A.A. into any public controversy (Tradition Ten: "Alcoholics Anonymous has no opinion on outside issues, hence the name of A.A. ought never be drawn into public controversy.")
- violate the anonymity of any A.A. member by linking their full name and A.A. affiliation at the level of press, radio or film (Tradition Eleven: "Our public relations policy is based on attraction rather than promotion; we need always maintain personal anonymity at the level of press, radio and films.") (Alcoholics Anonymous, 19821).

A third point is that groups claiming to be recovery support groups ought to also be held accountable by treatment facilities to certain basic standards, including the expectation that such groups be based on testable principles of personal change, are accountable for recovery outcomes, do not interfere with the medical treatment of its members, do not financially, sexually or emotionally exploit their members, and do not claim expertise for which they possess no education, training and experience (Nicolaus, personal communication, 2006). Recovery mutual aid group experiences are not universally positive, and some such experiences may be harmful. Professionals have a responsibility to understand the potential for such harm and injury, orient their clients to the potential risks as well as benefits of support group participation, link their clients to particular individuals and groups that have a reputation for integrity, and monitor each client's experiences within those groups that have been recommended. When a client is not experiencing positive benefits from their participation in a particular group or risks injury from such continued participation, then disengagement from that group and the exploration of alternative sources of recovery support are indicated and should be encouraged. Problems of attrition in recovery mutual aid groups are usually conceptualized as a failure of the individual, but such attrition should also be a source of feedback about and to the recovery mutual aid group.

A final point in this linkage philosophy is a reaffirmation of the earlier philosophy of choice that calls for respect for different relational styles of recovery and respect for the legitimacy of different recovery pathways (religious, spiritual, secular) and their respective support groups (White & Nicolaus, 2005). By relational style, we refer to how individuals in recovery relate or do not relate to others in recovery. There are acultural styles in which individuals recover without relationships with others in recovery, bicultural styles in which individuals have a balanced social network of people in recovery and "civilians" (those without addiction/recovery experience), and culturally enmeshed styles in which individuals are almost completely absorbed in relationships with other people in recovery (White & Kurtz, 2005). We recommend a linkage philosophy that includes tolerance for acultural styles of recovery (particularly for those with low problem severity and high recovery capital) as well as tolerance for very enmeshed styles of recovery. Persons with deep, prolonged involvement in cultures of addiction may require an enmeshed style of early recovery. There is recent evidence that these affiliation styles change for many people over the course of recovery (Kaskutas, et al, 2005).

Goals of Linkage Process: There are three primary goals for linking individuals in addiction treatment to recovery support groups and the larger communities of recovery: 1) to solidify recovery initiation (problem identification, recovery commitment, resolution of personal/environmental obstacles to recovery, beginning identity and lifestyle reconstruction), 2) to connect each individual/family to a community of recovered and recovering people with whom they can share their experience, strength and hope, and 3) to provide communal guidance for the transition from recovery initiation/stabilization to long-term recovery maintenance.

Linkage Principles: There are several scientifically and clinically grounded findings and principles that should guide the linkage of clients to recovery support groups.

- Assertive linkage (facilitating the connection between the client and a particular individual/group) is more effective than passive linkage (verbal encouragement) (Weiss, et al 2000).
- 40% of clients discharged from treatment do not participate in recovery support groups in the weeks and months following their discharge (Moos & Moos, 2005).
- Rapid entry into involvement with a recovery support group during treatment services generates better long-term recovery outcomes than delayed linkage (e.g., following treatment or at a period subsequent to treatment) (Moos & Moos, 2005).

- Broader patterns of recovery support group participation are more predictive of sustained remission than the more restrictive measure of meeting attendance (Montgomery, Miller & Tonigan, 1995; Humphreys, Moos & Cohen, 1997).
- The longer the participation in recovery support groups in the three years following primary treatment, the greater the probability of remission at 15+ years following treatment (Moos & Moos, 2005).
- There are high early dropout rates in recovery support group participation (in the 40-70% range)(Kelly & Moos, 2003; Moos & Moos, 2005).
- Sustaining and increasing recovery support group involvement over years 1-3 following treatment is associated with stable remission at subsequent follow-up (Moos & Moos, 2005).
- While some individuals disengage from recovery support groups after a period of recovery initiation and sustain stable remission (Kaskutas, et al, 2005), those who sustain recovery support group participation are more likely to be in remission at follow-up than those who disengage (Moos & Moos, 2005).

These findings suggest an assertive linkage process that begins immediately upon treatment initiation, is monitored over time and includes ongoing coaching for recovery support group participation and, when indicated, re-linkage to past or alternative groups following disengagement.

Measurable Benchmarks: The effectiveness of this linkage process can be reflected in two types of benchmarks. The first involves individual or collective process measures such as percentage of clients involved in recovery support meetings during the first 30 days following their discharge from treatment, the total and average number of weekly meetings attended in the first 90 days following discharge from treatment or the percentage of individuals referred to Twelve Step groups who have a temporary or permanent sponsor within 30 days of discharge. The second type of measurable benchmark involves collective changes in clinical/recovery outcomes that follow development of assertive linkage processes. Such hoped for outcome measures would include decreases in post-treatment relapse rates, extended lengths of time from discharge to first use, shorter episodes of lapse/relapse, reductions in treatment readmissions, lower post-treatment mortality rates and increases in quality of recovery measures.

Working with Mutual Aid Service Structures: Most recovery mutual aid groups have established service structures and procedures that guide the relationship between each group and treatment organization. The most formal of these guidelines are the Hospital and Institutions (H&I) Committees (also referred to as Treatment Facility [T.F.] Committees) developed within A.A. and replicated with minor adaptations in N.A., C.A. and other Twelve Step groups. A good orientation to H&I Committees and the relationship between Twelve Step programs and treatment organizations can be obtained by reviewing the following documents:

- *A.A. Guidelines: Treatment Facility Committees*
- http://www.alcoholics-anonymous.org/default/en_pdfs/mg-14_treatfacilcomm.pdf.
- *How A.A. Members Cooperate with other Community Efforts to Help Alcoholics* (A.A. Pamphlet)
- *A.A. and Treatment Facilities* (A.A. Pamphlet)
- *A.A. in Hospitals* (A.A. Pamphlet)
- *Basic H & I Guide of Narcotics Anonymous* http://www.na.org/h-i/hi-guidetoc05.htm
- *Narcotics Anonymous: In Cooperation with Therapeutic Communities Worldwide* (http://www.na.org/prespapers/in-cooperation.htm)

Some readers may respond that they have attempted to work with such committees but found them populated with "fundamentalists" who were not open to new ways of engaging and retaining individuals who have struggled to achieve stable recovery. Relationships with service committees are best approached as a long-term endeavor requiring tolerance, mutual respect and a process of mutual learning.

The service structure of recovery programs not based on the Twelve Steps can be found on the Internet websites of these organizations or by contacting them directly. Links to these sites and organizations can be found at http://facesandvoicesofrecovery.org/resources/support_home.php.

We would offer the following suggestions to build or renew the relationship between local treatment organizations and local recovery support groups:

- Respect the guidelines that each group has established for members who work or serve as volunteers in the addictions field (See *A.A. Guidelines for A.A. Members Employed in the Alcoholism Field.* (ND). New York: General Service Office, Alcoholics Anonymous.)
- Where possible, develop a single point of contact with each group (e.g., the chairperson of the H&I Committee).
- Establish at least annual meetings between your agency and the service committees of local recovery support groups to review such issues as support

meetings hosted at the treatment facility, transportation assistance to outside meetings, access to literature for clients, procedures for temporary sponsorship, use of speakers to make presentations about the group to clients, and any problems that have arisen in the relationship between the treatment facility, its clients, and the group.

- To help personalize the linkage process (in consultation with the service committee or representative), develop a cadre of reliable individuals with diverse characteristics and temperaments that will serve as temporary guides in getting a new person welcomed into the group.
- Avoid linkage practices that potentially violate the culture of the local group (e.g., bussing 30 new people in treatment to a small community meeting or linking heroin addicts without a history of alcohol use/problems to A.A. with narrow interpretations of A.A.'s tradition governing membership.)

In a process aimed at reconnecting treatment, recovery and community, treatment leaders are again beginning to define themselves as a part of the growing recovery community and see themselves as personally and institutionally accountable to this recovery community. Leaders and staff of progressive treatment organizations are again participating in communal meetings of local communities of recovery and opening the doors of their facilities to local recovery communities as a venue for social support and service. Leaders within American communities of recovery are also beginning to articulate the need for these communities to more effectively reach out to treatment organizations and the individuals and families they serve.

Encouraging Staff Exposure and Participation in Local Recovery Support Groups and Internet-based Recovery Resources: Assertive linkage to recovery support groups and the larger network of recovery community resources requires an in-depth knowledge of these local groups and resources. In the 1960s and 1970s, participation in local (open) meetings was expected of all staff, a practice that created an in-depth knowledge of different recovery support structures and something of the personality of each particular meeting. The shift from acute models of care to recovery management will stir calls for a renewal of this knowledge base. Programs can enhance this knowledge by encouraging service staff and volunteers to:

- Read the literature of the spectrum of recovery support groups,
- Visit open meetings of local recovery support groups,
- Visit Internet sites of the major recovery support groups and become familiar with various on-line recovery support meetings,

- Invite representatives of various recovery support groups to provide in-service training for clinical and support staff, and
- Participate in local recovery celebration activities either as a person in recovery or a friend of recovery.

Developing Recovery Volunteer Programs: One of the most vibrant recovery volunteer programs developed by an addiction treatment program was that developed at Lutheran General Hospital in the early 1970s. The hospital's alcoholism treatment unit recruited more than 200 volunteer A.A. and Al-Anon members who collectively provided more than 10,000 hours of volunteer service each year. The volunteers provided around the clock social support to the individuals and families going through treatment and helped link them to outside support meetings in the community (McInerney, 1970). Such dynamic volunteer programs dissipated amidst the growing professionalization of the field in the 1980s and 1990s, but efforts to restore them are increasing as part of the larger shift from acute models of treatment to models of sustained recovery management. Portrayed below are some of the functions that recovery volunteers can provide within the treatment milieu.[10]

---

[10] Those interested in developing or enhancing a recovery volunteer program will find the following resource helpful: *Successful Strategies for Recruiting, Training, and Utilizing Volunteers: A Guide for Faith- and Community-based Service Providers.* (2005). Rockville, MD: USDHHS, SAMHSA, CSAT. To order, call 1-800-729-6686.

Representative Functions of Recovery Community Volunteers
1. Offering themselves as "living proof" of the reality of recovery and the transformative power of recovery.
2. Sharing their recovery status and, when well-timed and appropriate, their recovery story.
3. Serving as a recovery lifestyle consultant, sharing practical tips on living as a person in recovery within one's family, school or workplace and larger community.
4. Helping staff and paid peer-support specialists guide the client/family into relationships with one or more local or virtual communities of recovery.
5. Providing support (e.g., information, transportation) and advocacy to each client/family to facilitate access to needed recovery services.
6. Providing face-to-face, telephone and email communications for purposes of monitoring, recovery coaching, and, when needed, early re-intervention.
7. Training family members (or persons in recovery) to run family education seminars and family support groups.

Developing or Renewing Recovery (Alumni) Associations: One of the dynamic bridges between treatment and the larger recovery community is provided through Recovery (Alumni) Associations that provide recovery support services in their own right to clients during and following treatment and who constitute an important pool from which volunteers can be drawn.

Profile of a Vibrant & Enduring Recovery Alumni Association

Group: Discovery (Alumni Association of New Day Center at Hinsdale Hospital, Hinsdale, IL)

Founded: Early 1980s

Founded by: John Daniels (aftercare director) and two graduates and their spouses.

Membership Size: Ranged between 250-500 over past ten years

Duration of Participation: 30-40% have participated for more than 5 years with some of founding members still participating

Meeting Frequency: Monthly social events and 2-3 organizational meetings each year

Social Event Activities: Potlucks, dinners out, bowling, weekend trips

Average Event Attendance: 60-70

Distinctiveness / Keys to Success: Involvement of partners/spouses and children; development of long-term relationships with individuals/families in recovery; autonomy of group from treatment organization (New Day only provides space and assistance with mailings)

Membership Fee: $5 per person per year

Association Assets: Approximately $10,000 used to support activities and participation of any members who cannot afford activities.

Greatest Challenge to Date: Engaging and retaining adolescents after treatment.

Source: Interview with Don Malec, Discovery Leader, January 19, 2006.

Recovery alumni associations can exist as a permanent recovery support structure or as a transitory support structure with its need diminishing as those completing primary treatment become more involved within and interact within local communities of recovery (Schwartz, personal communication, 2006). It is our experience that programs that most effectively link individuals to natural communities of recovery diminish the need for the treatment center alumni association as a support structure.

Developing Formal Peer-based Recovery Support Programs: There are a growing number of treatment and recovery support organizations experimenting with Peer-based recovery support services (P-BRSS) via new service roles (recovery coaches, peer assistants, recovery mentors, recovery support specialists). P-BRSS are non-clinical services offered on a paid or volunteer basis that guide individuals and families into a recovery-based lifestyle following severe alcohol and other drug problems. P-BRSS offer normative guidance on the recovery experience (stage-appropriate recovery education), linkage to communities of recovery, consultation on problems encountered in early recovery, on-going monitoring of recovery stability, assistance with lifestyle reconstruction (e.g., sober housing, sober leisure, etc.), and, when needed, a point of early re-intervention into lapses or relapses. P-BRSS are reflected in new roles going by such titles as recovery coaches, peer recovery mentors, recovery support specialists and recovery assistants. Peer-based recovery support services are being implemented under a variety of rationales (White, 2004).

1. Helpers derive significant therapeutic benefit from the process of assisting others (the "helper principle")(Riessman, 1965, 1990).
2. People who have overcome adversity can develop special sensitivities and skills in helping others experiencing the same adversity-a "wounded healer" tradition that has deep historical roots in religious and moral reformation movements and is the foundation of modern mutual aid movements.
3. The inadequacy of acute care models of treatment for people with high problem severity and complexity and low recovery capital is evident in low engagement rates, high attrition rates during treatment, low continuing care participation, and high re-admission rates.
4. Many addicted people benefit from a personal "guide" who facilitates disengagement from the culture of addiction and engagement in a culture of recovery.
5. Peer-based recovery support relationships that are natural, reciprocal, and enduring are not mutually exclusive of, but qualitatively superior to, relationships that are hierarchical, commercialized and transient.
6. P-BRSS are an attempt to re-link treatment and recovery, move the locus of treatment from the treatment institution into the natural environment of those seeking treatment services, and facilitate the shift from toxic drug dependencies to "prodependence on peers" (Nealon-Woods, et al, 1995).

P-BRSS are being piloted in some of the White House-initiated Access to Recovery Programs, within the Center for Substance Abuse Treatment's Recovery Community Services Program (RCSP), and within a growing number of programs experimenting with models of recovery management. The states of Connecticut, Arizona and Vermont have taken the lead in encouraging the development of recovery coach roles in treatment and recovery advocacy and support organizations, and there is a recent trend toward the privatization of recovery support services (e.g., Hired Power www.hiredpower.com).

Seen as a whole, the recovery coach role is comprised of multiple roles. The recovery coach is a:

- motivator and cheerleader (exhibits bold faith in individual/family capacity for change; encourages and celebrates achievement),
- ally and confidant (genuinely cares, listens, and can be trusted with confidences)
- truth-teller (provides a consistent source of honest feedback regarding self-destructive patterns of thinking, feeling and acting),
- role model and mentor (offers his/her life as living proof of the transformative power of recovery; provides stage-appropriate recovery education and advice),
- problem solver (identifies and helps resolve personal and environmental obstacles to recovery),
- resource broker (links individuals/families to formal and indigenous sources of sober housing, recovery-conducive employment, health and social services, and recovery support),
- advocate (helps individuals and families navigate the service system assuring service access, service responsiveness and protection of rights),
- community organizer (helps develop and expand available recovery support resources and affect policies that will support long-term recovery),
- lifestyle consultant (assists individuals/families to develop sobriety-based rituals of daily living), and
- a friend (provides companionship)(White, 2004).

It is also important to note what the recovery coach role is not. First, the recovery coach is not a therapist or counselor, although certain qualities and functions overlap with this role. This fact is reflected in the retraining that must occur when persons in recovery who are certified addiction counselors, psychologists and social workers volunteer to serve as addiction counselors. Such individuals must be retrained to eschew professional jargon and counseling techniques for a true peer support role (Ben Bass, personal communication). The recovery coach also is not a Twelve-Step sponsor and must not duplicate support activities that are being or could be provided by the larger recovery community. (White, 2006)[11]

---

[11]   Also see Loveland and Boyle (2005) for their recovery coach implementation manual.

There are many models of organizing P-BRSS. One model gaining increasing attention is that of the Recovery Community Center (RCC) developed by the Connecticut Community of Addiction Recovery (CCAR), which describes its RCC as follows:

> *A Recovery Community Center (RCC) is a recovery-oriented sanctuary anchored in the heart of the community. It exists 1) to put a face on addiction recovery, 2) to build "recovery capital" in individuals, families and communities and 3) to serve as a physical location where CCAR can organize the local recovery community's ability to care.* (From <u>Core Elements of A Recovery Community Center</u>, CCAR, 2006)

At CCAR, the RCC moves recovery from "the church basements to main street," provides a venue for sober socializing, a physical place for recovery development (linkage to recovery-conducive employment, recovery homes, recovery workshops, planned leisure activities, community service work) and as a medium for connecting people with recovery needs to people with recovery assets. CCAR sees its RCC as an organizational/human bridge between the professional treatment community and the recovery community. Where addiction counselors and Twelve Step sponsors view their service focus in terms of individuals/families that have sought their help, the RCC defines its "client" as the community—the WHOLE community. It is an innovative framework through which peer-based recovery support services can be delivered.

2006 Profile of the Vermont Recovery Center Network

Number of Recovery Centers (RC): 6

Usual Hours of Operation: 8 am to 10 pm

Average hours per week of Operation: 69

Number of Full- and Part-time Paid staff: 9

Primary Financial Support: Yearly grant from Vermont Department of Health / Division of Alcohol and Drug Abuse Programs

Secondary Financial Support: Local grants, local fundraising, membership fees

Number of Volunteers Per Center: Ranges from 7-50; average of 27 per center

Average Weekly Volunteer Hours per Center: Ranges from 20-225; averages 93 volunteer hours per week/per center

Number of Weekly Recovery Meetings: Range from 4-20; total of 66 recovery meetings per week at the 6 centers

Total Number of Participant Visits Past Quarter: 20,741

Average Age of Participants: 41

Average Length To Date of RC Participation: 1.75 years

% of Participant Evaluations Noting Role of RC in Finding Recovery: 55%

% of Participant Evaluations Noting Role of RC in Maintaining Recovery: 94%

% of Participants Who Have Participated in Treatment Programs in their Lifetime: 73%

% of Participants Who Have Participated in Treatment Programs in Past Year: 24%

Core RC Activities: Social support and fellowship, recovery meetings, recovery education (e.g., life skills training), linkage to specific services (e.g., treatment, housing, family services, employment, etc.), and social activities.

Future Vision: 12 recovery centers geographically dispersed across the state, enhanced linkage between professional treatment and local recovery support centers, and increased community awareness of recovery by making recovery visible on "main street."

Source: Personal Communication, Patty McCarthy, Executive Director, Friends of Recovery Vermont; Data from Vermont Department of Health / Division of Alcohol and Drug Abuse Programs

Peer-based recovery support services are not without potential pitfalls, including: the vulnerability of peer service providers and recipients; problems of role delineation among coach, counselor and sponsor; the lack of models for recruitment, orientation/training, and on-going supervision of P-BRSS specialists; and the lack of a code of ethics to guide the delivery of peer-based services (e.g., guidelines on such issues as self-disclosure, boundaries of competence, dual relationships, gifts, and level of accessibility, to name just a few).

The Process of Linking Clients/ Families to Recovery Support Groups and Communities of Recovery

Traditional "Aftercare" versus Assertive Approaches to Continuing Care (AACC): Revamping the process of linking clients to communities of recovery is part of the larger revamping of the traditional idea of "aftercare." In the traditional view, acute treatment initiates and stabilizes recovery and provides aftercare in the form of step-down treatment (outpatient sessions following discharge from residential). Participation in professionally directed "aftercare groups" and participation in A.A. or other recovery support groups would serve to maintain recovery. In this model, aftercare arrangements rely primarily upon verbal encouragement for such participation to each client by his or her counselor and are only available to those clients who have completed recommended levels of care.

In the new recovery management model, all care is part of a process of assertive continuing care. In contrast to traditional aftercare models, assertive approaches to continuing care:

- encompass all admitted clients/families, not just those who successfully "graduate," including those who terminated treatment against staff advice or were administratively ("therapeutically") discharged,
- place primary responsibility for post-treatment contact in AACC with the treatment institution, not the client,
- involve both scheduled and unscheduled contact (e.g., "I've been thinking about you today and thought I would call to say hi and see how things were going."),
- capitalize on temporal windows of vulnerability (saturation of check-ups and support in the first 90 days following treatment) and increase monitoring and support during periods of identified vulnerability,

- individualize (increases and decreases) the duration and intensity of check-ups and support based on each client's degree of problem severity, the depth of his or her recovery capital and the ongoing stability or instability of his or her recovery program,
- utilize assertive (see discussion below) linkage rather than passive referral to communities of recovery,[12]
- incorporate multiple media for sustained recovery support, e.g., face-to-face contact, telephone support and mailed and emailed communications,
- place emphasis on those combinations and sequences of services/experiences that can facilitate the movement from recovery initiation to stable recovery maintenance,
- emphasize support contacts with clients in their natural environments,
- may be delivered either by counselors, recovery coaches or trained volunteer recovery support specialists, and
- emphasize continuity of contact and service (rapport building and rapport maintenance) in a primary recovery support relationship over time (Dr. Mark Godley, Director of Research, Chestnut Health Systems, personal communication, February, 2006).

Building a Long-term Recovery Support Relationship: Clients receive mixed messages from those of us in the addiction treatment field. We TELL them that addiction is a chronic disorder and then treat them in ever-briefer episodes of treatment. We TELL them that recovery is a prolonged process rather than an event, but then we "discharge"/"graduate" and abandon them to pursue this process on their own. We TALK about the importance of post-treatment recovery support through peer-based recovery support groups, but we do not monitor the strength and durability of such connections. We TELL clients if they get in trouble after treatment to get back to us for additional help, but we all too often shame the returning client to the point that many stop seeking treatment or keep seeking help at new treatment centers. If we as addiction professionals really believe that addiction is a chronic disorder, then it is time our professional behavior matched our professional rhetoric.

Linking clients to recovery support groups and broader communities of recovery is best achieved within a long-term recovery support relationship, whether the person who initiates that relationship is a counselor or a paid or volunteer recovery coach.

---

[12]   Referral is not linkage; it is affirmation of the need for linkage and the hope that linkage will happen. Linkage is a process that assures that the connection between an individual and indigenous recovery support systems really happens.

As noted earlier, addictions researchers are investigating the power of post-treatment check-ups and support via face-to-face-interviews, mail and telephone contact and Internet-based monitoring and support. New research technologies, generating 90+% follow-up rates in longitudinal studies of addiction treatment, could be clinically adapted for use as ongoing recovery support interventions (Scott & Dennis, 2000). Such technologies create positive space in peoples' lives to forge long-term relationships that have meaning and value. Treatment centers such as the Betty Ford Center and Hazelden are trying to extend their support services beyond primary treatment through the use of telephone-based check-ups over the months following treatment.

Competing with the Culture of Addiction: Many clients with severe AOD problems are deeply enmeshed in cultures of addiction—an entrenched pattern of daily rituals and social relationships that sustain addiction. The fragileness of post-treatment adjustment is in part due to the resurging siren call of these rituals and relationships. To put it bluntly, representatives from the culture of addiction conduct aggressive post-treatment monitoring and re-intervention with individuals who have completed treatment, but we do not. What is wrong with this picture? If we are truly committed to helping our clients achieve long-term recovery and recognize that they are precariously balanced between recovery and re-addiction in the days, weeks, months and early years following treatment, then we must be in their lives as a positive influence on these daily recovery or re-addiction decisions that are made and help replace this culture of addiction with a culture of recovery (White, 1996).

Linkage Steps: Encouragement procedures can increase recovery support group affiliation and participation. Such procedures include:

- educating clients about the importance and potential benefits of post-treatment recovery support services ("Just as clients often minimize the severity of their AOD problems, they also tend to underestimate what will be required to successfully resolve those problems."),
- soliciting the client's past experience with solo experiments in sobriety
- soliciting client's past experience with and perceptions (stereotypes) of recovery mutual aid groups,
- reviewing the menu of post-treatment recovery support options (family, social, occupational, formal support groups),
- identifying important meeting characteristics (e.g., religious, spiritual, secular; smoking or nonsmoking; gender; ethnicity; age; geographical access) (Forman, 2002),

- using assertive rather than passive linkage procedures, e.g., orienting client about what to expect in his or her first meeting (As an example, see http://www. aa.org/default/en_about_aa.cfm?pageid=25, http://www.bma-wellness.com/ papers/First_AA_Meeting.html and http://www.bma-wellness.com/papers/First_ AA_Meeting.html#Locating%20a%20meeting)as a guide for what the client can expect at his or her first A.A. meeting),
- linking each client to a particular person (from a list of volunteer guides) to orient and guide the client into relationship with a local group and linking each client to a specific meeting for their initial exposure,
- demonstrating personal enthusiasm and optimism to the client about recovery support group participation,
- resolving obstacles to participation, e.g., day care, transportation,
- clarifying the role differences between the counselor, the recovery coach and the sponsor to avoid confusion, conflicting loyalties and manipulative splitting by the client,
- monitoring and evaluating each client's initial and ongoing responses to that person/meeting via follow-up phone calls, emails, or visits,
- providing support for continued contact or exploring alternatives in response to mismatches between person and group, and
- linking (where possible) family members to support structures congruent with the recovery framework of the client, e.g., referring spouses and children to Al-Anon and Alateen when the client is participating in A.A.[13]

In most cases, the addiction counselor will have explored the potential value of recovery support group participation by the end of primary treatment. When this is not the case, then the counselor or recovery coach responsible for post-treatment check-ups must begin this process anew. Reinforcing the importance of recovery support group participation can begin with helping the client re-assess his or her past efforts at solo problem resolution.

---

[13] For evidence of the effectiveness of encouragement procedures, see Mallams, et al, 1982.

Past Problem Resolution Efforts (Key Interview Questions)

1. How many times have you attempted on your own to cut down your alcohol or other drug use?
2. What is the longest time you were able to sustain your goal of cutting down?
3. How many times have you attempted on your own to stop your alcohol and other drug use?
4. What is the longest time you were able to sustain your goal of not drinking or using drugs?
5. Is there an average time that your efforts to cut down or stop use started to fail for you?
6. In your best past prior efforts to cut down or stop your drinking and/or drug use, what were you doing that helped make this effort more successful?
7. Which do you think is most achievable for you in the future: cutting down your alcohol and/or drug use or stopping all non-medical use of alcohol and drugs?
8. If you use your past experience as a guide, what can you do in the next year to make your current efforts more successful?
9. How will you know if what you are trying now is working for you?
10. What are the earliest signs that would tell you that the strategy you are using this time is not working?

Some clients will sustain their recovery without recovery support group participation, while others will come to see such participation as helpful or essential. The goal is not to get all clients to like going to recovery support meetings, although some will develop that sentiment. The goal is to draw from the client's own experience why he or she needs to participate in such groups and to use their experience to determine what type of group best meets that need. There is something almost mystical in the chemistry between the individual and a recovery support group/community.

When we speak of "recovery community," these qualities take on added significance because of the shared wounds its members bring to their membership in this community. It is here that those who have never experienced sanctuary often discover a place where they feel physically and psychologically safe for the first time. Here one is accepted not in spite of ones imperfectness but because of the very nature of that imperfectness. It is this shared "torn-to-pieces-hood" (as William James called it) that turns "people who normally would not mix" into a "fellowship." It is here that, in discovering one's self in the stories of others, people discover themselves and a "narrative community" whose members not only exchange their stories but possess a "shared story." Within such a community, one can find a deep sense of fit-a sense of finally discovering and connecting to the whole of which one is a part. The recovery community is a place where shared pain and hope can be woven by its members into life-saving stories whose mutual exchange is more akin to communion than communication. This sanctuary of the estranged fills spiritual as well as physical space. It is a place of refuge, refreshment and renewal. It is a place that defies commercialization-a place whose most important assets are not for sale. There is in this dynamic interaction [of person and group] as much a sense of having been chosen as there is a sense of choosing a particular framework of recovery. It is both a "you belong with us" connection between the group and the individual and a "this is where I belong" connection between the individual and the group. (White, 2001a)

That type of connection can be enhanced by reviewing each client's history of exposure to recovery support groups[14], his or her attitudes toward such groups, the factors most important to a positive group experience and his or her plans for immediate participation in such groups.

---

[14]   For a more detailed format for reviewing past support group experience, see Nicolaus, M. (2003). *Recovery by Choice*. Oakland, CA: LifeRing Press, pp. 235-241.

Which of the following are important for you in selecting a recovery support group? (Check all that apply) People who:

_____ have experience with my primary drug

_____ are the same gender

_____ are close to my age

_____ share my ethnic/cultural background

_____ share my views on religion, spirituality or secularity

_____ share my sexual orientation

_____ smoke tobacco

_____ do not smoke tobacco

_____ have tolerant attitudes toward mental illness

_____ have tolerant attitudes toward medications prescribed for addiction or mental illness

_____ have prior experience in the criminal justice system

_____ do not have prior experience in the criminal justice system

_____ have approximately the same income level

_____ have had very severe alcohol/drug problems

_____ have had mild to moderate alcohol/drug problems

_____ share my goal of complete abstinence

_____ share my goal of moderated use

Once a plan has been formulated, the addiction counselor or recovery coach can begin the process of assertively linking the client to a recovery support group and its larger community of recovery. There are two phases in this linkage process. The first phase, opening the referral, begins in the planning process and proceeds through two additional steps: 1) when necessary, orienting the client to the particular recovery support society he or she has chosen to explore and 2) providing a direct, human connection between the client and either a representative of a recovery support organization or his or her first exposure to meetings of that society. The second step can be achieved by facilitating a visit between the client and a recovery group representative or the recovery coach taking the client to his or her first meeting. Where a guide is used, an important point is that the connection between the client and the recovery group is not complete until the guide steps out of the middle of that formative relationship.

The second phase is closing the referral linkage. Where the first stage guided the client into relationship with a community of recovered and recovering people, the second stage is designed to ensure individual-group fit by assessing strength and durability of relationship between the client and the group. Such assessment can be incorporated into routine post-treatment check-ups.

    When Few Recovery Support Resources are Available: In communities with few recovery support resources it may be necessary for the addictions counselor or recovery coach to devote time to developing a broader pool of recovery support resources in the community. As an example, addictions counselors working in adolescent treatment programs often send adolescents back to local community and school environments with no indigenous recovery support services. The inevitable result is a high relapse rate—events that often occur within hours or days following discharge from treatment. An alternative approach is to supplement clinical services to the adolescent and family with time in the adolescent's community organizing school-based recovery support services and youth-oriented recovery groups and recovery activities.

    In communities where few specialized recovery support resources exist and clients are not affiliated with mainstream recovery groups, special supports may be organized that can evolve into more permanent recovery support structures. This strategy can exert an important role in the growth, diversity and vitality of the local recovery community.

Steps in Developing Special Recovery Support Groups

- Identify an area of unmet need for recovery support, e.g., the absence of women's meetings, young people's meetings, absence of secular recovery groups, etc.
- Sponsor an open-attend (attend as long as you like) continuing care group as an adjunct or alternative (for some).
- Continue the group until a strong core group of members coalesces.
- Recruit the strongest group members as peer-leaders, encourage and cultivate their leadership, decrease your role but not your presence as their leadership activities increase.
- Arrange for your peer-leaders to facilitate the group sometimes in your absence and process with the leaders and group members how this went in your absence.
- Raise the possibility of shifting the group from a professionally-directed continuing care group to a peer-sponsored and peer-led recovery support group.
- Provide info to assist group if they want to shift the group to a registered A.A., N.A., or other established recovery group.
- Monitor the status of the group and provide support to peer leaders.

NOTE: On-going cycles of this process may be required when established leaders relocate or mature out (in the case of young people's meetings).

Steps to Expand the Variety of Recovery Support Groups: Some communities lack Twelve Step recovery groups or alternatives to Twelve Step groups. Counselors and addiction counselors can also play important roles in enhancing the varieties of recovery support structures within their local communities.

Seeding Diversity in Local Recovery Support Groups

1. Remain personally knowledgeable and up to date on established and new recovery support groups.
2. Maintain a library of recovery support group literature and contact information that can be shared with your clients.
3. Encourage clients with computer resources and capabilities to explore the websites of various recovery support groups and to explore the world of Internet recovery support meetings. (Be prepared to provide cards with website listings.)
4. Invite guest speakers representing various recovery groups to visit your community and make presentations to clients and other interested parties.
5. Encourage individuals who are not responding to existing support structures to consider starting their own recovery support group.
6. Make clients aware of the growing movement to create broader recovery support structures, e.g., recovery homes, recovery schools, recovery work co-ops, etc.
7. Serve as a consultant to recovering individuals/families who want to explore development of a special recovery support group.

PROVIDING LONG-TERM RECOVERY MANAGEMENT

Linking clients from addiction treatment to communities of recovery has the greatest impact when this activity is imbedded within a large framework of long-term recovery management and support that encompasses pre-treatment engagement and recovery priming (motivational enhancement), in-treatment recovery support services (to enhance engagement, strengthen recovery initiation, and reduce treatment attrition) and post-treatment recovery support services. Our focus will be on the latter of these service categories.

Post-treatment recovery management begins at the point of discharge from primary treatment. In the emerging recovery management model, this period is considered the key to fully transferring what the client learned in treatment to his or her natural life in the community. The steps in this process include 1) ongoing check-ups and support, 2) stage appropriate recovery education (recovery coaching), 3) validating or reinitiating assertive linkage to recovery support groups and the larger network of community recovery activities, 4) resolving personal and environmental obstacles to recovery, and, 5) when needed, early re-intervention and re-linkage to recovery support group resources or professional treatment. The following discussion focuses primarily upon the check-up and linking functions.

Monitoring involves mutually agreed upon contact between the client and a recovery coach so that both may assess the client's status and explore the recovery process. The monitoring process usually begins with a higher frequency of contact in the first 90 days following treatment and decreases in frequency and intensity after that, with the proviso that check-up frequency can increase by mutual agreement at any time the client enters a period of heightened vulnerability. In most cases, clients with lower problem severity and higher recovery capital require shorter and lower intensity monitoring than do those with higher problem severity and lower recovery capital.

The major factor that compromises recovery from chronic health care problems is failure of the individual to adhere to recovery maintenance protocol, e.g., following medication directions, diet restrictions, exercise recommendations and other self-care prescriptions (McLellan, et al, 2000). Sustained monitoring is a powerful tool to enhance adherence to recovery maintenance protocol, a fact revealed in the addictions field from the discovery that research follow-up contacts actually generate their own therapeutic effects (Sobell and Sobell, 1981).

The following table illustrates the range of interventions that are indicated across five different circumstances the client may be in at the time of follow-up contact.

Status at Follow-up	Intervention Options
No Problems Reported	-Expressions of regard & concern -Identify sources (decisions, actions, people) of successful recovery maintenance -Identify positive consequences of recovery -Praise success -Maintain routine check-up schedule
Instability/distress, no alcohol/drug use but high risk of relapse (e.g. cravings, thoughts of using)	-Expressions of regard & concern -Elicit positive effects of sobriety & potential negative consequences of returning to AOD use -Intensify peer recovery supports -Enlist support from significant other -Explore option of contact with professional helper -Linkage to sober living environment -Increase check-up contact in next 30 days
Slip with return to abstinence	-Expressions of regard & concern -Evaluation of the slip (& lessons learned) -Evaluation of the strength of peer recovery supports (Re-linkage or linkage to alternative group) -Elicit positive effects of sobriety & potential negative consequences of sustained return to AOD use -Elicit recommitment to recovery -Increase frequency of check-ups for next 60 days to verify recovery stability

Alcohol/drug use without reported negative consequences	--Expressions of regard & concern -Review of past consequences of AOD use -Evaluate abstinence goal & client's commitment to continue AOD use or return to sobriety goal -Elicit positive effects of sobriety & potential negative consequences of sustained return to AOD use -Explore earliest ways client would know that AOD use was becoming a problem again -Enlist significant other in monitoring and support -Option of re-linkage to peer and professional support -Apply test of moderation ground rules, e.g., Miller & Munoz, 2005 -Increase check-ups for next 90 days
Alcohol/drug use with negative consequences	-Expressions of regard and concern -Elicit duration & intensity of negative consequences and future problems if use continues -Elicit how these problems would change if sobriety re-initiated -Assertive linkage to peer recovery supports -Assertive linkage to professional supports -Support to family/significant other -Increase monitoring of response to peer & professional suppor

Source: Adapted and amplified from Stout, et al, 1999.

A Brief Note on Early Re-intervention: In the routine process of post treatment monitoring and assessing individual responses to post-treatment mutual aid involvement, counselors and recovery coaches will experience encounters in which the client is on the brink of lapse/relapse or has already experienced lapse/relapse. We would offer several points to consider regarding the process of early re-intervention. *First*, re-intervention is important because it provides a point of recovery restabilization when problem severity has not fully re-escalated and when the client still has recovery assets that can facilitate long-term recovery (assets that are depleted over time with re-addiction). The goals of re-intervention are to reduce the client's immediate threat of injury to self and others, shorten the length and intensity of the lapse/relapse experience and use the lapse/relapse experience to elevate the commitment to recovery and strengthen relationships with the community of recovery.

Second, many clients experience intense shame following relapse and that shame is a major barrier to recovery restabilization. That shame can be diminished by providing normative data on relapse and recovery, praising the continued commitment to recovery, and re-affirming the recovery support partnership. *Third*, not everyone who lapses or relapses needs readmission to primary treatment. Those who do need treatment may not need the same level of care they most recently experienced. The problem may lie, not in the mechanics of recovery initiation, but in the transition from recovery initiation to recovery maintenance in the client's natural environment. The focus should be on building recovery supports into this environment to facilitate the development of a sobriety-based lifestyle and skills in the sobriety-based resolution of problems in daily living. Thus, a call to a sponsor and re-linkage to a support group may be more appropriate than readmission to treatment for some clients. Where treatment is needed, that linkage process must be direct rather than simply verbal encouragement. *Finally*, while post-treatment re-intervention is part of the process of sustained recovery management, the clinical strategies contain many of the elements essential to effective brief interventions: empathy, feedback, emphasis on personal responsibility, clarification of choices, professional advice, and expressions of confidence in client's ability to change (Miller and Rollnick, 1991).

Styles of Long-term Recovery Mutual Aid Affiliation: It is important to understand the varieties and styles of recovery maintenance and the evolution of these styles over time. For example, everyone who stops regularly attending recovery support meetings is not on the verge of relapse and re-addiction. A recent study of patterns of A.A. attendance concluded that, "contrary to A.A. lore, many who connect only for a while do well afterwards" (Kaskutas, et al, 2005). This does not diminish the importance of A.A.; in fact, it suggests measuring the impact of A.A. and other recovery support groups solely by current membership statistics results in a gross underestimate of the total contributions such groups make to addiction recovery. While some people will need or profit from lifelong attendance at A.A. meetings, others will disengage from or decrease meeting participation while sustaining stable recovery. Research on what distinguishes the "maintainers" from the "disengagers" is limited; we suspect that cumulative studies will reveal that the former are made up of those with addictions of greater severity and complexity and fewer recovery supports, as well as people who shift the primary focus of their recovery group participation to social fellowship and spiritual development. Recovery stability and vulnerability for relapse must be measured by looking at the whole person and their recovery environment, rather than solely on meeting attendance or non-attendance.

LINKAGE SKILLS: A BRIEF REVIEW

To bring these discussions to closure it might be helpful to briefly review the core knowledge and skills that addiction counselors and recovery coaches require to perform the services we have described. Those critical skills include:

- Developing and sustaining a supportive, non-exploitive, recovery-focused relationship with each individual and family seeking services,
- Assessing each client, family and community's recovery capital and recovery resource needs,
- Remaining aware of all national and local recovery support resources
- Empowering each client to make choices related to their recovery pathway/style,
- Maintaining relationships with key individuals/groups within local communities of recovery,
- Matching the needs and preferences of clients to particular recovery support resources,
- Linking (guiding into relationship with) each client to an identified person/group,
- Monitoring each person's response to a chosen pathway/style of recovery and their need for amplified clinical or peer-based recovery support resources,
- Offering feedback and support related to recovery pathway/style choices,
- Providing, when needed, early re-intervention and recovery re-initiation services, and
- Facilitating the development of needed recovery support resources.

SUMMARY

In this essay, we have tried to:

1) describe the emergence of a recovery paradigm as a new organizing concept for treatment and recovery support services,
2) summarize the scientific evidence supporting post-treatment check-ups and assertive linkage to peer-based recovery support groups,
3) describe the growing diversity of American communities of recovery,
4) outline strategies for building/strengthening relationships between treatment organizations and local recovery societies, and
5) offer suggestions on how, within a larger framework of post-treatment monitoring and support, addiction counselors and recovery coaches can link individuals/families to recovery support groups.

It is our hope that this effort adds momentum to the movement to shift addiction treatment from an acute care model to a model of sustained recovery management.

About the Authors: William White is a Senior Research Consultant at Chestnut Health Systems and author of *Slaying the Dragon: The History of Addiction Treatment and Recovery in America* and *Pathways from the Culture of Addiction to the Culture of Recovery*. Ernie Kurtz's books include *Not-God: A History of Alcoholics Anonymous* and *The Spirituality of Imperfection* (with Katherine Ketcham).

REFERENCES

Alcoholics Anonymous (1982). *Twelve Steps and Twelve Traditions*. New York: A.A. World Services, Inc.

Anglin, M. D., Hser, Y., & Grella C. E. (1997). Drug addiction and treatment careers among clients in DATOS. *Psychology of Addictive Behaviors, 11*(4), 308-323.

Anthony, W., Gagne, C., & White, W. (in press). Recovery: A common vision for the fields of mental health and addictions. *Psychiatric Rehabilitation Journal.*

Biernacki, P. (1986). *Pathways from Heroin Addiction: Recovery Without Treatment.* Philadelphia, PA: Temple University Press.

Borkman, T. (1997). Is recovery planning any different from treatment planning? *Journal of Substance Abuse Treatment, 15*(1), 37-42.

Broffman, T., Fisher, R., Gilbert, B., & Valentine, P. (in press). Telephone recovery support & the recovery model. *Addictions Professional.*

Chappel, J. N. (1993). Long-term recovery from alcoholism. *Psychiatric Clinics of North America, 16*(1), 177-187.

Coyhis, D. (2000). Culturally specific addiction recovery for Native Americans. In J. Krestan (Ed.), *Bridges to Recovery* (pp. 77-114). New York: The Free Press.

Dakis, C., & O'Brien, C. (2005). Neurobiology of addiction: Treatment and public policy ramifications. *Nature Neuroscience, 8*(11), 1431-1436.

Dawson, S. A., Grant, B. F., Stinson, F. S., Chou, P. S., Huang, B., & Ruan, W. J. (2005). Recovery from DSM-IV alcohol dependence: United States, 2001-2002. *Addiction, 100*(3), 281-292.

Dennis. M. L., Scott, C. K., & Funk, R. (2003). An experimental evaluation of recovery management checkups (RMC) for people with chronic substance use disorders. *Evaluation and Program Planning, 26*(3), 339-352.

Dennis, M. L., Scott, C. K., Funk, R., & Foss, M. A. (2005). The duration and correlates of addiction and treatment careers. *Journal of Substance Abuse Treatment, 28*(Supplement 1), S51-S62.

Dennis, M. L., Scott, C. K., & Hristova, L. (2002). The duration and correlates of substance abuse treatment careers among people entering publicly funded treatment in Chicago [Abstract], *Drug and Alcohol Dependence, 66*(Suppl. 2), 44.

De Soto, C.B., O'Donnel, W.E., & De Soto, J.L. (1989) Long-term recovery in alcoholics. *Alcoholism: Clinical and Experimental Research*, 13:693-697.

Donovan, D. (1998). Continuing care: Promoting maintenance of change. In W. R. Miller, & N. Heather (Eds.), *Treating Addictive Behaviors* (2nd ed., pp. 317-336). . New York: Plenum Press.

Else, D. (1999). Recovering recovery. *Journal of Ministry in Addiction And Recovery, 6*(2), 11-23.

Emrick, C. D. (1989). Alcoholics Anonymous: Membership characteristics and effectiveness as treatment. *Recent Developments in Alcoholism, 7,* 37-53.

Emrick, D. C., Tonigan, J. S., Montgomery, H. & Little, L. (1993). Alcoholics Annonymous: What is currently known? In B. McCrady and W. R. Miller (Eds.), *Research on Alcoholics Anonymous: Opportunities and Alternatives* (pp. 41-78). Brunswick, NJ: Rutgers Center of Alcohol Studies.

Fiorentine, R. (1999). After drug treatment: Are 12-step programs effective in maintaining abstinence? *American Journal of Drug and Alcohol Abuse, 25*(1), 93-116.

Fiorentine, R., & Hillhouse, M. (2000). Drug treatment and 12-step program participation: The additive effects of integrated recovery activities. *Journal of Substance Abuse Treatment, 18*(1), 65-74.

Forman, R. F. (2002). One AA meeting doesn't fit all: 6 keys to prescribing 12-step programs. *Psychiatry Online, 1*(10), 1-6.

Fransway, R. (2000). *12-Step Horror Stories.* Tucson, AZ: See Sharp Press.

Gilliam, M. (1999). *How A.A. Failed Me.* New York: William Morrow.

Godley, S. H., Godley, M. D., & Dennis, M. L. (2001). The assertive aftercare protocol for adolescent substance abusers. In. E. Wagner & H. Waldron, (Eds.), *Innovations in Adolescent Substance Abuse Interventions* (pp. 311-329). New York: Elsevier Science Ltd.

Granfield, R., & Cloud, W. (1999). *Coming Clean: Overcoming Addiction Without Treatment.* New York, NY: New York University Press.

Grella, C. E., & Joshi, V. (1999). Gender differences in drug treatment careers among the National Drug Abuse Treatment Outcome Study. *American Journal of Drug and Alcohol Abuse 25*(3), 385-406.

Hser, Y., Anglin, M., Grella, C., Longshore, D., & Prendergast, M. (1997). Drug treatment careers: A conceptual framework and existing research findings. *Journal of Substance Abuse Treatment, 14*(3), 1-16.

Hser, Y., Grella, C., Chou, C. & Anglin, M. D. (1998). Relationship between drug treatment careers and outcomes: Findings from the National Drug Abuse Treatment Outcome Study. *Evaluation Review, 22*(4), 496-519.

Hser, Y., Hoffman, V., Grella, C., & Anglin, D. (2001). A 33-year follow-up of narcotics addicts. *Archives of General Psychiatry, 58*(5), 503-508.

Hubbard, R. L., Flynn, P. M., Craddock, G., & Fletcher, B. (2001). Relapse after drug abuse treatment. In F. Tims, C. Leukfield, & J. Platt (Eds.), *Relapse and Recovery in Addictions* (pp. 109-121). New Haven: Yale University Press.

Hubbard, R. L., Marsden, M. E., Rachal, J. V., Harwood, H. J., Cavanaugh, E. R., & Ginzburg, H. M. (1989). *Drug abuse treatment: A national study of effectiveness.* Chapel Hill, NC: University of North Carolina Press.

Humphreys, K. (2004). *Circles of Recovery: Self-Help Organizations for Addictions.* Cambridge: Cambridge University Press.

Humphreys, K., Mankowski, E., Moos, R., & Finney, J. (1999). Do enhanced friendship networks and active coping mediate the effect of self-help groups on substance abuse? *Annals of Behavioral Medicine, 21*(1), 54-60.

Humphreys, K., Mavis, B. E., & Stoffelmayr, B. E. (1994). Are twelve-step programs appropriate for disenfranchised groups? Evidence from a study of posttreatment mutual help group involvement. *Prevention in Human Services, 11*(1), 165-180.

Humphreys, K., & Moos, R. (2001). Can encouraging substance abuse patients to participate in self-help groups reduce demand for health care? *Alcoholism: Clinical and Experimental Research, 25*(5), 711-716.

Humphreys, K., Moos, R. J., & Cohen, C. (1997). Social and community resources and long-term recovery from treated and untreated alcoholism. *Journal of Studies on Alcohol, 58*(3), 231-238.

Humphreys, K., Wing, S., McCarty, D., Chappel, J., Galant, L., et al, (2004). Self-help organizations for alcohol and drug problems: Toward evidence-based practice and policy. *Journal of Substance Abuse Treatment, 26*(3), 151-158.

Ito, J., & Donovan, D. M. (1986). Aftercare in alcoholism treatment: A review. In W. R. Miller, & N. Heather (Eds.), *Treating Addictive Behaviors: Process of Change* (pp. 435-452). New York: Plenum.

Jason, L. A., Davis, M. I., Ferrari, J. R., & Bishop, P. D. (2001). Oxford House: A review of research and implications for substance abuse recovery and community research. *Journal of Drug Education, 31*(1), 1-27.

Jason, L. A., Olson, B. D., Ferrari, J. R., & Lo Sasso, A. T. (in press). Communal Housing Settings Enhance Substance Abuse Recovery. *American Journal of Public Health.*

Jin, H., Rourke, S. B., Patterson, T. L., Taylor, M. J., & Grant, I. (1998). Predictors of relapse in long-term abstinent alcoholics. *Journal of Studies on Alcohol, 59*(6), 640-646.

Johnson, E., & Herringer, L. (1993). A note on the utilization of common support activities and relapse following substance abuse treatment. *Journal of Psychology, 127*(1), 73-78.

Kaskutas, L. A., Ammon, L., Delucchi, K., Room, R., Bond, J., & Weisner, C. (2005). Alcoholics Anonymous Careers: Patterns of AA Involvement Five Years After Treatment Entry. *Alcoholism: Clinical and Experimental Research, 29*(11), 1983-1990.

Kelly, J. F., & Moos, R. (2003). Dropout from 12-step self-help groups: Prevalence, predictors, and counteracting treatment influences. *Journal of Substance Abuse Treatment, 24*(3), 241-250.

Kirkpatrick, J. (1986). *Goodbye Hangovers, Hello Life* NY: Ballantine Books.

Kurtz, E. (2002). Alcoholics Anonymous and the disease concept of alcoholism. In T. McGovern, & W. White (Eds.), *Alcohol Problems in the United States: A Twenty Year Treatment Perspective* (pp. 5-40). New York: Haworth Press.

Kurtz, E., & White, W. (2003). Alcoholics Anonymous. In J. Blocker, and I. Tyrell (Eds.), *Alcohol and Temperance in Modern History* (pp. 27-31). Santa Barbara, CA: ABC-CLIO.

Lash, S. J. (1998). Increasing participation in substance abuse aftercare treatment. *American Journal of Drug and Alcohol Abuse 24*(1), 31-36.

Loveland, D., & Boyle, M. (2005). *Manual for Recovery Coaching and Personal Recovery Plan Development.* Posted at http://www.bhrm.org/guidelines/addguidelines.htm

Mäkelä, K., Arminen, I., Bloomfield, K., Eisenbach-Stangl, I., Bergmark, K., Kurube, N., et al. (1996). *Alcoholics Anonymous as a Mutual-Help Movement: A Study in Eight Societies.* Madison: University of Wisconsin.

Mallams, J. H., Godley, M. D., Hall, G. M., & Meyers, R. J. (1982). A social-systems approach to resocializing alcoholics in the community. *Journal of Studies on Alcohol, 43*(11), 1115-1123.

McInerney, J. (1970). The use of Alcoholics Anonymous in a general hospital alcoholism treatment program. *Medical Ecology and Clinical Research, 3*(1), 22.

McKay, J. R. (2001). Effectiveness of continuing care interventions for substance abusers: Implications for the study of long-term treatment effects. *Evaluation Review, 25*(2), 211-232.

McKay, J. R. (2005). Is there a case for extended interventions for alcohol and drug use disorders? *Addiction, 100*(11), 1594-1610.

McKay, J. R., Lynch, K. G., Shephard, D. S., & Pettinati, H. M. (2005). The effectiveness of telephone-based continuing care for alcohol and cocaine dependence. *Archives of General Psychiatry, 62*(2), 199-207.

McLellan, A. T. (2002). Have we evaluated addiction treatment correctly? Implications from a chronic care perspective. *Addiction, 97*(3), 249-252.

McLellan, A.T., Lewis, D. C., O'Brien, C. P., & Kleber, H. D. (2000). Drug dependence, a chronic medical illness: Implications for treatment, insurance, and outcomes evaluation. *Journal of the American Medical Association 284*(13), 1689-1695.

Mertens, J. R., Weisner, C. M., & Ray, G. T. (2005). Readmission among chemically dependent patients in private, outpatient treatment: Patterns, correlates and role in long-term recovery outcome. *Journal of Studies on Alcohol, 66*(6), pp. 842-847.

Miller, W., & Kurtz, E. (1994). Models of alcoholism used in treatment: contrasting AA and other perspectives with which it is often confused. *Journal of Studies on Alcohol, 55*(2), 159-166.

Miller, W.R. & Munoz, R.F. (2005). *Controlling Your Drinking: Tools to Make Moderation Work for You*. New York: Guilford Publications, Inc.

Miller, W. R., & Rollnick, S. (1991). *Motivational Interviewing: Preparing People to Change Addictive Behavior*. New York: Guilford Press.

Miller, W. R., Walters, S. T., & Bennett, M. E. (2001). How effective is alcoholism treatment in the United States? *Journal of Studies on Alcohol, 62*(2), 211-220.

Montgomery, H. A., Miller, W. R., & Tonigan, J. S. (1995). Does Alcoholics Anonymous involvement predict treatment outcome? *Journal of Substance Abuse Treatment, 12*(4), 241-246.

Moos, R. & Moos, B. (2005). Paths of entry into Alcoholics Anonymous: Consequences for participation and remission. *Alcoholism: Clinical & Experimental Research. 29*(10), 1858-1868.

Morgan, O.J. (1995a). Extended length sobriety: The missing variable. *Alcoholism Treatment Quarterly, 12*(1), 59-71.

Morgan, O. J. (1995b). Recovery-sensitive counseling in the treatment of alcoholism. *Alcoholism Treatment Quarterly, 13*(4), 63-73.

Morgenstern, J., Kahler, C. W., Frey, R. M., & Labouvie, E. (1996). Modeling therapeutic response to 12-step treatment: Optimal responders, nonresponders, partial responders. *Journal of Substance Abuse, 8*(1), 45-59.

Nealon-Woods, M., Ferrari, J., & Jason, L. (1995). Twelve-Step program use among Oxford House residents: Spirituality or social support for sobriety? *Journal of Substance Abuse, 7*(3), 311-318.

Nicolaus, M. (2003). *Recovery by Choice*. Oakland, CA: LifeRing Press.

Office of Applied Studies. (2005). *Treatment Episode Data Set (TEDS): 2002. Discharges from Substance Abuse Treatment Services* (DASIS Series S-25 No. DHHS Publication No. (SMA) 04-3967). Rockville, MD: Substance Abuse Mental Health Services Administration. *Retrieved from http://wwwdasis.samhsa.gov/ teds02/2002_teds_rpt_d.pdf* .

O'Brien. C. P., & McLellan, A. T. (1996) Myths about the treatment of addiction. *Lancet 347,* 237-40.

Riessman, F. (1965). The "helper-therapy" principle. *Social Work, 10,* 24-32.

Riessman, F. (1990). Restructuring help: A human services paradigm for the 1990s. *American Journal of Community Psychology, 18*(2), 221-230.

Room, R. (1989). The U.S. general population's experiences of responding to alcohol problems. *British Journal of Addiction, 84*(11), 1291-1304.

Scott, C. K., & Dennis, M. L. (2000). A cost-effective approach to achieving over 90% follow-up in outcome monitoring with substance abuse treatment clients. *Drug and Alcohol Dependence, 60*(Suppl. 1), s200.

Scott, C. K., Foss, M. A., & Dennis, M.L. (2005). Pathways in the relapse— treatment—recovery cycle over 3 years. *Journal of Substance Abuse Treatment, 28*(Supplement 1), S63-S72.

Simpson, D. D., Joe, G. W., & Broome, K. M. (2002). A national 5-year follow-up of treatment outcomes for cocaine dependence. *Archives of General Psychiatry, 59*(6), 539-544.

Simpson, D. D., & Marsh, K. L. (1986). Relapse and recovery among opioid addicts 12 years after treatment. In F. Tims, & C. Leukefeld (Eds.), *Relapse and Recovery in Drug Abuse* (NIDA Monograph 72, pp. 86-103). Rockville, MD: National Institute on Drug Abuse.

Smith, J. (2005). Commentary: Alcoholism and free will. *Psychiatric Times, 41*(4), 1-7.

Sobell, L. C., & Sobell, M. B. (1981). Frequent follow-up as data gathering and continued care with alcoholics. *International Journal of the Addictions, 16*(6), 1077-1086.

Sobell, M.B., Sobell, L.C., Bogardis, J., Leo, G.I. and Skinner, W. (1992). Problem drinkers' perceptions of whether treatment goals should be self-selected or therapist-selected. *Behavioral Therapy,* 23, 43-52.

Stout, R. L., Rubin, A., Zwick, W., Zywiak, W., & Bellino, L. (1999). Optimizing the cost-effectiveness of alcohol treatment: A rationale for extended case monitoring. *Addictive Behaviors, 24*(1), 17-35.

Substance Abuse and Mental Health Services Administration, Office of Applied Studies (2002). *Treatment Episode Data Set (TEDS): 1992-2000. National Admissions to Substance Abuse Treatment Services.* (DASIS Series: S-17, DHHS

Publication No. (SMA) 02-3727). Rockville, MD: Substance Abuse and Mental Health Services Administration.

Tiebout, H. (1949). The act of surrender in the therapeutic process, with special reference to alcoholism. *Quarterly Journal of Studies on Alcohol, 10*, 48-58.

Tonigan, J. S., Miller, W. R., Chavez, R., Porter, N., Worth, L., Westphal, V., Carroll, L., Repa, K., Martin, A., & Tracy, L. A. (2002). *AA participation 10 years after Project MATCH treatment: Preliminary findings.* Poster presentation, Research Society on Alcoholism, San Francisco, July.

Tuchfeld, B. S. (1981). Spontaneous remission in alcoholics: Empirical observations and theoretical implications. *Journal of Studies on Alcohol, 42*(7), 626-641.

Wesiner, C., Matzger, H., & Kaskutas, L. A. (2005). How important is treatment? One-year outcomes of treated and untreated alcohol-dependent individuals. *Addiction, 98*(7), 901-911.

Weiss, R. D., Griffin, M. L., Gallop, R., Onken, L., Gastfriend, D. R., Daley, D., Crits-Christoph, P., Bishop, S., & Barber, J. (2000). Self-help group attendance and participation among cocaine dependent patients. *Drug and Alcohol Dependence 60*(2), 169-177.

White, W. (1996). *Pathways from the culture of addiction to the culture of recovery: A travel guide for addiction professionals* (2ⁿᵈ ed.). Center City, MN: Hazelden.

White, W. (1998). *Slaying the Dragon: The History of Addiction Treatment and Recovery in America.* Bloomington, IL: Chestnut Health Systems.

White, W. (2000). *Toward a new recovery movement: Historical reflections on recovery, treatment and advocacy.* Presented at Recovery Community Support Program (RCSP) Conference, April 3-5, 2000. Retrieved July 31, 2004 from http://www. facesandvoicesofrecovery.org/pdf/toward_new_recovery.pdf.

White, W. (2001a). A lost vision: Addiction counseling as community organization. *Alcoholism Treatment Quarterly, 19*(4), 1-32.

White, W. (2001b). Pre-AA Alcoholic Mutual Aid Societies. *Alcoholism Treatment Quarterly 19*(1), 1-21.

White, W. (2002). The treatment renewal movement. *Counselor, 3*(1), 59-61.

White, W. (2005). Recovery: Its history and renaissance as an organizing construct. *Alcoholism Treatment Quarterly, 23*(1), 3-15.

White, W. (2005). Recovery Management: What if we <u>really</u> believed addiction was a chronic disorder? *GLATTC Bulletin.* September, pp. 1-7.

White, W. (2006). *Sponsor, Recovery Coach, Addiction Counselor: The Importance of Role Clarity and Role Integrity.* Philadelphia, PA: Philadelphia Department of Behavioral Health.

White, W., Boyle, M., & Loveland, D. (2002). Alcoholism/addiction as a chronic disease: From rhetoric to clinical reality. *Alcoholism Treatment Quarterly, 20*(3/4), 107-130.

White, W., Boyle, M., & Loveland, D. (2004). Recovery from addiction and recovery from mental illness: Shared and contrasting lessons. In R. Ralph, & P. Corrigan (Eds.), *Recovery and Mental Illness: Consumer Visions and Research Paradigms* (pp. 233-258). Washington DC: American Psychological Association.

White, W., & Hagen, R. (2005). Treatment, recovery, community: A call for reconnection. *Counselor, 6*(6), 52-56.

White, W., & Kurtz, E. (2005). *The Varieties of Recovery Experience*. Chicago, IL: Great Lakes Addiction Technology Transfer Center.

White, W., & Nicolaus, M. (2005). Styles of secular recovery. *Counselor, 6*(4), 58-61.

White, W., and Sanders, M. (2004). Recovery management and people of color: Redesigning addiction treatment for historically disempowered communities. Posted at www.bhrm.org and http://www.facesandvoicesofrecovery.org/resources/overview.shtml#publications

White, W., & Taylor, P. (in press). A new recovery advocacy movement. *Recovery Magazine*.

White, W., Woll, P., & Webber, R. (2003). *Project SAFE: Best Practices Resource Manual*. Chicago, IL: Illinois Department of Human Service, Office of Alcoholism and Substance Abuse.

Wilbourne, P., & Miller, W. (2003). Treatment of alcoholism: Older and wiser? *Alcoholism Treatment Quarterly, 20*(3/4), 41-59.

Zweben, J. E. (1986). Recovery oriented psychotherapy. *Journal of Substance Abuse Treatment, 3*(4), 255-262.

APPENDIX A

Resources to Contact about How to Organize a Recovery Community Center

Asian Pacific American Community Recovery
Network (ACORN)
Kelly Thao, Community Outreach Specialist
720 8th Avenue South, Suite 200
Seattle, WA 98104
(206) 695-7649
kellyt@acrs.org

Connecticut Community for Addiction
Recovery (CCAR)
Phillip A. Valentine, Executive Director
530 Silas Deane Highway Suite 220
Wethersfield, CT 06109
(860) 571-2985
phillip@ccar.us
http://ccar.us/

Detroit Recovery Project (DRP)
Andre Johnson, Program Manager
1151 Taylor Street, Room 417C
Detroit, MI 48202
(313) 876-0770

Easy Does It, Inc.
Dave Reyher, Executive Director
1300 Hilltop Road
Leesport, PA 19533
(610) 373-2463
dreyheredi@comcast.net

El Paso Alliance
Ben Bass, Executive Director
6000 Welch No. 7
El Paso, TX 79905
Phone: 915-594-7000
http://www.recoveryalliance.net/
BBass@RecoveryAlliance.net

Friends of Recovery – Vermont (FOR-VT)
Patty McCarthy, Executive Director
PO Box 1202

Montpelier, VT 05601
(802) 229-6103, 1 (800) 769-2798
RecoveryVT@aol.com http://www.
friendsofrecoveryvt.org/

Pennsylvania Recovery Organization-Achieving
Community Together (PRO-ACT)

Bev Haberle, Project Director

Women's Community Recovery Center

Bailiwick Office Complex Suite 12/14

Doylestown, PA 18901

(215) 345-6644 Bhaberle@bccadd.org

Recovery Association Project (RAP)
Kathy Brazell, Executive Director
1100 NE 28th Avenue, Portland, OR 97232
Phone 503.493.9211 Fax 503.493.9249
http://www.rap-nw.org/**Error! Hyperlink
reference not valid.**
kb@rap-nw.org

RECOVER Project
Laurie Kamansky, Project Manager
55 Federal Street, Suite 125
Greenfield, MA 01301
(413) 774-5489
lkamansky@wmtcinfo.org

Walden House, Inc.
Demetrius Andreas, Project Director
149 West 22nd Street
Los Angeles, CA 90007
(213) 741-3731
dandreas@waldenhouse.org
http://www.waldenhouse.org/

Great Lakes (HHS Region 5)

ATTC   Addiction Technology Transfer Center Network
Funded by Substance Abuse and Mental Health Services Administration

Perspectives on Systems Transformation: How Visionary Leaders are Shifting Addiction Treatment Toward a Recovery-Oriented System of Care

Interviews with:
H. Westley Clark, MD, JD, MPH, CAS, FASAM
Thomas A. Kirk, Jr., PhD
Arthur C. Evans, PhD
Michael Boyle
Phillip Valentine
Lonnetta Albright

WILLIAM L. WHITE, MA

Published by the Great Lakes Addiction Technology Transfer Center

Great Lakes Addiction Technology Transfer Center
Jane Addams College of Social Work
University of Illinois at Chicago
1640 West Roosevelt Road, Suite 511 (M/C 779)
Chicago, Illinois 60608-1316

2007

At the time of publication, Terry Cline, PhD served as the SAMHSA Administrator. H. Westley Clark, MD, JD, MPH, CAS, FASAM served as CSAT Director, and Catherine D. Nugent, MS served as the CSAT Project Officer.

PRODUCED UNDER A GRANT FUNDED BY THE CENTER FOR SUBSTANCE ABUSE TREATMENT, SUBSTANCE ABUSE AND MENTAL HEALTH SERVICES ADMINISTRATION

U.S. DEPARTMENT OF HEALTH AND HUMAN SERVICES

Center for Substance Abuse Treatment, 5600 Fishers Lane

Rockwall II, Suite 618, Rockville, Maryland 20857, 301.443.5052

Its contents are solely the responsibility of the authors and do not necessarily represent the official views of the agency.

Grant No. 6 UD1 TI13593-02-3

CSAT
Center for Substance
Abuse Treatment
SAMHSA

Perspectives on Systems Transformation How Visionary Leaders are Shifting Addiction Treatment Toward a Recovery-Oriented System of Care

PREFACE

Dear Colleague,

The Great Lakes Addiction Technology Transfer Center (Great Lakes ATTC) is part of a national network of Addiction Technology Transfer Centers funded by the Substance Abuse and Mental Health Service Administration's Center for Substance Abuse Treatment (SAMHSA, CSAT). The ATTC's primary goal is to help elevate the quality of addiction treatment by designing and delivering culturally competent, research-based training, education, and systems-change programs for addiction treatment and allied health professionals.

In 2006, the Great Lakes ATTC published a monograph entitled Recovery Management, by William White, Ernest Kurtz, and Mark Sanders. Months later, the Northeast Addiction Technology Transfer Center published a companion monograph by William White and Ernest Kurtz entitled Recovery: Linking Addiction Treatment & Communities of Recovery—A Primer for Addiction Counselors and Recovery Coaches. There was an overwhelming response to these publications, raising many questions about how to implement a redesign of addiction treatment that focused on sustained recovery support. Those questions prompted development of this third monograph.

The interviews in this monograph provide the most detailed discussions to-date of the ways in which leaders at all levels are transforming addiction treatment into a truly recovery-oriented system of care.

The opening interview with Dr. H. Westley Clark, Director of the Center for Substance Abuse Treatment, describes the emergence of recovery as an organizing paradigm for the addictions field and discusses CSAT's numerous recovery initiatives.

The second interview with Dr. Tom Kirk details the recovery-oriented system-transformation efforts of the Connecticut Department of Mental Health and Addiction

189

Services. This discussion details system-change efforts initiated at the state level and ways in which they have altered addiction treatment and recovery in local communities in Connecticut.

The third interview with Dr. Arthur Evans outlines the stages of the recovery-focused system-transformation efforts launched in 2005 by the Philadelphia Department of Behavioral Health and Mental Retardation Services.

The fourth and fifth interviews describe implementation of recovery management pilots at local community levels. Michael Boyle describes the radical revamping of service philosophies and practices within the behavioral health units of Fayette Companies in Peoria, IL. Phil Valentine reports on ways in which peer-based recovery support services and a network of recovery community support centers were developed by a grassroots recovery community organization.

The final interview with Lonnetta Albright discusses the role of the ATTCs in helping extend the acute care model of addiction treatment to a model of sustained recovery management.

It is our hope that this monograph will provide at least tentative answers about the implementation of recovery management at state and local levels. Recovery management pilots are progressing all over the country. We will continue to monitor these efforts and periodically report to the field on the lessons learned in these projects, projects that deserve wide replication.

William L. White, MA
Senior Research Consultant
Chestnut Health Systems
Consultant, Great Lakes Addiction Technology Transfer Center

RECOVERY AS AN ORGANIZING CONCEPT

An Interview with H. Westley Clark, MD, JD, MPH, CAS, FASAM
By William L. White, MA

INTRODUCTION

The effort to achieve a more recovery-focused system of care in the design and delivery of addiction treatment services has received considerable impetus from the Substance Abuse and Mental Health Services Administration's (SAMHSA) Center for Substance Abuse Treatment (CSAT). Through programs such as National Recovery Month, the Recovery Community Support Program (RCSP), Access to Recovery (ATR), and the Recovery Summit, to name just a few, CSAT has moved recovery to the conceptual center of its efforts to enhance the availability and quality of addiction treatment in the United States. I conducted the following interview with Dr. H. Westley Clark, Director of CSAT, January 12, 2007, on behalf of the Great Lakes Addiction Technology Transfer Center (GLATTC). The interview provides one of the most compelling statements to-date on this shift toward a recovery paradigm.

GREAT LAKES ATTC: Dr. Clark, could you highlight your professional background and the circumstances that brought you to CSAT?

DR. CLARK: I'm a psychiatrist and addiction medicine specialist and have worked in the addictions field off and on for the past 30 years. Before coming to CSAT in 1998, I had most recently worked for the Department of Veterans Affairs in San Francisco, serving vets with substance use disorders, psychiatric disorders such as Post-Traumatic Stress Disorder, and medical disorders such as HIV. I also have a degree in Public Health and a degree in Law, which have increased my sensitivity to some of the policy issues germane to the substance abuse arena. My professional interests before coming to CSAT included such diverse areas as substance use among pregnant women, workplace drug testing, and working with substance use in the criminal justice system. I also worked as a senior policy advisor for the Robert Wood Johnson Foundation's Substance Abuse Policy Research Program.

GREAT LAKES ATTC: During your tenure at CSAT, recovery has emerged as a central organizing concept, both at SAMHSA and at CSAT. Could you describe the background of this shift in emphasis?

DR. CLARK: Recovery has been a key construct in the substance use disorder arena for some time. Recovery, as you know, is an integral construct of 12-Step and other self-help programs. It became clear to me as a clinician that it is not simply acute intervention that helps a person. It's the ability to receive ongoing contact and support from others, either through professional support or through a community of recovering peers. Recovery is more than an abstinence from alcohol and drugs; it's about building a full, meaningful, and productive life in the community. Our treatment systems must reflect and help people achieve this broader understanding of recovery.

A few things happened at SAMHSA that facilitated the evolution of the recovery construct over the past five years. SAMHSA adopted recovery as its central vision. Our vision is a life in the community for everyone, and our mission is one of building resilience and facilitating recovery. CSAT, in turn, developed the vision of "Making the hope of recovery a reality...." Prior to 2002, we had a Recovery Community Support Program (RCSP) that organized people in recovery to advocate for themselves at the state and local community levels. We then translated that into a focus on peer-based recovery support activities within local communities. We made significant strides in building relationships in the community and expanding local recovery support services. The next major milestone was Access to Recovery (ATR), a Presidential initiative that provided a hundred million dollars a year for further expanding recovery support services provided by grassroots recovery community organizations and faith-based organizations. The new SAMHSA and CSAT missions and these two CSAT programs helped push recovery to the forefront of our activities at CSAT.

GREAT LAKES ATTC: CSAT's Recovery Month activities have grown exponentially in recent years. What do you see as their collective goal, and to what do you attribute such phenomenal growth?

DR. CLARK: Communities across the country have been concerned about the misuse of substances and the wide range of people affected by such misuse. National leaders and local community leaders recognize that we need the community benefits of recovery, and we need local communities to support people in recovery. And we want to provide a framework through which people in recovery can help others in need of recovery. That's what I've been promoting. We want support for those in recovery. We want people in every community to know that treatment works, that recovery is possible, and that long-term recovery is a reality. We want recognition for those in recovery, for their service providers, and for the efforts of local communities. Recovery Month provides such recognition through an ever-widening range of activities, including ballgames, picnics, pow wows, recovery celebration walks, and educational events. These events reward the hard work of people in recovery, their families, and the various organizations that have supported the recovery process. Seeing thousands of people in recovery gathered together reinforces the possibility and promises of recovery.

These events also provide a venue for organizing community response to new or resurging drug problems. A recent issue is methamphetamine. Large numbers of communities are seeing a drug that they hadn't seen before. In the beginning of the methamphetamine phenomenon, a number of people proclaimed that those affected were hopeless. What that meant for the community was that they would have to write off their sons and daughters. I think the community at large is loath to do that. Recovery Month offers an antidote to such pessimism by offering living proof of long-term recovery and its blessings to individuals, families, and communities.

GREAT LAKES ATTC: CSAT recently sponsored its first national Recovery Summit. What do you think was most significant about this event?

DR. CLARK: We are facilitating multiple discussions about recovery as a construct. We think that through the ATR and RCSP programs we can play a critical role in championing the impact of the holistic community-based system aiding recovery. The Recovery Summit helped articulate principles and guidelines that can guide our work. If we are going to foster recovery, we need to have a clear understanding of the range of recovery experiences and the elements that go into long-term recovery. We need the participation of the recovery community, the treatment community, and the research community to do that. I was quite happy with the Summit and our work to begin this dialogue across communities that often have little contact with one another.

William L. White

GREAT LAKES ATTC: One of the most significant initiatives under your leadership at CSAT has been the Recovery Community Support Program. What do you think are some of the most significant contributions of the RCSP?

DR. CLARK: The RCSP program has demonstrated that people in recovery can in fact participate in offering assistance to other people who either are beginning the recovery process or need to have their long-term recovery efforts supported. The RCSP program is designed to help reduce stigma and barriers to service. We have two models. We have professionally facilitated recovery and peer-based recovery. Both models operate on the principle that the consumer can play a critical role in the recovery process. The peer support model offers several examples of services that are consumer driven and that can serve as important adjuncts to formal substance abuse treatment and prevention efforts. Peer-based recovery support services build on and extend the effects of acute intervention.

I think one of the things coming out of our ATR program is the understanding that the outcomes of acute intervention can be enhanced and sustained. We don't want to just describe the substance use disorder as a chronic relapsing disease and just leave it at that. What our peer support services, facilitated support services, and recovery model do is to stretch the effects of our interventions, while at the same time reducing the frequency of such acute episodes. We don't have to wait until a person completely relapses, with all the attendant problems with the family, the workplace, and the law. Recovery support services provide a vehicle to prevent relapse or to prevent lapses from progressing into full relapses. And we don't have to wait for people to hit bottom. What peer support efforts do is lift the bottom, so that individuals can find recovery before they've alienated their families, their employers, and the legal system.

GREAT LAKES ATTC: What do you envision in terms of the future of the RCSP program?

DR. CLARK: Well, as with all of our programs, we are tied to available funds. We are currently collecting performance data on the RCSP program, to make sure that we're achieving our goals and objectives. I'd like to continue to support the RCSP program, because it does represent the efforts of individuals in recovery. We would like to see if we can get the state agencies to acknowledge the utility of recovery support services as a part of their continua of care. We hope to demonstrate that peer-based recovery support services are more cost effective for individuals, families, and the community, and that they complement rather than compete with professionally directed treatment services. In fact, peer-based recovery support services enhance the impact of professional care by sustaining the effects of such care long after the intervention is

194

completed. When I used to run a 28-day program, I would ask myself, "What happens on day 29?" Then, when I worked in an intensive outpatient program, I saw somebody 3 or 4 times a week, but I only saw them a few hours out of a 24-hour day. What did they do the rest of the time? You quickly learn—especially early in the process— that from a neuropsychological point of view, people are a lot more vulnerable in the early stages of recovery, after acute treatment. So I wanted something that would help me do my job. Recovery support services help me do my job, and they help the professional's patients build a life in recovery after the professional has helped initiate that recovery process.

GREAT LAKES ATTC: There have been recent calls to shift addiction treatment from a model of acute biopsychosocial stabilization to a model of sustained recovery management. To what extent does this represent a fundamental change in the historical design of addiction treatment?

DR. CLARK: Substance use disorder treatment in the United States is being scrutinized from multiple perspectives, and the whole notion of sustained recovery management is consistent with the notion of disease management that you find elsewhere. The chronic disease model recognizes that there is no acute solution. You break your leg, you put a cast on it; it heals, and you go on with an otherwise unchanged life. You don't have a problem—unless, of course, you're into extreme sports. But if you've got asthma, you're going to have asthma off and on for awhile. If you've got diabetes, your diabetes is going to require different management strategies over a prolonged period of time, if not for the rest of your life. Some strategies are just diet and careful monitoring of what you eat. Other strategies include oral pills. Another strategy is insulin. These are different strategies, but they all require a fervent effort. Like long-term management of any other chronic disease, the substance use disorder recovery management strategy offers a framework for sustaining and actively managing recovery over a lifetime.

What recovery management does is allow you to differentiate and titrate the intervention. Not everybody needs an intervention at the same time or at the same level of intensity. Relapse is a common event early in the treatment and recovery process, and there are points of heightened vulnerability later in the recovery process. The recovery management model acknowledges this vulnerability but posits that relapse is not inevitable if the ongoing recovery process is actively managed.

We also have people with multiple problems, such as co-occurring depression or anxiety disorders. We've got complex medical issues, like HIV, Hepatitis, and AIDS. We've got other issues in the recovery process, like homelessness or involvement with the criminal justice system. So a recovery model says, "Okay, from the public's point of view, we have to deal with all of these complexities." We've got individuals who've been physically and sexually abused, or are victims of domestic violence or other kinds of violence and stress. So we need to have support for individuals depending on their unique situations, and that support must extend beyond the point of crisis stabilization. Beyond detox, beyond medical maintenance, what else happens in that person's life? We need to be doing aggressive post-treatment monitoring and support—in part, because drug dealers are interested in having people buy their products, and they will be doing aggressive post-treatment monitoring and marketing.

Our data at the Substance Abuse and Mental Health Services Administration shows that 73 percent of the people who meet criteria for needing treatment for drugs perceive no need for treatment. Eighty-eight percent of people who meet criteria for needing treatment for alcohol use perceive no need for treatment. Now, they endorse all of these things, saying, "My life is adversely affected as a result of my alcohol or my drug use." But these are people—73 percent, 88 percent—who are not seeking treatment. They see no need for treatment. So when we talk about recovery being a community phenomenon, my question is this: "How is it that a person on a self-administered test can endorse 'I'm having problems with alcohol and drugs and with my job, my family, my health, the law, my life, but I don't need treatment'?" In many cases it's because their environment is saying, "You don't need treatment," whether it's because of stigma, whether it's because of denial for other reasons, whether it's because there's a conspiracy of silence. This person is already endorsing, "I'm having problems." This isn't somebody who's just using alcohol casually, or occasionally using an illicit drug. These are people who endorse a sufficient severity of their substance use that treatment is warranted. So, if that's the case, we need a recovery management strategy that helps promote the notion that the individual needs to be in recovery. The community needs to be in recovery. They need to work together on that.

GREAT LAKES ATTC: One of the things that is coming out of CSAT's recovery support initiatives is a more assertive approach toward actually identifying and engaging these people and altering that perception.

DR. CLARK: Right. We also believe that the recovery process needs to be a part of an integrated health care delivery system—one in which substance use problems are perceived as health issues and not simply as a mental health issue or an issue of concern only to substance use disorder treatment practitioners. The message we are trying to promulgate throughout the whole health care delivery system is the value of brief intervention and referral to treatment. We are trying to help healthcare providers talk about substance use in nonjudgmental ways and intervene skillfully when they encounter substance-related problems. We are trying to get these practitioners to intervene early and to sustain their support, just as they would in response to hypertension, diabetes, or other chronic disorders.

GREAT LAKES ATTC: Do you envision a much closer integration of primary healthcare and addiction treatment in the future?

DR. CLARK: That is our hope. That is what our screening/brief intervention effort is trying to facilitate. The recovery process, as you know, is plagued with problems of compliance similar to those found with hypertension and diabetes. What we are doing is promoting a one-stop shop, meaning that the health centers would be authorized to provide early intervention. We don't have to wait until the person crashes and burns and finally arrives at the doors of substance use disorder treatment, usually via the criminal justice system. By the time you get into the criminal justice system or the child welfare system as a result of drug use, you've usually got a long list of severe and complex problems. We believe that issues with alcohol and drugs adversely affect the person's health and the person's well-being, given that these problems have to manifest elsewhere. Early intervention will allow us to respond to these problems early and to begin to work with the person from a motivational point of view. The goal is to deal with these problems before they're exacerbated to more severe levels.

GREAT LAKES ATTC: There are recovery-oriented systems transformations underway in states like Connecticut and in cities like Philadelphia. Do you see such efforts as the wave of the future?

DR. CLARK: Connecticut has done a brilliant job with the recovery model. Tom Kirk has a very good theoretical model, which could be widely replicated. I applaud the visionary efforts of Connecticut and Philadelphia and others who are leading this recovery-focused transformation of substance use disorder treatment. The field of substance use disorder treatment will have better outcomes as we move towards a recovery-oriented service system. What is emerging in these frontier efforts is the development of an integrated system that mobilizes both the formal and informal resources of a community toward the goal of widening the doorways of entry into recovery and providing the support needed for people to move from a community's problems to a community's assets.

William L. White

Great Lakes ATTC: There is growing evidence that sustained post-treatment monitoring and support, assertive linkage to recovery communities, and early re-intervention enhance long-term recovery outcomes. Do you think such services will become standard practice in most addiction treatment programs?

Dr. Clark: The real question is how we define post-treatment monitoring. We need to be careful about characterizing post-treatment monitoring. We know that some people, particularly those with more severe problems, need ongoing support following primary treatment, and the evidence confirms that post-treatment recovery support services can help reduce relapse and facilitate early re-intervention. We could also use toxicology screening as feedback to an individual and an opportunity for early re-intervention. Post-treatment monitoring and support need to be recovery focused, with an emphasis on support as opposed to simply a policing function. That gets us back to recovery management. The question is, "Is the recovery management service that is monitoring the individual also supporting and helping the individual?" From assertive community treatment, we recognize that these are things that have to be put in place. Recovery support services will offer you the same dynamic and can be tailored to individual problem severity and recovery support needs. But the whole key is the experience that you are part of a community and the community cares about you. The community is supporting you. Monitoring sounds like an externally imposed mandate. What I'd like to see is recovery support services conceptualized as a voluntary phenomenon—something that is chosen because it is in the best interest of the individual.

Great Lakes ATTC: Several of the states and cities are committed to the development of ongoing recovery support services but are wrestling with the challenge of finding the best financing models to get these services into the field. "Do we enhance existing rates for inpatient and outpatient treatment that include recovery support services? Do we bill these as separate services?" Do you have any thoughts about future financing of post-treatment support services?

Dr. Clark: Part of a performance-driven system is looking at what we are getting from our existing system. That accountability becomes a key variable in what we're doing. As I pointed out, our delivery system addresses the needs of only a small minority of the individuals who need our services. If the majority of people who suffer from alcohol and drug problems presented for treatment, we would truly be overwhelmed. Our existing waiting list is miniscule compared to the potential demand. So the question for political leaders and those charged with managing behavioral health care systems is,

"How do I determine service priorities?" You can look at recovery services in isolation, or you can ask what such services will mean to other costs that substance use disorders impose on the community. What will these services mean to demands upon the mental health system, the child welfare and the criminal justice systems? If I collect one dollar for taxes, I can spend that dollar any number of ways. The savings that accrue within the criminal justice system and the child welfare system can be used to support the recovery of people who no longer demand the resources of those systems. We need to take the long view.

We're trying to get people to 5 years out. If I can get you to 5 years out in recovery, the chances of your getting to 10 years of recovery goes up dramatically. You see the potential. If you see the dollar as only the dollar from Medicare or the Block Grant, people will fight over that dollar. If you see the dollar as a whole dollar, a taxpayer's dollar, then people must ask how we can enhance recovery outcomes while minimizing demands for repeated episodes of high-cost services. If we can stabilize and support people in recovery, they won't need repeated episodes of such higher-cost interventions. What we pay for repeated episodes of detox and inpatient treatment will pay for a lot of post-treatment recovery support services. We will come to see the recovery support services as a good financial investment.

GREAT LAKES ATTC: What do you think are some of the most significant obstacles to treating severe alcohol and other drug problems in a manner similar to the management of other chronic illnesses?

DR. CLARK: As we begin to integrate substance use disorder treatment and primary health care, such parallels will become more obvious. What Tom McLellan and others are trying to do is to promote the parallels between other chronic health conditions and their treatment and substance use disorders and how they can best be treated. We're just beginning to understand the chronic care model in primary health care. What we will be doing in substance use disorder treatment is finding better ways to shorten and actively manage the prolonged course of many substance use disorders. Our message in Recovery Month to individuals, parents, friends, relatives, and employers is that these are solutions to these problems, and resources need to be mobilized to deal with these problems until they are brought under control. Our screening and brief interventions can help resolve these problems before someone crashes and burns. And with a recovery-oriented system of care, we can mobilize resources for those with the most severe and complex substance use disorders.

We want service providers to recognize that they have a sustained obligation to such clients, and that we have an obligation to use the best science and the best clinical strategies to promote long-term recovery.

GREAT LAKES ATTC: How is CSAT helping the treatment field make the transition toward more recovery-oriented systems of care? What do you see as the role of the ATTCs in helping the field through this historic transition?

DR. CLARK: CSAT recently hosted a Recovery Summit that brought together multiple stakeholders, including the major professional associations from the substance use disorder field, as well as leading substance use disorder researchers and key recovery community organizations. The focus was on how to use this new recovery orientation to enhance our research knowledge about recovery and how to improve the quality of substance use disorder treatment. We'll periodically consider whether we need additional recovery summits to guide our future efforts. We are continuing to work with visionaries like Tom Kirk in Connecticut to disseminate working models to other states and local communities. We have funded the Legal Action Center to document issues related to recovery barriers, social stigma, and confidentiality issues in the delivery of recovery support services. One of our primary functions continues to be bringing together diverse stakeholders such as recovering individuals, family members, mutual aid organizations, system professionals, and those providing peer support services for policy review and systems planning. The systems transformation we envision goes two ways: the bottom to the top, and the top to the bottom. Our ATTCs are playing an important role in disseminating new information as it becomes available.

GREAT LAKES ATTC: Some of the organizations that CSAT has funded, such as White Bison, Inc., are integrating a recovery orientation with primary prevention activities. Do you think this growing recovery orientation will lead to a greater integration between treatment and prevention?

DR. CLARK: I think SAMHSA will increasingly move toward an integrated model that bridges and integrates primary prevention, early intervention, treatment, and recovery support services. The issue with early intervention is to bring evidence-based practices to bear on the human manifestations of our prevention failures—to reach those who didn't receive or heed our prevention messages. So rather than seeking a dichotomy between prevention and treatment, I think it is best to see these as a single continuum. A message common to all is that, once you start using, drug use is powerfully reinforcing and can quickly escalate out of control. With the strategies we develop and employ, we need to be able to reach people across this continuum of drug involvement—from people who have never used to people who are in long-term recovery, and all points in between. We need interventions that reach people who have diminished control over their decision-making. We know brains are in transition once drug use begins. We need to continue to make sure that the prevention and treatment interventions we employ are appropriate for each individual, family, and community.

GREAT LAKES **ATTC:** CSAT has done a wonderful job of reinforcing the idea that the recovery support services need to be nuanced across developmental age and gender and cultural context. That seems to be a very important contribution in what you've done the last several years.

DR. CLARK: Thank you. This is the product of a conscious and sustained effort on the part of many dedicated staff.

CREATING A RECOVERY-ORIENTED SYSTEM OF CARE

An Interview with Thomas A. Kirk, Jr., PhD
By William L. White, MA

INTRODUCTION

Across the country, references to the State of Connecticut pepper discussions about behavioral health systems transformation. Many states are attempting special recovery-focused initiatives and pilots, but Connecticut stands at the forefront of attempts to totally transform a state behavioral health care system into one permeated with this recovery orientation. I conducted the following interview with Tom Kirk, Commissioner of the Connecticut Department of Mental Health and Addiction Services, on September 26, 2006, on behalf of the Great Lakes Addiction Technology Transfer Center. This interview provides one of the most probing examinations to-date of the process of behavioral health systems transformation.

> William L. White, MA
> Senior Research Consultant
> Chestnut Health Systems

GREAT LAKES ATTC: Could you summarize your background before becoming Commissioner of the Connecticut Department of Mental Health and Addiction Services (DMHAS)?

DR. KIRK: My graduate training in psychology was at Catholic University in Washington, DC, after which I joined the faculty of Virginia Commonwealth University (VCU) in

Richmond, Virginia. While still on faculty, I did some part-time consulting work at one of the larger adult prisons in Virginia. It was around this time that drug use and related offenses were placing extraordinary pressure on correction systems. I eventually left my tenured position at VCU and established a private consulting practice which emphasized criminal justice system and addiction-related issues. Thereafter, my professional journey included increasingly responsible public-sector positions focusing on the design and management of services for persons with substance use and co-occurring (mental health) disorders in the Washington, DC area.

GREAT LAKES ATTC: When and how did you first come to Connecticut?

DR. KIRK: I came to Connecticut in 1990 to direct Liberation Programs, Inc., a rather large substance abuse prevention and treatment agency in Stamford. In that position I interacted with my colleagues in other community-based addiction service agencies who were under contract with the Single State Addiction agency. In July of 1995, John Rowland became governor of Connecticut and proposed to merge or create a new agency that combined mental health and addiction services. My concern, frankly, was that the mental health component (Department of Mental Health) was so much bigger that the addictions component would be neglected. After I had voiced my concerns about this, some people asked me whether I would be interested in being considered for a Deputy Commissioner's position in this new department, to oversee addictions services. One thing led to another, and in October of 1995, I became the Deputy Commissioner for addiction services in this new Department of Mental Health and Addiction Services (DMHAS). When the Deputy Commissioner for Mental Health subsequently left and the Commissioner retired, I was asked to be the Commissioner and assumed this role in May of 2000.

GREAT LAKES ATTC: When would you pinpoint the beginning of the recovery initiative in Connecticut?

Dr Kirk: When you are interviewed for appointed positions, you must go before the legislature, who will then vote on your nomination. During that process you provide written testimony and are queried about the service philosophy you will bring to the agency for which you are being considered. In my interview and testimony in October, 1995, I talked about the need for recovery as a driving force for service design—and have done so in every subsequent reappointment session with the legislature, and I periodically read those testimonies to remind myself of that focus. At the same time, the heavy emphasis really didn't take hold until around 1997.

GREAT LAKES ATTC: Were there conditions in the late 1990s in the addiction and mental health fields that really contributed to this, sort of ramping this up as a major initiative?

DR. KIRK: One such condition was the sense in both mental health and addiction services that a lot of people were repeatedly going in and out of this system without achieving stable, long-term recovery. One of the things that I wanted to do was to identify persons who were high service utilizers—people who were recycling in detox and rehab—and to see what we were missing in our work with them. One of the strategic goals that we worked on, beginning in 1998 and heavily through 2002, was to revamp services for those who were either poorly served or underserved in our service system. The recognition of high service utilizers and the dollars we were investing in them without positive outcomes was prompting legislators and staff from the Governor's Office of Policy Management to suggest restrictions on how many times someone could be admitted in a year. These were difficult fiscal times in Connecticut, so the pressure to cut or restrict services was intense. That forced us to look at what we were doing and how to respond better to people with severe problems and long and complex service histories. The fiscal pressures created extraordinary challenges but, in retrospect, were opportunities for changes in the system.

GREAT LAKES ATTC: How did you respond to these challenges?

DR. KIRK: Rather than batten down the hatches or just close things down, we began to ask, "How do we rethink what we are doing and move forward in an informed way?" So the fiscal pressures forced us to examine quality-of-care issues and conclude, "What we are doing is just not good enough; something has to be done." So we started moving from the acute-care mentality and the acute-care funding system to what some people are calling a chronic-care or recovery-management model.

GREAT LAKES ATTC: You seem to have involved the recovery advocacy organizations very early in this process.

DR. KIRK: In late 1998 and early 1999, we started asking the question, "What does recovery really mean?" and we involved our DMHAS-funded addictions and mental health advocacy organizations to help us answer that question and to help us formulate core recovery values and principles. Those groups started out like oil and water but eventually came together under the leadership of Bob Savage, the founder and first director of the Connecticut Community for Addiction Recovery, Inc. (CCAR) and Yvette

Sangster of Advocacy Unlimited, Inc. (AU), to create the Recovery Principles and Core Recovery Values that have been the foundation of our subsequent work.

GREAT LAKES ATTC: It is amazing the role that service consumers have played in reshaping behavioral health services in Connecticut.

DR. KIRK: One of the things I've learned, and I don't pay as much attention as I should, is to listen to the people who actually are the recipients of services and those who've moved on to long-term stable recovery. They'll give you a better idea what it is that you should be doing or could be doing. They may not always be right or have the complete picture, but they can help keep you focused on the things that are important. I remember presenting some really complicated structural proposals—fancy PowerPoint presentations and all that sort of stuff—to a mental health consumer group in the northwest part of the state, in the Danbury area, and when I was finished a guy in the front row says, "All I want to know is, am I still going to have a case manager?" From his point of view, his case manager was the system.

GREAT LAKES ATTC: How did you go about the process of planning the kind of system transformation you have led in Connecticut?

DR. KIRK: There were several key steps. The first one was to refine our vision and our plan. We came up with an initial strategic plan that had four major goals. The first goal—to promote an infrastructure that would support quality services—was based on the belief that service quality is the driving force of recovery. The second strategic goal was to focus on underserved, poorly served populations, including a stronger emphasis on cultural competence. The third goal was to enhance the management effectiveness of DMHAS. And the last goal was to be aggressive in our development of resources and partnerships.

Let me elaborate on some of these. Our work on the first goal included identifying recovery values and principles in collaboration with Bob Savage and Yvette Sangster. This in turn led to discussions about quality measures, recovery outcomes, and how to assess an agency's degree of recovery orientation.

One component of the second goal involved several strategic decisions. We made informed decisions to focus our attention on four or five issues that we felt could quickly elevate service quality. The issues we chose to focus on were culture, gender, trauma, and co-occurring disorders. We believed a focus on these issues in terms of information, training, service enhancement, etc. would produce a measurable improvement in the quality of the system. Our work in these areas has been significant and sustained, and has achieved that goal

The third goal, to enhance our management capability, involved a major change in our system that had begun with a decision made by my predecessor. That decision was to not turn over management of the contractual funds that drove our service system to a private managed care company. We decided to use managed care principles, but to administer that process ourselves. We chose not to lose 20 percent of our funds via an outside management contract. But that meant we needed to recruit a different caliber of player into the state agency system. We needed and found individuals who had managed care experience in the private sector, but who were open to administering such a system within the framework of public sector values.

The fourth goal, aggressively pursuing additional funding, led to sophisticated approaches to garnering increased federal dollars to support our system. Since 1998, we've brought in over $120 million in federal grant awards to help build and sustain parts of our service system. We hired people to help us procure that money, with the understanding that we would never go after grant dollars for the sake of grant dollars, but to strategically seek dollars that would support our larger vision.

GREAT LAKES ATTC: Creating that vision at the same time you were forging a new agency must have been an incredible challenge.

DR. KIRK: My predecessor had a great line. He said, "We are not merging mental health and addictions. We're creating a new agency, and one plus one is going to give us three." We had to create a new culture. The addictions and mental health cultures are both so strong. It wasn't a surprise to us that shaping this new culture took some time, but through this effort we ended up with a new culture that not only respects the best and brightest and most sensitive components of each of the two systems, but also moved us to a new level. We redefined ourselves as a healthcare agency, not a social service agency. People with substance use disorders and psychiatric conditions have a healthcare condition. They share illnesses with behavioral components rooted in the chemistry of the brain. Seeing ourselves as a healthcare agency helping people manage and recover from these illnesses served as a bridge between the mental health and addiction cultures. It gave us a common platform. Our mission is to promote wellness and health and to help people with behavioral health disorders regain their health and reclaim their lives.

GREAT LAKES ATTC: How were you able to transform your system and still maintain its maintenance functions?

DR. KIRK: That's the key. You're trying to reengineer the system at the same time you have to keep it running. One of the things that I did was to say to Arthur Evans, PhD, my Deputy Commissioner at the time: "I want you to run a research and development component within DMHAS." I freed him of most operational responsibilities and asked him to form work groups to look at everything we had done in recent years, including the federal initiatives, and to pick the best ideas and practices. I asked him take the recovery values that our advocacy groups had put together and to translate them into DMHAS policies. So we created a draft Commissioner's Recovery Policy outlining the move toward a recovery-oriented service system, and then met in retreats with boards, providers, consumers, our own staff, and all sorts of other groups to complete our foundational recovery policy. (See www.dmhas.state.ct.us, then click on "Recovery" under "Major Initiatives.") That statement is as valid and important now as when we first signed it in 2002. Arthur Evans skillfully created and guided much of this development effort, and also added Dr. Larry Davidson from Yale University and others within DMHAS to help us implement this new recovery vision. Dr. Evans eventually left his position to assume responsibility for a large public entity in Philadelphia, while Dr. Davidson subsequently established and staffed at Yale a special program on recovery. Both of these professionals were critical to driving the changes we were implementing

GREAT LAKES ATTC: How did this R & D unit relate to your operations staff?

DR. KIRK: We made a mistake early in the process in keeping Arthur's group separated from operations a bit longer than we should have. We had one track that was improving service operations and a separate track with our recovery initiative. They were both progressing so well that they almost took on lives of their own. You had two different focuses in the agency, and people were not necessarily tying the two of them together. So we reached an awareness that we needed to bring these two tracks together. I brought together all of our key leaders in the agency, as well as the private non-profits, and said, "We're not moving away from the four major goals, but we're going to come up with one single overarching goal that integrates our work on these goals." And that overarching strategic goal was to develop and maintain a value-driven, recovery-oriented service system. We had to convince our own staff and the service providers that this was not a "flavor of the month" thing but an overriding philosophy that would shape everything in the coming years.

We had to stop people from thinking, "It's the *project du jour.* Don't spend too much energy here, because it's going to be something different a year from now." We had to convince everyone that we were going to seek the highest quality of service at the most realistic cost. And we had to help people operationalize their understanding of what a recovery-oriented system would mean for their programs and their roles. To do that, we had to promote recovery-oriented concepts such as recovery capital, recovery supports, sober housing, recovery-conducive employment, etc. We said, "We want you to continue to focus on co-occurring, on gender, on culture, on trauma, and on some other areas that truly are improving the overall value index of the service system, but we want you to place all of these initiatives within this larger recovery orientation." We did that in 2002-2003.

Staying the course with some basic core elements is extraordinarily important, and the recovery practice guidelines that we just recently put together form a crucial piece that has defined our recovery policy in practice terms.

GREAT LAKES **ATTC:** As you went from the conceptual to changes in practice, what obstacles did you encounter, both inside DMHAS and with your provider community?

DR. KIRK: The first challenge was people saying, "We're already doing that; this is not new." There were two variations on this. First, there were people who really had been pushing this and had not been heard. Some of these people were angry that it took us so long to get to this orientation. Some said, "I've been talking about this for 10 years, and no one has listened, and you come along in 2000 and talk about recovery as if this is the latest and best thing. I've been championing this for years before you ever got here." So we had to listen to these people and get them on board with us. This was a group who did believe in this orientation and were already doing it to the best of their abilities. Others said, "We're doing it," but when we looked at the way they ran their agencies and the way their services were provided, they were a long way from the recovery values we were extolling. For them, we had to define these recovery values at a practice level, so they could see the ways in which they were really not providing recovery-oriented care.

GREAT LAKES **ATTC:** Helping agencies self-evaluate their recovery orientation must have been a crucial part of this process.

DR. KIRK: Yes. Larry Davidson worked with us to develop a scale that could help agencies measure their degree of recovery orientation. This work ("Findings from the DMHAS Recovery Self Assessment") is posted on the DMHAS website (www.dmhas.

state.ct.us) under "Major Initiatives," "Recovery," "Reports and Position Papers." We built recovery orientation into the language of all our contracts, along with a contractual requirement that each agency had to conduct a recovery self-assessment process. We are currently working on further refining recovery outcome measures. We followed that self-assessment process with coaching and technical assistance to move toward greater recovery orientation. We also created something called "The Recovery Institute," a training curriculum consisting of a series of recovery-focused courses designed particularly for people working in private non-profit service agencies. More than 5,000 people have attended one or more of these courses. After establishing "The Recovery Institute," we set up what we call "Centers of Excellence." This consisted of a competitive process that would provide funding for agencies to receive consultation in one of six areas, such as outreach, strength-based assessments, culturally informed services, and so on. We picked agencies that either saw themselves as particularly good in these areas or really wanted to become excellent in their competencies in these areas. Considering we were only paying for consultation services through the financial assistance of SAMHSA technical assistance, we were amazed at how many applicants responded to this RFP. We made a big to-do out of it, recognizing those we selected as Centers of Excellence in Connecticut. They ranged from hospitals to private addiction or mental health agencies, to some of the state-operated mental health components.

GREAT LAKES ATTC: Did you also take steps during this early period to support recovery advocacy and support organizations, and to ensure their involvement in the system-transformation process?

DR. KIRK: We increased funding to such groups, to allow them to expand their operations on a statewide basis. There was federal money supporting some of their activities, e.g., CCAR, and we added state dollars to supplement this. We've since increased our state funding of these advocacy organizations. This has helped strengthen consumer involvement in our system and expand peer-based recovery support services. We also met with the executive director and board representatives of each of the person–in–recovery/consumer groups under contract with DMHAS. We discussed their contract requirements, listened to their vision and goals, and focused on affirming our joint vision and mission.

GREAT LAKES ATTC: How did you manage the system-transformation process inside DMHAS?

DR. KIRK: A couple of different ways. The communication strategy was very important. In late 2000, we started putting out "Messages from the Office of the Commissioner." This communication piece came out every two weeks or so and was sent to everybody in the service system, external and internal, including all of our 3,500 DMHAS staff. The messages the first couple years were typically from me, but then we involved other people in crafting these messages, such as a message from Bob Savage (who was then Director of the Connecticut Community of Addiction Recovery) or a message from members of my executive staff. To-date, there have been over 130 such Messages. So there was a steady emphasis on this recovery initiative and what it would mean to everyone in the system and in DMHAS. A second communication piece started in 2000 was "INFORMATION... foundation of good policy." It is a one-page brief, based on data and released several times a year. Approximately 80 have been published since 2000. The "Messages from..." and the "INFORMATION" documents cover numerous angles—recovery management, recovery support services, our work with high-service utilizers, linkage to care, employment, housing, and new approaches to public managed care. We used these communications to highlight what we were doing and the kind of problem solving we were trying to do. All are at www.dmhas.state.ct.us.

GREAT LAKES ATTC: Could you provide some examples of such problem solving?

DR. KIRK: We have a state-operated facility in Hartford that provides detox and residential services, and in the same neighborhood a private non-profit treatment agency that provides similar services. I kept hearing that people couldn't get into either facility. I put in place a daily census count that each facility needed to call in to the central office, and we continued to get complaints that people couldn't get in, even when our counts showed empty beds. So we did a review and came up with something called SATEP: Substance Abuse Treatment Enhancement Project. We reconfigured the beds and added some supplemental services, such as a 24-hour access telephone line and transportation funds that allowed people in need to get transported by taxi to treatment, or from one service component to another. These strategies increased service access.

Another problem we had was with people who were opiate dependent who would repeatedly use primary treatment services but fail to follow through on any continuing-care services. We started OATP, an Opiate Agonist Treatment Program that identified these individuals and assigned them a recovery specialist, who tracked them through the system and assertively linked them to continuing-care services. This service also increased service utilization rates within many of our funded agencies. We took the same capacity and increased access and improved linkage to follow-up care. This lowered the admissions of our high service utilizers and opened up beds for other people. To achieve that system wide meant we had to confront various bureaucratic stupidities. For example, we had one of our state-operated programs that had a policy that they did not admit on Friday afternoons. Needless to say, we changed such policies that had emerged as roadblocks to people's recoveries.

A third area involved our use of alternative living centers. These are not treatment centers but sober living environments used by long-term substance users who had achieved sobriety. Providing such sanctuaries helped these people achieve stable recovery and became an important step-down level of care within our system that further decreased admissions by our high service utilizers. And we did it for a fraction of the cost of a detox or residential treatment day. Staff heard so much about recovery and these recovery-focused problem-solving efforts that it just became a part of the internal culture.

GREAT LAKES **ATTC:** It sounds like the whole understanding of levels of care changed through this process.

DR. KIRK: We dramatically expanded the range of services. This is really important. We modified ASAM criteria, what we call Connecticut ASAM, to get providers as well as the people seeking services more focused on what people needed rather than what was available. We pushed a widened definition of levels of care with more precise admission and continued-stay criteria. Our goal was to get out of a situation where, if you showed up at a clinic that does A, B, and C, you would get A, B, C, even when you needed D, E, F. Our efforts to expand the service menu and refine the process of matching people based on their needs helped shape a service system in which both service providers and consumers made more informed choices about levels of care. Adding some really good measures helped that. One of our most critical measures was continuity of care, e.g., was each client actually linked (not just referred) to follow-up care within 7 days of his or her discharge? This had a significant influence on our readmission rates.

GREAT LAKES **ATTC:** You have made a significant investment in Connecticut in developing non-clinical recovery support services within your behavioral health care system. Could you describe the impact these services have had?

DR. KIRK: The recovery support services have had a significant impact on decreasing repetitive use of acute high-cost services. Recovery support services have served as an important vehicle for reaching out and engaging people in treatment and recovery processes. They have also served as an effective bridge in moving people across different levels of care within the clinical service system. Recovery support services have represented a relatively low-cost means of sustaining people's recovery without the need for sustained treatment or the multiple treatment episodes that might otherwise be required.

GREAT LAKES ATTC: What would you recommend to directors in other states who don't currently have recovery advocacy and support organizations?

DR. KIRK: I would recommend that a director and his or her staff get to as many forums as possible that provide opportunities to interact with people in recovery. And I would suggest they keep a log of what they have heard in these forums. I gave a talk last year at the annual meeting of the National Alliance on Mental Illness. I had someone help me put it together, and I junked a good part of it because it just wasn't people oriented enough. Instead I added "What I heard along the way." Let me just give you a couple examples, because I think that this is something that anybody could do. One of the things I heard along the way is, **"when I get too functional, I lose my services."** In the acute-care system of addiction treatment, people actually get penalized via loss of support when they get better. Another message I heard was, "When I come to this clinic, I feel like I'm a junkie, and I'm not a junkie anymore." What does that say about our service system? I asked another person I met in one of our clubhouses, "If you could ask for something, what would you ask for?" He said, "I just wish people had more time to talk to me." These are things that any state director and his or her staff can get by going into these situations and listening and asking themselves the implications of such comments for the design changes needed in the service system.

You have to work with and nurture the development of peer advocacy and support organizations, and you have to help them mature beyond the "us against the world" stance that often characterizes the early days of such organizations. As I told one advocate, "You have to understand when you're beginning to win something and stop chasing windmills all the time, because, after a while, people don't pay any attention to you anymore." It's not only working with these organizations; it's helping them mature as organizations. I'm more comfortable with an approach that doesn't place the advocates as employees of the state agency. We've shifted from these groups being our watchdogs to these groups being our partners in transforming our system of care.

GREAT LAKES ATTC: How do you think financing models are going to have to change to become congruent with this recovery model?

DR. KIRK: Great question, and an interesting one, because we're in the midst of that issue right now. I'll give you one example. We just had a needs assessment. We asked some folks to conduct a survey for us that, in part, identified about 850 service consumers who were having significant problems of one type or another. One of the striking findings was that a significant percentage of these people were assigned to services judged to be what they needed, but in which the people were not participating. For whatever reasons, they were not engaging in what others saw them needing. This is a clinical question, but it is also a fiscal question. If the services we are paying for are not engaging those they are intended to serve, perhaps it is time we altered the service menu. And that may include paying for things, such as peer support services, which have not been historically reimbursable services. We need funding guidelines that allow us to think outside the box and support services that are responsive to recovery needs. If post-treatment recovery support is critical to long-term recovery outcomes, we need to fund such services, as we recently did by funding our recovery advocacy agency to provide telephone-based recovery support services to people for 12 weeks following their discharge from primary treatment.

We have to ask: What are the components that would serve to engage people and link them between different levels of care more effectively? What new levels of care do we need to add to the existing service system? What are the components that would dramatically increase access to and utilization of existing services? If sober housing is critical to recovery maintenance, then we need to think about supporting housing initiatives. Tying recovery support services with existing levels of care challenges traditional funding mechanisms, through which the former were not reimbursable services. We're looking at different ways of combining components into a service level of care, to achieve good continuity of care. In short, we are building on the work of Tom McLellan, Bill White, and others to shift towards treating severe addiction as a chronic or continuing-care disorder like my high cholesterol or somebody else's high blood pressure. What would that mean? You could move toward a system that was not based solely on fee-for-service and that redefined an episode of care.

Let's say that Tom Kirk shows at agency X, and based on an assessment it is determined that I will likely need involvement in formal treatment across multiple levels of care for the next year. And the formal treatment might be—I don't know—detox. It might be intensive outpatient. Based upon that, we say that we will fund the agency to have responsibility for providing this episode of care for me during the year, up to a set dollar value. They can spend the money on services for me at their discretion, as long as it supports my recovery process.

This new definition of an episode of care could involve different combinations of clinical and recovery support components that I could benefit from, and that my service provider or I could purchase on my behalf. We could tie outcome measures to my entering and remaining in what I call a "recovery zone"—sober and stable functioning in the community. What are being paid for are services that support my stability, not just high-cost crisis interventions. What does that mean in terms of financing? One of the approaches we're looking at for the future is the idea of "covered lives"—paying agencies to provide comprehensive services for a given number of people per year, rather than paying for delivered service units.

GREAT LAKES ATTC: Do you see primary healthcare integrated into this vision of sustained recovery support?

DR. KIRK: This is an extraordinarily important issue. One of the things I'll pay attention to over the next year is the primary healthcare needs of the people we have in our private non-profit and state-operated service system. On the mental health side, the lifespan of a person with psychiatric disability is something like 15 years less than other persons, and when we look at the data for people we have in our service system, they're not dying of suicide; they're not dying of drug overdoses. They're dying of cardiac conditions, respiratory conditions, and the kinds of things that the rest of us suffer from. So if we're really going to talk about a recovery-oriented holistic system, we have to pay attention to primary healthcare needs.

One of the major priorities for my medical director is to focus on a greater linkage between the physical healthcare needs of our people and their substance abuse or mental health needs. We have what's called PARS. PARS is our Performance Assessment Reviews for all of our managers. I just finished identifying the things that I would expect them—including the 10 CEOs of the major state-operated facilities—to focus upon this year. One of them relates to addressing the physical healthcare needs of the people we have in our service system. Co-occurring disorders, employment, physical healthcare, and recovery orientation are the four major initiatives that we are focusing upon this year in terms of improved services.

GREAT LAKES ATTC: Did you run into regulations inside DMHAS, or federal regulations, that actually got in the way of the system transformation that you've been attempting?

DR. KIRK: Yes, particularly licensing authorities. The program licensing authority in the State of Connecticut is the Department of Public Health (DPH), which is very medically oriented. Here's the kind of situation that comes up. In the programs for women and children that we run, a mother may come in for services, and she might have one or two young children come with her, and other women may watch her children while she is in group or meeting with her counselor. Public Health looks at this and declares that we must have separate therapeutic childcare for such situations, which is extraordinarily expensive. Those are the kinds of conflicts we're trying to work through with DPH. It's a conflict in philosophies. They may cite a program for not being medical model oriented at the same time we are trying to move that program from a medical model to a more peer-based recovery model. I meet with the Public Health Department once a month to work out such issues. There have been dramatic changes in some ways, yes, but it's a process. Being in a process, we still have a long way to go.

GREAT LAKES ATTC: Have the federal agencies that you work with been supportive of the directions that you're going?

DR. KIRK: We've gotten good support from CSAT and CMHS as well as CSAP in the recovery focus. We're one of the Mental Health Transformation states, as well as an Access to Recovery state and one of the Strategic Prevention Framework states. Between the technical assistance they gave us in support of the Centers of Excellence and the Strategic Prevention Framework grant we have from CSAP, the federal agencies have been supportive of our system-transformation efforts. The real challenge is with Medicaid regulations. We've had site visits where their philosophies and ours conflict, and we've had to balance our recovery orientation with meeting the regulations that flow from their medical model.

GREAT LAKES ATTC: When you look back over the history of the recovery initiative, what do you personally feel best about?

DR. KIRK: I feel best about the direction we set and the fact that the resulting focus and energy are producing real change in the way people who receive services in our system think about themselves and their hope for recovery. I feel good that our recovery philosophy is filtering throughout the system. You hear people talking about things today that we talked about two years ago, but they've made it a part of them. There's a bumper sticker that says, "When people lead, their leaders will follow." I think in an interesting sort of way we've been able to create a movement where people— service consumers and people in recovery—are becoming more and more energized, and they're guiding the system-transformation process in ways that the service professionals could never do by ourselves. If I got fired tomorrow, I would feel real comfortable that the movement would continue long after I left the system.

The question is, "How do you institutionalize things so that people take ownership of these innovations and carry them forward?" I strongly believe that we all stand on the shoulders of the people who came before us. I talk about the recovery stuff so much, and I spend so much time talking with the Governor and legislators about it, that I now hear them using the words. It's something to listen to the Governor talking about behavioral health systems transformation in her own words.

GREAT LAKES ATTC: As you look ahead, what do you see as the next steps in the system-transformation process in Connecticut?

DR. KIRK: As much progress as we have made, we still have a long way to go in the recovery-oriented focus, because it involves total system change, not just one program. So we will continue to identify "lessons learned" from our experiences—how Access to Recovery or related activities can be embedded into the service system versus being the latest grant. I also believe that we have to work on identifying and cultivating staff—management and line staff—whose leadership and other skill sets can serve to model what a recovery-oriented system really is like. We will be intensely focusing on things like employment, the addition of recovery support services to the basic service menu, and physical healthcare and co-occurring disorder services. Another focus will be on pushing the service design toward wellness promotion and recovery support services that groups of people in different areas of the state need, rather than toward what the historical structures dictate that we continue to fund. A third area will be shifting the financing of the overall system to support a continuing-care model. We must change the financing mechanisms.

GREAT LAKES ATTC: As a final question, are there any tips you would offer your counterparts on how to manage similar efforts at systems transformation?

DR. KIRK: One tip would be to focus the transformation process through an overall message that allows people to see the individual initiatives as fitting into a whole. System transformation will fail if it is just seen as a bunch of discrete initiatives. You have to continue to hammer away about how existing things and new initiatives tie into this larger picture. You also have to honor what people have done in the past and not inadvertently demean their efforts. The message is, "We want to take the gems that we can learn from you, based upon your experience, and elevate them within what we are building." When I was at the agency in Stamford talking about some of this, a guy who had been running our methadone program from day-one said, "Sometimes when I hear you talk about this, it's as if I've been doing the wrong stuff for the last 20 years." That's not the message we want to convey. We need to understand what they've been doing in the trenches, what they've learned, and build on that.

The Recovery-Focused Transformation of an Urban Behavioral Health Care System

An Interview with Arthur C. Evans, PhD
By William L. White, MA

Introduction

Beginning with Dr. Benjamin Rush's eighteenth-century writings on chronic drunkenness as a medical disease, the City of Philadelphia has held an honored position in the history of addiction treatment and recovery in America. That history of innovation continues today in a bold vision of integrating mental health and addiction services within a conceptual framework of long-term recovery. Leading that innovation is Dr. Arthur Evans, Director of the Philadelphia Department of Behavioral Health and Mental Retardation Services. The following is an interview I conducted with Dr. Evans in November, 2006 on behalf of the Great Lakes Addiction Technology Transfer Center. In this wide-ranging interview, Dr. Evans eloquently describes the behavioral health system-transformation process that is underway in the City of Philadelphia. In my writings I have posed the question, "How would we treat addiction if we <u>really</u> believed that addiction was a chronic disorder?" Answers to that question are emerging in Philadelphia in a way that will influence the future of addiction treatment in America.

Great Lakes ATTC: Could you summarize your professional background and the circumstances that brought you to Philadelphia?

Dr. Evans: I'm a clinical and community psychologist and have been working in the addictions field for the last 19 years, first as a practitioner and program manager, then in policy-level positions in the State of Connecticut. I served as the Director of Managed Care and then Deputy Commissioner for the Connecticut Department of Mental Health and Addiction Services. In that role, I was very much involved in strategic planning and leading system-transformation efforts in Connecticut. I was then invited to come to Philadelphia to fill a newly created position following the city's decision to combine all of its behavioral health services into an integrated system. I was recruited to continue building on the history of innovation in Philadelphia's behavioral health system.

GREAT LAKES ATTC: Provide an overview of how behavioral health services are organized in Philadelphia.

DR. EVANS: Pennsylvania has a county-based delivery system, with all dollars flowing through each single county authority. On the mental health side, our single authority is an Office of Mental Health, which receives all statewide grant dollars allocated for the city of Philadelphia and is one of three units within the Department of Behavioral Health/Mental Retardation services (DBH/MRS). The Office of Metal Health is responsible for services to primarily indigent individuals who have problems related to serious mental illness. There's also an Office of Addiction Services, which receives state dollars and federal grant dollars for people with addictive disorders. And then there is Community Behavioral Health (CBH), which is a private, non-profit, 501(c)(3) managed behavioral healthcare organization that is fully owned and run by the City. I'm the president of the Board of CBH, and the executive director of CBH reports to me. CBH administers behavioral health payments for practically all of the Medicaid populations that are served in the city. So those three entities allow us to manage practically all of the behavioral health dollars in Philadelphia as a single public system.

GREAT LAKES ATTC: How did the vision develop to redesign mental health and addiction services toward greater recovery orientation?

DR. EVANS: When I came into this position, the city had a fairly long history of innovation, particularly around how it has organized and administered behavioral health services. Through our initial discussions with multiple community constituencies, there was a desire to move our system of care toward greater recovery orientation, which was consistent with national policy directions as indicated by the New Freedom Commission Report and recent Institute of Medicine reports. What emerged from these discussions was a clear vision: *an integrated behavioral health care system for the City of Philadelphia that promotes recovery, resiliency, and self determination.*

GREAT LAKES ATTC: You made a decision early on to use the recovery orientation as the bridging concept between mental health and addiction services. How has this vision guided your work?

DR. EVANS: It is clear that many of the people we serve have co-occurring mental illness and substance use disorders. As we listened to the stories of people in recovery, it quickly became clear that we needed to find a way to serve these people more holistically. It was critical for us to have a vision of recovery that really incorporated both addiction and mental health, and an integrated vision through which we could plan and allocate funds for both mental health and addiction services. Because of the unique structure of the Department of Behavioral Health in Philadelphia, we have been presented with an incredible opportunity to make this integration real at every level. Our goal is to move toward a unified framework of behavioral healthcare. Two early steps were important in this process. First, we brought together representatives from the mental health and addiction fields, including recovery advocates, people in recovery and family members, and providers of services, and we developed the following shared understanding of recovery:

> *Recovery is the process of pursuing a fulfilling and contributing life regardless of the difficulties one has faced. It involves not only the restoration but continued enhancement of a positive identity and personally meaningful connections and roles in one's community. Recovery is facilitated by relationships and environments that provide hope, empowerment, choices, and opportunities that promote people reaching their full potential as individuals and community members.*

Second, we developed a set of nine core recovery values that would guide our system-transformation process in both mental health and addiction service settings. Those values were *hope, choice, self-direction/empowerment, peer culture/peer support/peer leadership, partnership, community inclusion/opportunities, spirituality, family inclusion and leadership, and a holistic/wellness approach.*

GREAT LAKES ATTC: You've described the ongoing system-transformation process as unfolding in three overlapping stages: aligning concepts, aligning practices, and aligning context. Could you describe those stages?

DR. EVANS: Our goal is systemic and lasting change in the design and delivery of behavioral healthcare services. As a result, we made a conscious effort to think about: 1) how we want thinking to change, 2) how we want people's behavior to change, and then 3) how we want to change the policy, fiscal, and administrative contexts to support the behavior and thinking that we ultimately would like to see in the system. All of our system-transformation activities keep these three areas of focus in mind. For example, if we focus only on trainings that introduce a particular area of behavioral change—let's say the increased use of motivational interviewing—but we haven't aligned our policies and funding decisions to support that shift, this behavioral change won't be able to be sustained over time. Alternatively, if we focused on trainings that promoted a certain philosophical viewpoint without giving people practical ways that their behaviors needed to change in order to reflect this new viewpoint, those trainings would not effectively support systems transformation. These three areas—concept, practice, and context—are interrelated and cyclical. Our ability to obtain conceptual clarity influences our ability to successfully operationalize our transformation values. The manner in which recovery-oriented practices are defined and implemented shapes the regulatory and fiscal support necessary for lasting change. Regulatory and fiscal policies in turn have an immediate impact on the kinds of services and supports we can develop for people seeking recovery.

GREAT LAKES ATTC: There are growing calls to transform behavioral health care agencies into truly "recovery-oriented systems of care." How did you convey to your service providers exactly how service practices would change within such systems of care?

DR. EVANS: We engaged service consumers and providers in dialogue about how practices would change, and in our published plan for system transformation we outlined twelve areas in which we expected services to change and outlined the direction of such changes. The chart below illustrates our summary of those changes within our *Blueprint for Change.*

City of Philadephia's Blueprint for Change

Service Engagement: Expand outreach services to reach people (individuals, families, communities) at earlier stages of problem development.

Service Access: Continue the rapid level of service access that has long-characterized some components of the Philadelphia behavioral health service system (e.g., substance abuse treatment services) and increase the ability to access services in other areas (e.g., psychiatric access, housing with community supports, etc.)

Recovering Person's Role: Emphasize the rights of people in recovery to participate in and direct service decisions, plan for services, and move toward self-management of their own recovery journeys in collaboration with the people who serve them.

Service Relationship: Shift the primary service relationship from an expert-patient model to a partnership/consultant model.

Assessment: Move toward assessment procedures that are global (holistic), strengths-based (rather than pathology-based) and continual (rather than an intake activity).

Clinical Care: Move to clinical care services that are recovery-focused, evidence-based, developmentally appropriate, gender-sensitive, culturally competent and trauma informed. These services recognize that excellent clinical care is critical but is only one aspect of service needed among others in a recovery-oriented system.

Service Retention: Enhance service retention rates (reducing rates of service consumer disengagement and rates of administrative discharge) by increasing the quality of clinical services and enhancing in-treatment recovery support services.

City of Philadephia's Blueprint for Change

Locus of Service Delivery: Increase the delivery of community integrated, neighborhood- and home-based services and expand recovery support services in high-need areas. This enhances normalization and the effectiveness of skill teaching and skill retention, and decreases stigma.

Peer-based Recovery Support Services: Dramatically expand the availability of non-clinical, peer-based recovery support services and integrate professional and peer-based services.

Dose/Duration of Services: Provide doses of services across levels of care that are associated with positive recovery outcomes. The intent is that intensity of services will naturally decrease over time as recovery stability and quality increase, but that recovery checkups and, when needed, early re-intervention will continue for a considerable period of time. The system will develop innovative means for this connection (e.g., assertive phone follow up). Our vision is continuity of contact in a primary recovery-support relationship over time.

Post-treatment Checkups and Support: Shift the focus of service interventions from acute stabilization to sustained recovery management via post-treatment recovery check-ups. Support the use of Peer Specialists for post-treatment follow up, stage-appropriate recovery education, assertive linkage to recovery communities and, when needed, early re-intervention. Shift from passive aftercare to assertive approaches to continuing care.

Relationship to Community: Greater collaboration with indigenous recovery support organizations (e.g., faith community), more assertive linkages of clients to local communities of recovery, greater role in recovery education/celebration in larger community and greater role in recovery advocacy (e.g., issue of stigma and discrimination).

Source: *Recovery-Focused Transformation of Behavioral Health Services in Philadelphia: A Declaration of Principles and a Blueprint for Change,* Philadelphia Department of Behavioral Health and Mental Retardation Services

What we tried to achieve in our *Blueprint for Change* was to outline how the practices of our Department and our service providers would change through the system-transformation process, and how consumers and family members and other community resources could play important roles in this process.

GREAT LAKES ATTC: How did you plan the system-transformation process, and what constituencies did you involve in this process?

DR. EVANS: We think an inclusive, "big tent" approach is very important. From the very beginning, we engaged a variety of stakeholders, including people in recovery, providers, our staff, diverse community groups, and the faith community, because we had to find ways that the concept of recovery would resonate with all of those various constituencies. We created a Recovery Advisory Committee (RAC) that spent several months developing the consensus definition of recovery and core recovery values that all of those various groups could embrace. We continue to host regular community forums where people from across the city can come and share their thoughts and ideas about the system-transformation priorities. We believe that such partnering and ongoing input are critical for the long-term success of systems transformation.

GREAT LAKES ATTC: What are the early priorities that emerged out of that process?

DR. EVANS: For the next two years, we will be focusing our change efforts within seven priority areas: community inclusion/opportunity, holistic care, peer culture/peer support/ peer leadership, family inclusion and leadership, partnership, extended recovery supports, and quality of care.

GREAT LAKES ATTC: In your presentations describing the system transformation, you have talked about the importance of parallel process. What do you mean by this?

DR. EVANS: What I mean by this is that the relationship we want to see between our direct-care providers and those they serve must be mirrored inside our department, both in the relationship between our department and the treatment providers and in our relationship with other community organizations. This realization has forced us to think about our own behavior and how it helps or hurts our system-transformation efforts. An early and ongoing priority for us was to make sure that the way we were doing business was consistent with the way we wanted our service providers to do business. For example, in planning new initiatives, we are involving the provider and recovering community in the early stages of thinking and development of ideas, rather than "telling them" what we want them to do. In the same way we are hoping that providers will tap the expertise of people in recovery, we are also trying to tap the expertise of providers in solving the problems that confront us both. Also, stressing the importance of dignity and respect in how we interact with one another has been a cornerstone of these efforts.

Great Lakes ATTC: How are you continuing to work at system transformation at the same time you have to maintain much of the system's functioning?

Dr. Evans: When you're running a billion-dollar organization, most of your energy and the organization's energy is focused on keeping the organization going, and relatively little of that energy is directed towards strategic planning, visioning, and taking the organization in a new direction. So first we had to build an infrastructure. We had to develop roles that allowed people to devote time to conceptualizing where we wanted to go, working on new initiatives, engaging various stakeholders, and developing the many products that were crucial to the system-transformation process. We did this by hiring a director of strategic planning, who would work in partnership with the director of policy and planning to develop and move system-change efforts forward. We created an internal steering group, the Systems Transformation Steering Committee, composed of representatives in key positions across the department. This group is also charged with developing and moving system-change initiatives forward. We have used national and local consultants to add expertise to the already existing skills of our staff and to support our major change initiatives. We developed specific targeted projects to implement our vision. Right now, for example, we are transforming our maintenance partial hospitalization system into a recovery-oriented, community-integrated system of services and supports. In order to do this, we are introducing all the transformation priorities into these transformed programs. We are working in partnership with people in recovery and providers in all aspects of the development of these programs. We are working with the State to break down regulatory and funding barriers to the provision of recovery-oriented services. This same process is happening in many new initiatives.

Great Lakes ATTC: Describe your use of workgroups to plan and implement change for particular service areas.

Dr. Evans: That's an example of where we had to behave in ways that were consistent with the recovery philosophy. One of the first things we did was to identify those areas where we thought it was important to have concentrated work—issues that we felt were critical to achieving a recovery orientation. Spirituality, for instance, is important to many people in recovery, and yet the linkages between the Department and the vast faith community in Philadelphia were weak. We developed our faith-based task force to work at developing these partnerships, which are envisioned to be reciprocal in nature. We bring resources to the table for the faith-based organizations, and they bring resources to us.

We know that, in a recovery-oriented environment, expert clinical care is critical. The Evidence-Based Practices (EBP) workgroup was developed to review the current state of the science and to develop recommendations for current EBPs, promising practices, and support structures for their implementation and installment in organizations. One outcome of our work in this area is the development of a new partnership with Dr. Aaron Beck and the Beck Center for Cognitive Therapy. This will have a direct impact on clinical care as we introduce cognitive therapy throughout our service system.

The Trauma Task Force is looking at the critical role that trauma plays in many addiction and mental health disorders, and is developing creative ways to incorporate trauma-informed services into our provider organizations.

The content of these workgroups is important, but the process for developing them is equally important. We staffed the workgroups by opening them up to everyone in the organization. I sent out an email that basically said, "We have a variety of workgroups. Anyone in the organization, regardless of your role, has the opportunity to be a part of the workgroups." Well, one of the interesting things we found out is that people who were in non-programmatic administrative and support positions signed up to help with these groups. We found out that many people in our organization were in recovery or had family members who were in recovery or struggling with addiction or mental health problems. They wanted to be a part of this service-improvement process, and they brought a very important perspective that the programmatic staff didn't always bring. The message their inclusion sent was that, if we truly believe in partnership at all levels, if we truly believe in the idea of people rising to their highest level of potential, we had to create opportunities like that internally, as a way of modeling what we wanted our providers to do. This engaged a whole layer of the organization who, quite frankly, had been underutilized in the past. It engaged them and got them really excited about the work we were doing.

This same process is happening at provider organizations across the city. As they catch the vision, or feel freer to pursue the vision they have been developing in the past few years, they are reaching out to new people within their organizations. They are engaging community partners, working with faith-based organizations in new ways, looking at the evidence for their clinical practices, and increasing their trauma awareness and capacity for intervention.

GREAT LAKES ATTC: You developed a very close relationship with the Pennsylvania Recovery Organization—Achieving Community Together (Pro-Act) and other recovery advocacy organizations. How important do you think those relationships have been to the transformation process?

DR. EVANS: Engaging the recovery community, and engaging the recovery community in new ways, has been one of the most important things that we have done. Pro-Act has been terrific in the process. They have been out front in helping to put a face on recovery, something that we support tremendously. They have helped us engage the recovery community in a variety of activities, and they've been able to carry the message of recovery and the hope of recovery to communities that we may not have been able to reach as a department. They have pushed our thinking about what we should be doing as a department, both with our funded service organizations and with the larger community. It is hard to imagine having done this work without the partnership with Pro-Act.

GREAT LAKES ATTC: In relationship to the broader community, you made a decision early on to involve the faith community in this initiative. How did you come to that decision, and what has been the outcome of that involvement?

DR. EVANS: There are several reasons we felt it was important to involve the faith communities. First was our recognition that many people recover within the perspectives, beliefs, and contexts generated from their faith. As a result, we felt it was important to recognize the potential role of spirituality in the treatment and long-term recovery process. We also knew that there are many people who will not engage in treatment without the blessing of their faith communities. People often seek help initially from within their faith communities, and we wanted to build connections between these communities and our behavioral health service system. We felt the faith community, particularly the clergy, was in a position to help us achieve our goals, and at the same time that we could be of service to them. We were particularly interested in the support that faith communities could provide to people during and following addiction treatment. We wanted to help those entities in the community that were there to support people coming out of prison and out of treatment, and to help them do that work on a long-term basis.

GREAT LAKES ATTC: How did you prepare the existing addiction treatment agencies for the changes that would be coming through the system-transformation process? There must have been considerable anxiety about what this would mean for everyone.

DR. EVANS: We did a number of things. First, we engaged them from the very beginning, articulated the vision of where we wanted to go, and invited them along on the journey.

We brought in top people from around the country, people like Bill White and Mike Hogan, to help articulate and legitimize our vision and to generate excitement about where we were going. We continue to involve the provider community in the major decisions we have made and are making as part of the whole transformation effort. For most major efforts we have cross-system workgroups that involve providers, people in recovery, and family members, as well as DBH staff. We've tried to be very transparent about our decision-making. Finally, we've tried to make sure that what we are promoting is clearly reflected in the Requests For Proposals for funding that we issue. We have tried to be consistent in our messaging and catch ourselves when we are doing things out of old habits that violated those core messages.

GREAT LAKES ATTC: Do you think that the fundamental relationship with the provider community has changed through this process?

DR. EVANS: I think that they are becoming more trusting of and more open with us. We are trying to move away from a policing role—the "gotcha mentality" that we in government can drift into. We are trying to move toward a partnership model that emphasizes our need to work together toward a shared recovery vision. Through developing workgroups that involve all stakeholders on different topics, we are tapping into the expertise of the provider community as we plan and develop new initiatives, practices, and vision. Our addictions group is currently involved in a process that involves all stakeholders in planning the next steps in transforming this segment of the system.

GREAT LAKES ATTC: What are some of the changes that you've seen already through the system-transformation process?

DR. EVANS: The thing I get the most satisfaction from is the fact that people have a voice now who historically have not had a voice within our system. Foremost among these are people in recovery and their family members who are not a part of the "professional" advocacy groups and had not historically participated in the

Department's planning efforts. We have hired people in recovery in the Department to help us in this transformation. We are training and mentoring them to assume leadership roles in the future. We recognize that, while many organizations have people in recovery on staff or on boards, it takes additional support and training to have them assume true leadership roles. We are committed to this process.

We have also opened ourselves to input from the larger non-professional community in ways that are unprecedented. These are just people in the community, including faith leaders and leaders of grassroots community-based organizations, who now are engaged with us in very important ways. There are also several other things that come to mind.

We have committed to train and hire 100 peer specialists in the system over the next year. These are people who have mental illness and/or co-occurring disorders who have moved to a place in their recovery where they are ready to "reach back a hand" to someone else. Hiring these trained people into our provider organizations will be a huge step forward in advancing the voice and leadership of people in recovery.

We are moving our "monitoring process" to one which is less focused on adherence to regulation and more focused on recovery and recovery outcomes. We're redoing our evaluation process with a focus on recovery outcomes, as opposed to traditional process measures. We are developing funding models that support recovery-oriented services and incentivize recovery outcomes. We're looking at how to create funding mechanisms where dollars follow the client. We're looking at funding mechanisms that provide people with a menu of services, as opposed to site-based services where people don't have those kinds of options.

GREAT LAKES ATTC: You've taken people inside your organization who for years have seen themselves in a policing function and transformed them into technical consultants and partners with agencies. That is a radical change in the monitoring process.

DR. EVANS: That is a huge change that we are still working on. An example of progress that we are making in this area is with our monitoring and credentialing process. Providers have often complained that this process is too focused on minor details (e.g., a missing signature), rather than on the bigger picture of quality of care. Recently I have had a number of providers share with me that they had a great credentialing visit—that it was very helpful. This is something we'd never heard before. This is a credit to our staff, who are really focusing on quality and making a variety of important changes to move the system forward and improve care. Providers are starting to see us as collaborators in this process—as people who are trying to help them provide a better service. We've still got a long way to go, but we're clearly making progress.

GREAT LAKES ATTC: As you look back over this process, are there any lessons that you think you would share with other cities or states wanting to pursue a similar system-transformation process?

DR. EVANS: I can't say enough about the issue of parallel process that we touched on earlier. Consistency—walking the talk—is very important. You can't have a singular external focus of telling the providers what they need to do in order to be more recovery oriented. It has to be, "What do we collectively need to do to conduct our business in a way that is consistent with these values? And then how do we help and partner with our providers and consumers and other stakeholders to make this transformation happen?" To me, the most important aspect of this is having a mindset that is collaborative, that is supportive, and that is consistent with the values of recovery. After that, there are a number of things we've learned. First of all, transparency is very important. You can't promote a recovery-oriented system and then make decisions about how you're going to fund and who you're going to fund with opaque processes that people don't understand. That doesn't work. I think the other thing that we've learned is: communication, communication, communication. You have to keep putting the message out, letting people know what you're doing and why you're doing it. I think it's also important to give people practical examples of what you want them to do. So you're not only articulating that a recovery orientation is important, but you're also providing people with opportunities to get training and support around how they're going to change their practice.

Another key lesson is the role that relapse plays in this systems-transformation work. This is another example of our parallel process. Providers, people in recovery, and families are all used to doing things one way, and the pull back to the familiar is always there. "Relapses" of many kinds will happen. We are learning to plan for them, to learn from them, and hopefully to build in supports to lessen their occurrence.

GREAT LAKES ATTC: You've made an incredible investment in training through this process, both local training and bringing outside people in for training. Could you comment on that?

DR. EVANS: We've had to do that. The training that most behavioral health professionals get offers no consistent recovery orientation. You can't assume people have been trained from this perspective, so it must become part of everyone's orientation and training within the field. We felt that we needed to put a significant amount of resources into training, to help people have a different way of thinking about the work, but also help them have a different way of behaving. The trainings are designed to give people different options in terms of how they design and deliver high-quality services. We also made an important strategic decision about the nature of this training. People in recovery, providers, and staff from the Department are trained together. This format has modeled the kind of partnerships we are working to develop and has definitely increased the impact of the training. Training in this way is another example of the parallel process.

In the next 12-18 months we are going to build on this basic training through providing training that advances, not just our collective understanding of recovery, but also the implementation of recovery-oriented practice across the behavioral health system.

Great Lakes ATTC: As you look back over this process, what are some of the areas of system transformation that you feel you've had some of the greatest success in?

Dr. Evans: I think we have a considerable amount of buy-in from multiple constituencies at this point in the process. We try to keep our ear to the ground in terms of what people are really saying, and we create opportunities for people to tell us what they're really thinking, through focus groups and other mechanisms. We now have almost universal acceptance of our core ideas by our stakeholders. I think that's huge.

One other area that really excites me is what I see happening among the communities of people in recovery. We have people in recovery now working as consultants within DBH on major projects. There are people involved in change-management teams at provider organizations. There are people sharing their recovery stories in many public venues; and there is a new energy, enthusiasm, and emerging leadership capacity within that community. This is critical in terms of moving us toward a "consumer-directed" system.

We also are developing new initiatives that are true partnerships. We recently funded several prevention initiatives but required that the applicants for those funds demonstrate partnerships between providers and local grassroots organizations. We are providing seed-grant funding for enhancement of programs over the next year to providers who are willing to commit to moving our system-transformation priorities forward in innovative ways.

William L. White

All these seemingly separate initiatives create a synergy of vision, energy, and momentum that will support moving this transformation forward.

GREAT LAKES ATTC: One of the obstacles that people often cite in discussions of moving toward greater recovery orientation and shifting from models of acute care to sustained recovery management is the question of financing. Do you have any thoughts about where service financing models will go in the coming years to support this recovery orientation?

DR. EVANS: We are going to need different kinds of funding models, because many of the things that support recovery are not what we are reimbursing in the fee-for-service rates through which we currently pay service providers. We're going to need to move to more risk-based financing models that give people more flexibility in how to use the dollars that they receive and place the emphasis more on service outcomes and less on units of service delivery. The other thing we need to think about is how we can support giving people a menu of options, and how providers can offer those options in ways that are financially viable. We're attempting to do that with a major redesign of our partial hospital programs and our day-treatment programs. We're attempting a radical redesign based on the notion of giving people a menu of choices, having fewer site-based services, and providing more services in the community. We're working with the state to develop a financing model through Medicaid that will allow us to do that. We have to invest energy, time, resources, and commitment to work on those issues.

GREAT LAKES ATTC: Have federal programs and regulatory guidelines helped or hindered the transformation process in Philadelphia?

DR. EVANS: Medicaid policies have been the most difficult. With State grant dollars, we have more flexibility to purchase services that are more supportive of people's long-term recovery. The biggest impediment for us is the medical necessity criterion that is required through Medicaid, and how narrowly that's defined. If I were to identify one barrier, that would be it.

There could be many other examples, but another one that impacts us daily is the division between mental health and addictions funding and regulations. This division stands in the way of a truly unified behavioral health system organized around the needs of the person in recovery.

Another is Medicaid's perspective that "treatment services" are best provided on site, when in actuality people's lives happen in their communities. This presents

232

an obstacle to providing resources to support true learning in people's natural environments.

Both of these barriers are being worked on now with key policy makers at the State.

But it's not just external obstacles. Our own regulations have sometimes been an obstacle. We're constantly fighting them. We can be our worst enemy at times, by doing things because of tradition and history. We are involved in an internal process to continue to move toward flexibility and a base of regulations that promotes recovery and support for the person's recovery plan. One project that is assisting with this is our Unit Recovery Planning Initiative. Each unit within the Department is going through a process to explore the implications that our system-transformation priorities have on their daily work and decision making. As a system, we have spent a significant amount of time developing a shared vision. Now internally we are examining what that vision means for our internal practices, policies, and fiscal strategies. Consistent with the collaborative and inclusive approach that we have taken thus far, each member of each unit is a part of this process. Through engaging in this work, staff are developing an increased sense of ownership in the transformation. They are also identifying the tension between our current practices and our envisioned system of care, and as such helping us prioritize our focus.

GREAT LAKES ATTC: How are you planning to evaluate the system-transformation processes that are underway?

DR. EVANS: We're going to do a number of things. One of them is that we've established a recovery baseline assessment of our whole system. We basically required all of our providers to complete a recovery assessment that collected information about the perception of the recovery orientation of each program from the viewpoint of the management staff, the director, the staff, and service consumers and their families. We scored them and rated them, and we will reassess the system after a year or so to see how these key dimensions have changed. We are doing ethnographic studies of the processes we have used to implement the change process. And we are also looking at recovery outcome measures at individual, program, and system levels.

GREAT LAKES ATTC: What do you see as the next major steps in the system-transformation process in Philadelphia?

DR. EVANS: One of the exciting but challenging things about this process is that it has so many facets. I think there are several key things we need to focus on in this next stage. One critical area is continuing to build on the momentum that we created thus far around increasing, not only the involvement, but also the leadership of people in recovery in the system. As such we will continue to support people in recovery in achieving and maintaining diverse leadership roles and having opportunities to participate in policy decisions going forward. To advance this goal, we are currently exploring a partnership with a local community college to develop a leadership program for people in recovery that will lead to an Associates degree. We will also be exploring the development of more consumer-operated services.

A second major area that I think we have to continue focusing on is changing our own internal policies to be more consistent with a recovery orientation. I think we still have some work to do internally to be an organization that conducts its business within a recovery-focused framework. In order for this transformation to take root and lead to sustained change, we are going to have to be even more consistent in walking our talk and creating policies that will support the transformation. We have begun this next phase in partnership with providers and people in recovery. One of our system-transformation priorities, for instance, is community integration. As providers have begun to change their practices to facilitate increased opportunities for people to become fully integrated into their communities, they have expressed concerns about balancing consumer choice with their professional assessment of an individual's readiness to engage in certain activities. They want to know, when there is a discrepancy between the two, what should they do? They have also asked how their liability as providers is factored into all decision making. To address tensions such as this, we are developing ad hoc workgroups such as our risk assessment workgroup. This consists of a diverse group of stakeholders who are exploring together what risk assessment should look like in a recovery-oriented system of care, and what monitoring policies and practices need to be changed within our department to support the providers' movement in this direction.

In addition to tackling some of the tensions that emerge as we increasingly strive to operationalize and implement recovery-oriented care, we are also seeking to develop demonstration projects which can be models of recovery-oriented care for the rest of the system. Right now we are in a competitive application process to award mini grants to providers and community-based organizations. Innovative projects that result from this and other initiatives will be highlighted and celebrated at a one-day conference early next year. We believe that a critical part of this phase of the transformation process will be creating opportunities for the development of a learning community where our department, people in recovery, family members, and providers can come together to share lessons learned and celebrate successes.

This next phase will also involve an increased focus on enhancing naturally occurring recovery supports in the broader community. We have people in recovery coming to us right now wanting to start mutual-help groups that don't currently exist in their neighborhoods. We are developing a training program for these leaders on how to develop, implement, and sustain mutual-support groups. These groups will be in the community, drawing from the community and giving back to the community. We are also increasing our focus on supporting grassroots community-based organizations and faith-based organizations where many people in recovery turn for help, and ensuring that linkages between this informal "treatment" system and the formal treatment system are strengthened.

Finally, in this next phase of the transformation, we are going to increase our focus on delivering more services and supports that are evidence based. The people we serve deserve the best, and we need to get tooled up to deliver it.

We have much to do, but we are very excited about these new directions that the stakeholders in the system have chosen.

Frontline Implementation of Recovery Management Principles

An Interview with Michael Boyle
By William L. White, MA

INTRODUCTION

Many of the core recovery management principles and practices were piloted and refined within the Behavioral Health Recovery Management (BHRM) project. This collaborative effort of Fayette Companies in Peoria, Illinois, Chestnut Health Systems in Bloomington, Illinois, and the Center for Psychiatric Rehabilitation at the University of Chicago was funded by the Illinois Department of Human Services, Division of Alcoholism and Substance Abuse. Since the inception of the BHRM project, Fayette Companies has served as a model of recovery-oriented systems transformation in a community-based behavioral health organization. I conducted the following interview with Michael Boyle, President and CEO of Fayette Companies and Director of the BHRM project, September 29, 2006, on behalf of the Great Lakes Addiction Technology Transfer Center.

GREAT LAKES ATTC: Mike, could you begin by summarizing your background and how you came to your current position?

MIKE BOYLE: I've been with Fayette Companies and its predecessor organizations here in Peoria, Illinois my whole career. I started as a youth outreach worker and then ran an alcoholism treatment center that consolidated in 1976 with four other organizations to form what is now the Human Service Center. Fayette Companies serves as the parent management corporation of a family of behavioral health service units that include the Human Service Center; White Oaks; Human Service Center Foundation, a 501(c)(2) property investment company; and Behavioral Health Advantages, providing Employee Assistance Programs and consultation services to businesses and industry.

Each year, Human Service Center (HSC) provides mental health treatment and recovery support services to about 1,600 people with serious mental illness. HSC also operates a methadone treatment program, a work release program, a transitional housing program for federal probation, and a long-term women's addiction treatment program. White Oaks offers a full array of addiction treatment services, from a medical detoxification unit to gender-specific residential programs for men and women, as well as gender-specific intensive outpatient and day programs serving over 2,000 people per year. We offer a specialized program for older adults who are in need of in-home substance use disorder (SUD) treatment services, and we have youth programs that provide both mental health and SUD treatment services, as well as prevention services. We presently have 18 service locations and more than 380 staff. Our programs are supported primarily through state contracts, Medicaid reimbursement, and corporate insurance. The mission of the Human Service Center is to "Engage people in a life of recovery and assist them to live their lives well."

Over the past 32 years, I have served as Vice President of Operations, as Executive Vice President, and currently as President and CEO. In recent years, I have focused on implementing an integrated vision of mental health and addiction treatment services and evidence-based treatment practices. I have also been fortunate to be a participant in the Network for the Improvement of Addiction Treatment (NIATx), which has taught me how to use process-improvement techniques to impact quality of care in addressing addictions.

GREAT LAKES ATTC: Describe how the behavioral health recovery management program came into existence.

MIKE BOYLE: Ten years ago, behavioral health leaders were scrambling to prepare for or implement managed care. During this time, I found myself drawn to national conferences on managed care that included presentations from primary care physicians on disease management. Organizations like Kaiser Permanente were often presenting on what they were doing to deal with chronic medical disorders. That's when I started thinking, "We say addiction and serious mental illness are chronic conditions; why are we using such an acute-care model to treat them?" I wondered why we were not using disease-management approaches like those that were emerging in primary medicine. Then in 1999, my local state representative approached me and asked if we had any legislative needs that he could help with. We began to discuss some of the needs of the field, and that led to writing legislation that would support the development of a disease-management approach to addictions and serious mental illness. We put together a legislative bill for a three-year project that would fund the development of this approach, and it passed the House and Senate and—with a little negotiation—was signed by the Governor.

We asked for a million dollars over a three-year period to support the project. In the course of moving the legislation through, the Secretary of the Illinois Department of Human Services became very interested in the project and offered to fund the idea if the legislation was passed. This was very helpful, since the bill would then not need an appropriation tied to it. As this came to fruition, I approached Chestnut Health System's Lighthouse Institute and recruited Bill White as an Associate Director of the project. David Loveland, now Director of Research at Fayette Companies, became the other Associate Director, with a specialty in serious mental illness and co-occurring disorders. Pat Corrigan from the University of Chicago, Center for Psychiatric Rehabilitation later joined as a third partner in the Behavioral Health Recovery Management project.

GREAT LAKES ATTC: What distinctions were you making between recovery management and disease management as this project developed?

MIKE BOYLE: It was Bill White who came up with the concept of recovery management rather than disease management. I remember at the time, I said, "Well, everybody knows now what disease management is. It's been around for a decade. No one has ever heard of recovery management." And Bill said, "In three years, they will." That was enough to sell me. Disease management (DM) has basically been built on the foundation of evidence-based practice—what science says will generate the best outcomes for specific chronic diseases. DM emphasizes science-based clinical guidelines for service practitioners, and DM also tries to actively engage each individual in managing his or her own illness rather than leaving everything to the physician and other health care professionals. Recovery Management (RM) incorporates the DM approach, but shifts the focus from the disorder to the person, from symptom management to building a life in recovery. RM approaches also place greater emphasis on natural supports within the family and community that can be aligned to enhance recovery initiation and maintenance. RM asks: "How can we build recovery support within the larger community? How can we assertively link the individual to such recovery support resources?" RM, because it focuses on the whole life rather than the disorder, is also broader in its scope, encompassing such areas as social and recreational activities, employment, education, housing, and life meaning and purpose. It is about making recovery a very enjoyable and positive experience.

GREAT LAKES ATTC: For readers unfamiliar with recovery management, could you briefly summarize how traditional clinical practices change in this model?

MIKE BOYLE: Thresholds of engagement are lowered, with a considerable emphasis placed on outreach services. Motivation is viewed as an important factor but seen as an outcome of treatment rather than a precondition for treatment admission. There is an emphasis on assessment processes that are global, continual, strengths-based, person- and family-centered, and culturally grounded. The service menu is broadened, and the eventual locus of services shifts to homes and neighborhoods. The service relationship is based on a partnership model that is much longer in duration and less hierarchical. Perhaps most distinguishing is the shift in emphasis from acute bio-psychosocial stabilization to long-term recovery monitoring and support; assertive linkage to communities of recovery; and, when needed, early re-intervention.

GREAT LAKES ATTC: Was the RM approach a natural progression in the overall development of Fayette Companies and its service units?

MIKE BOYLE: Actually, it's really ironic. We formed our first organization, Human Service Center, by consolidating four mental health, drug, and alcohol treatment programs in the 1970s, but we had never really integrated care. So, in the late '90s, I started an initiative to fully integrate co-occurring disorders. We'd already been making some progress in trying to integrate the treatment of serious mental illness with primary healthcare by establishing a primary care clinic within our outpatient mental health center. We really needed to address co-occurring substance use disorders and all mental illnesses, particularly serious mental illness. About half of the population we serve have both disorders. People with serious mental illness were often abusing or addicted to substances, and our addiction programs were filled with people suffering from serious mental illness, mood disorders, and anxiety disorders, including post-trauma effects and Posttraumatic Stress Disorder. We formed a quality improvement committee with multi-disciplinary representation across the functions of the organization, with the mission of fully integrating treatment services across the continuum of care. That's when, in 1998, we really started implementing evidence-based practices. The recovery management project shared that objective, and it was a natural evolution from the integration of treatment for co-occurring disorders to a more comprehensive vision of assisting people with the long-term recovery process. This moved us beyond thinking about biopsychosicial stabilization to the broader issues involved in recovery maintenance and enhancement of quality of life. Our focus began to shift toward long-term recovery and the role we could play in that.

GREAT LAKES ATTC: How did you begin to prepare staff for some of the changes that were implemented through this process?

MIKE BOYLE: Early on in our co-occurring project, we realized that we had to address staff's values and beliefs, their attitudes, and the different cultures of our mental health and addictions programs. We took all our clinical staff and divided them into small groups (12-15 staff each) that gathered in brown-bag lunch meetings every week. These meetings were facilitated by members of our co-occurring committee. We developed a list of statements we called "fire starters," to elicit and discuss beliefs and feelings about particular issues. Examples of our fire-starter statements include:

- Addictive and psychiatric disorders are both significant chronic conditions often characterized by episodes of exacerbation, remission, and relapse.
- All persons should be retained in service and treated with great respect in spite of non-adherence with treatment plan recommendations, including not taking prescribed medications or a return to use of the drug of choice.
- Addiction and mental illness are both no-fault disease categories.
- No behavioral health problem is so grave that an individual cannot be engaged in the recovery process.
- It is more important to convey caring and concern than to avoid being manipulated or conned—even at the cost of "enabling."
- Medication can be an effective strategy in the treatment of both disorders.
- Recovery begins with hope, not abstinence from drug use or reduction of psychiatric symptoms.

GREAT LAKES ATTC: Did this help "unfreeze" the cultures across programs?

MIKE BOYLE: It worked very well. We had intense debate over issues such as whether somebody who was on methadone treatment could be considered to be in recovery. One staff member would declare, "You couldn't be in recovery on methadone; You're still using an addictive drug!" That would trigger counter-responses from other staff: "Wait a minute. I've got people who are on methadone who are not using any alcohol or non-prescribed drugs. All the urine drug screens are clean. They have a family and a job, and they're doing great. What do you mean, they're not in recovery?" That type of interaction opened people's eyes and their minds. Here's another example. A person who worked in our detox program said, "People with addictions make a conscious choice to go back to using. They go to the bar. They go buy some marijuana or cocaine, whereas people with serious mental illness really don't make a choice when they relapse." Mental health staff responded, "People make a conscious choice to not take their medications any longer. That's analogous to making a choice to drink or use a drug. Both populations know the risks and the likely events that will follow."

GREAT LAKES ATTC: Were there staff people who couldn't make this transition?

MIKE BOYLE: We made it clear to everyone, "We're going west, and the wagon train is leaving. We don't know exactly where we're going to end up. We're not sure if it's going to be in California or Oregon, but if you want to stay with this organization, you've got to get on board the train and make this journey with us." We made our expectations explicitly clear in written documents that outlined the attitudes, values, knowledge, and skills that we saw as the core of this shift toward recovery management and behavioral health service integration. Not all made it, but most did.

GREAT LAKES ATTC: Training seems to have been a crucial part of your system-transformation process.

MIKE BOYLE: Yes. All of this involved bringing outside trainers into the organization. In fact, we started the co-occurring initiative by bringing in Dr. Ken Minkoff to conduct a full day's training that was the largest clinical training in the history of the organization—with more than 120 staff. He does a great job of motivating people and getting them laughing at some of the stupid things we do. And then we followed up with a lot of evidence-based training for both mental health and substance abuse. We started with Motivational Interviewing (MI), which led to a major cultural change in our service units. That training was a milestone in shedding the culture of confrontation that had long-pervaded some of our service units. Rather than verbally beating people into superficial compliance, we redefined our jobs as helping people take a look at the pros and cons of the choices they have and the discrepancies between their life goals and their behaviors. That was probably the most important cultural change we made in both our mental health and addiction services.

We followed the MI training with a series of other trainings. The manualized treatments covered included Community Reinforcement training provided by Bob Meyers, Contingency Management training provided by Nancy Petry, Strengths-Based

241

approaches by Leigh Steiner, Illness Management and Recovery from Kim Mueser, and Supportive Employment from Pat Corrigan and associates. We also provided basic training on recovery management principles. These trainings collectively moved us closer to evidence-based practice and toward a stronger recovery orientation. We also moved to person-centered care that required us to give up some of our delusions that we had control over people's individual decisions that impacted their lives. Rather than prescribing techniques, we had to engage individuals as partners in the pursuit of recovery.

GREAT LAKES ATTC: It seems like there was an interesting relationship between the BHRM project and Fayette, in which you used the service programs as a kind of laboratory to test out emerging ideas and approaches. Is that accurate?

MIKE BOYLE: That's very accurate. I'll give you one example. Four years ago, the local state-operated psychiatric hospital in Peoria closed. We took that opportunity to look at how we could improve services as some of the savings from the hospital closing were provided to us to expand our community-based services. One of the services we developed was recovery coaching. We said, "Wait a minute. If we're going to keep people coming through the front door, we need to open a back door for sustained recovery support." One of the evidence-based practices we were using at the time was assertive community treatment, the ACT model from Madison, Wisconsin. The ACT model, as it was widely implemented, was a life sentence of case management. We rethought that position. We hired two people to be recovery coaches, and we went through all of our case management caseloads to identify people who were doing well whom we could graduate from case management and put on this other team that would provide ongoing recovery support and monitoring. That was probably our first foray into recovery coaching and ongoing monitoring. Many are coming here only because they need to see the doctor every 90 days to continue to monitor their psychotropic medications. They don't need anything else from us. So we've developed criteria, and we're trying to link these people to primary care, particularly a federally qualified health center that we work with, and totally graduate them from the organization, saying, "If you ever have a return of symptoms, or you need help, we'll always be here. Call any time. You are no longer a mental health client." The primary care physician can monitor their psychotropic medication while he or she is treating other physical disorders like diabetes and hypertension.

GREAT LAKES ATTC: Mike, describe your changing philosophy about client access to services and the importance of retention.

MIKE BOYLE: Recovery management can increase access by lowering barriers to entry, but our access was pretty open even before the BHRM project, with one exception. We did have exclusionary criteria that resulted in our rejecting people with co-occurring disorders for both our mental health and addiction services. We had to work to eliminate these service-entry barriers, which we were able to do with considerable success. Our bigger issue was retention. We were fine bringing people back who had had previous treatment episodes, but we were throwing a lot of people out for lack of motivation or for petty rule violations. Particularly in addiction treatment, if people didn't say the right things and do the right things, we were throwing them out or making them feel unwelcome enough that they'd leave. Our philosophy had been that they were not ready for recovery and that they needed to get back to the streets and accumulate some more pain in their lives. This is an area in which we saw dramatic change in staff attitudes.

GREAT LAKES ATTC: Elaborate on that change.

MIKE BOYLE: We started accepting people for where they were and respecting them for telling us the truth. Our new position was, "You don't have to say that you're here because you really want to stop using all drugs. It's okay to be ambivalent. It's okay to say, 'I'm only here because the court's forcing me to be here, or because I have to be here to get my kids back'." Training on motivational interviewing changed the culture. We grew from blaming people for their lack of motivation to attempting to understand their current circumstances and desires. This change in philosophy was enhanced through our involvement over the past three years with the Robert Wood Johnson Foundation's Network for the Improvement of Addiction Treatment. We have tried to make the environment in our treatment programs very welcoming, rather than conveying the feeling that you're being processed into jail. In fact, we're trying to use the term "engagement" rather than "retention." You can retain people in jail or a locked psychiatric unit. Engagement implies the establishment of a relationship in which the person wants to be involved in the services. The whole atmosphere has changed.

GREAT LAKES ATTC: That must have generated a significant change in the nature of the service relationship.

MIKE BOYLE: One of the BHRM principles is development of a recovery partnership rather than a hierarchical dominance by the treatment program and the treatment professional over the individual. That has been a huge, huge change across the whole organization and reflects the strengths-based approach that Charles Rapp endorses for people with serious mental illness. Our messages are clear: We're here to work together. We want to understand what your goals are. What do you need to start and sustain your recovery? How can we help you achieve that? Our focus extended beyond treatment to each person's goals for his or her life. Often, a "non-treatment" goal will help the person realize that participating in treatment activities will assist them in reaching their goals. For example, obtaining and maintaining employment may be a primary goal, and taking psychiatric medications and reducing use of alcohol or drugs may be an important step toward meeting the goal of employment.

GREAT LAKES ATTC: You have argued that administrative discharge is a form of clinical abandonment.

MIKE BOYLE: A decade ago, we discharged people because they were violating our numerous rules and because we determined that they just weren't really ready to change. Our first step was to get rid of a lot of stupid rules that had little to do with someone's recovery. We've had to step back and ask, "Why are we doing this?" Many times, it's because we've always done it that way, and we can't even remember how the policy or practice started. I'll give you an example. We had a blackout period in our residential programs during which individuals weren't allowed to make phone calls or have visitors for a period of time. The clients were saying, "Hey, I really wanna call my kids and let them know how I'm doing." I remember a young woman who had a very close and supportive relationship with her father saying, "I really want to call my dad. I just want to talk to him." We finally said, "Okay. Let's do away with this blackout period. See what happens." The myth was that people would get homesick or hear the call of the streets and leave. Well, guess what? They stayed. Our average length of stay went up significantly as our AMA (leaving against medical advice) rate dropped after we changed this policy. In one of our programs, the AMA rate dropped from 30 percent to between 11 and 12 percent. And that happened by changing how we treated people. That's what it comes down to. Listening to our customers. Listening to what they want. Taking the strengths-based, Motivational Interviewing approach and avoiding confrontations and power struggles with our clients. We were often discharging people because we were picking fights with them. We had to abandon our philosophy of "It's our way or the highway." Our administrative discharge rate is now about 4 percent, a fraction of the national average, and usually results from someone bringing drugs into the program, or from violence.

GREAT LAKES ATTC: It seems you've found effective clinical alternatives to administrative discharge.

Mike Boyle: Today we're more likely to move someone to an alternative level of care than to sever the service relationship with the agency, and to stay involved with someone who wants to pursue a decision we think may not be a good one. Today, if someone says, "I don't want to stay longer in residential care," we work with them to find an outpatient alternative. We stopped dictating what people "should" do and started offering them choices at every step in the process. As a result, we're minimizing treatment dropout, and we've substantially increased the number of people involved in step-down care following residential treatment. For a recent 18-month period, the percentage of clients continuing in outpatient treatment following completion of residential care increased to 94 percent from 69 percent for the previous 18-month baseline period. Furthermore, participation in outpatient increased from 19 percent to 34 percent for those who didn't complete residential care.

A few years ago, if somebody used while they were in one of our outpatient programs, it would be an immediate administrative discharge. That whole attitude has changed. Now, if somebody comes in and says "I had a relapse over the weekend," we work with that experience. What went wrong? How can you prevent that from happening again?

Great Lakes ATTC: The changes you describe in the service relationship are striking.

Mike Boyle: We've learned how very important it is to empower the individual. We've shifted from, "How do we keep this person out of the hospital?" to "How do we enhance this person's quality of life in the community?"

Great Lakes ATTC: Another area of innovation in which you've invested considerable time and resources is the integration of primary healthcare and behavioral health treatment.

Mike Boyle: Another key recovery management principle is the importance of moving beyond the integration of mental health and addiction treatment toward the larger integration of behavioral health with primary healthcare. A large number of the individuals with serious mental illness and with severe drug and alcohol problems whom we serve have co-occurring physical health problems and needs. The medications we use, the new atypical antipsychotics, have side effects that can include weight gain. This may contribute to the potential development of hypertension, diabetes, and other weight-related disorders. For another example, on the addiction side, the attending physician for our women's program tested all of the women for Hepatitis C and found that 25 percent were positive for Hepatitis C; but, of that population, only 40 percent of those who were positive knew they were positive. It's time we started looking at the whole person—looking at global health.

GREAT LAKES ATTC: What strategies have you found effective to link people to primary healthcare in your programs?

MIKE BOYLE: We work very closely with a federally qualified health center (FQHC) that was established here in Peoria about three years ago. In fact, we were a sponsor in getting the organization started. They have assumed responsibility for the primary care clinic that is operated within our mental health center. Our goal is to enroll everyone in the FQHC who doesn't have an ongoing primary care relationship. On the addiction side, we work closely with the FQHC to link clients to the FQHC, other clinics, or primary healthcare providers. We are also increasing our referrals to primary health care from our detox program. Also, with client consent, we have standard letters that we can use to inform someone's primary physician of his or her admission to addiction treatment, letters that request the support of the physician in the patient's ongoing recovery. Examples of these forms can be found on the BHRM web site at www. bhrm.org in a guideline for linking addiction treatment with primary care. Our recovery coaches also play a major role in linking people to primary health care.

GREAT LAKES ATTC: How do you currently view the importance of recovery coaches in recovery management?

MIKE BOYLE: Let me describe what we've done with recovery coaching in our addiction treatment units. Two years ago, we took some existing funding and hired two women, both of whom were in addiction recovery, to pilot a recovery coaching program for women in our residential addiction programs. When women are within 4 to 6 weeks of completing treatment, we ask them if they would like to have a recovery coach, and we explain that the recovery coach will work with them to develop their own personal recovery plan as part of their transition out of residential treatment. We have guidelines, and the forms we use are all on the BHRM website; people are welcome to adapt them to their own programs. The recovery coaches work with women on 8 domains:

- Recovery from substance use disorders
- Living and financial independence
- Employment and education
- Relationships and social support
- Medical health

- Leisure and recreation
- Independence from legal problems and institutions
- Mental wellness and spirituality

This plan is developed before they leave residential treatment, and recovery coaching remains available to them even if they leave AMA, or for any other reason before they complete treatment. When they do leave, the recovery coach transitions with them into the community, to help them implement their personal recovery plans and also to evaluate and modify their recovery plans as necessary.

What we found is that half of the women who accepted the recovery coach— and most do want it—were homeless upon leaving. One of the first efforts of the recovery coach is often linking our women to a local shelter or recovery home so that, on the date of discharge, they have a place to go that's safe and recovery-conducive. A lot of attention is also focused on helping clients gain employment, so they can get into their own apartment or sober living situation. Whatever their goals are, we help them pursue what they want.

At six-month follow-up, the results have been very encouraging. Seventy percent of the women have improved their living situations. At admission to drug treatment, only 4 percent of the women were employed. At six-month follow-up, we have 54 percent employed. Also noteworthy is the fact that 36 percent are involved in some type of educational activity. We're looking at adding some type of supportive education services to the recovery coach program that would help people with three levels of education: providing pre-GED, for people who need to improve their math and writing skills to get in a GED program; helping getting people enrolled in a GED adult diploma program; or helping people get enrolled in secondary education, particularly at our junior college. A big goal of many of the women we serve is to improve their education. We are also putting computer labs into our residential facilities so people can start building computer expertise while they're in residential treatment. This will also provide access to web-based resources and recovery supports that will expand significantly in the next few years. In fact, we're working on the development of these web-based recovery treatment and support interventions with the Innovations to Recovery project headed by Dr. David Gustafson at the University of Wisconsin.

GREAT LAKES ATTC: You've referenced some efforts to evaluate your shift toward a recovery management model. Could you describe some of these efforts in more detail?

MIKE BOYLE: In the past four years, there has been tremendous synergy between the implementation of Recovery Management and our participation in the Network for the Improvement of Addiction Treatment (NIATx). NIATx has taught us methods of process improvement for increasing access and retention, essential goals of Recovery Management.

One of the principles of BHRM is lowering the threshold to treatment. We have a central assessment unit for women that had an average length of one to fourteen days between the date of her calling and the date of her assessment. We simply did away with scheduling appointments and offered next-day assessment on demand. The time between the call and receipt of the first service dropped to an average of 2 to 3 days. Furthermore, the percentage of calls that resulted in a competed assessment increased from 50 percent to 70 percent.

Another BHRM principle is establishing a recovery partnership with those we serve. We used the NIATx rapid-change process to make treatment welcoming and engaging. For two women's residential programs, the rate of discharges against medical advice dropped from 30 percent or greater to 11-12 percent.

There is also a "business case" for these changes. For example, in one residential program, earnings increased by $274,000 annually, compared to the baseline period one year earlier.

GREAT LAKES ATTC: One of the comments elicited from presentations on recovery management is, "Nobody will ever fund this. Who's going to pay?" How have you funded the innovations you have described?

MIKE BOYLE: For recovery coaching, we can bill those services either to the Division of Mental Health or to the Division of Alcoholism and Substance Abuse as case management services. Medicaid covers mental health case management services in Illinois. Unfortunately, case management services linked to addiction treatment are not funded in our state by Medicaid. As far as potential funding through insurance is concerned, we haven't approached that yet. I suspect it will be easier to sell this concept to corporations and insurance companies than to the public funders because of the former's experience with new approaches to the management of chronic medical disorders. Our recovery management project was only supposed to be three years in length, but the Division of Alcoholism and Substance Abuse was so impressed with the results that they extended the project for two more years and then converted the grant to a fee-for-service contract two years ago. We funded the recovery coaches by taking some of the former BHRM development money and using it to fund the salaries of the recovery coaches and then billing out those services.

GREAT LAKES ATTC: Do you have a vision of how funding changes will help support this transition from an acute care model to a recovery management model of addiction treatment in the next 10 years?

MIKE BOYLE: I think our first step is to prove that this model is effective and to study the cost implications and potential cost offsets and cost benefits. We need that data to approach the funders, both private and public. At this point in time, all we have is the pilot data that looks very good, but it is weak from a research perspective. We are getting indications that are confirming the value of this approach. These include positive impact on engagement and retention, demonstrated through our work with the Network for the Improvement of Addictions Treatment, and the well designed studies of the Assertive Continuing Care and the Recovery Management Check-ups that have been conducted by Lighthouse Institute. We need additional studies that confirm the value of post-treatment monitoring, support, and early re-intervention. We need formal studies of recovery coaching and its effects on relapse and recovery rates. We know anecdotally that recovery coaches provide a level of support that can help some people overcome a lapse without having to return to structured treatment. Our traditional response to relapse has been readmission for another treatment episode. Why do we continue to put people back through the same treatment they've been through multiple times and think this time it's going to work? We need studies that illuminate how to deal with the problem of post-treatment relapse in the client's natural environment.

GREAT LAKES ATTC: What are some of the obstacles you've encountered in implementing the recovery management model, whether that's inside your agency; in the community; or at the federal, state funding, or regulatory levels?

MIKE BOYLE: There were several such obstacles. Let's start with the external ones. We've already referenced issues related to funding and regulatory compliance, but an obstacle we didn't anticipate was the attitudes of our referral sources. It took some time to orient them to what we were doing and why. On the criminal justice side, they like to mandate residential treatment whether people need it or not, and the same is often true of the child welfare system. It took us some time to demonstrate the value of less intensive services such as recovery coaching. As long as a person is staying engaged in a service process, our referral sources are supportive of our new service philosophies.

GREAT LAKES ATTC: Did the recovery management efforts that you've initiated open the doors to other projects and areas of innovation for the agency?

MIKE BOYLE: I believe the Recovery Management project was a key factor, along with our participation in the Network for the Improvement of Addiction Treatment, in our being selected for a United Nations project, the International Network of Drug Treatment Resource Centers. One of the four UN workgroups is focused on sustainable livelihoods for rehabilitation and reintegration, and the workgroup is using the principles of BHRM as well as Cloud and Granfield's concept of recovery capital as a foundation for the manuscript we're developing on how we can support recovery. The other project that ties in with our recovery management work is our involvement in the Innovations for Recovery project being developed by the University of Wisconsin, which involves the application of technology to treatment and recovery support. Its primary focus at the present time is on post-treatment recovery support, so this was a natural complement in the shift toward recovery management. Through this project, Dave Gustafson and his engineers are taking Alan Marlatt's relapse prevention schema and looking at technological applications we can use to help people when they're in various risk situations. For example, GPS technology might be used to identify people entering their high-risk environments and provide support through an avatar counselor on a PDA-type device. Our field is far behind other areas of health care in the use of new technologies to provide treatment. These technologies might make ongoing recovery support and monitoring affordable while providing an efficient means of ongoing outcome monitoring. We are even considering developing a recovery support "island" in a virtual world that can be accessed for support and information 24 hours a day.

GREAT LAKES ATTC: Are there pitfalls that other agency directors should be aware of if they want to consider implementing a recovery management philosophy at their agencies?

MIKE BOYLE: First and foremost is how to counter staff resistance or inertia. Recovery management challenges a lot of traditional service thinking and service practices, so there will be resistance. We worked through that by involving everyone in the process and through our training and supervision activities. An equally difficult challenge is the question of time. Many staff like the concept of recovery management and ongoing support, but they uniformly say, "We don't have time to do it. We'd love to be able to keep in contact with individuals when they leave and know how they're doing and provide them support, but we can't do it. As soon as somebody walks out the door,

I've got somebody new on my caseload." That's a big barrier to overcome. The time problems flow from the fact that funding streams are primarily designed to support the acute-care model.

In regards to funding, I believe providers will have to partner with funding and regulatory agencies to make necessary changes in the rules that control the provision and purchasing of addiction treatment services. This will have to occur on an individual basis with each state, due to the variations among states. Some states are already changing their funding mechanisms to support some aspects of a Recovery Management approach. In Arizona, for example, peer-delivered recovery support services are covered through their Medicaid funding stream.

GREAT LAKES ATTC: It does seem like the financial interests of addiction treatment programs work against providing long-term recovery support.

MIKE BOYLE: There are opportunities to incent service providers for providing such services. Pay-for-performance experiments in Delaware and Philadelphia are focusing on access and keeping people in treatment once they've begun. If we really move toward paying for recovery outcomes, that could change the whole world.

GREAT LAKES ATTC: What do you personally feel best about related to the work you've done in recovery management over the past six years?

MIKE BOYLE: The question probably should be, what do "we" feel best about, as BHRM has been a team effort of folks, obviously including Bill White, as well as folks like David Loveland, Pat Corrigan, and Mark Godley. What I feel best about is changing the entire culture of my organization for clients and staff. If somebody who worked here ten years ago walked in here today, they wouldn't recognize us as the same organization. Now everybody talks about using evidence-based practices. Our staff members' learning plans are based on evidence-based practices. Everybody's looking at recovery. I mean, recovery wasn't even a word we used on the mental health side ten years ago.

On a national level, it has been a thrill to watch more and more providers, states, and federal organizations become interested in Behavioral Health Recovery Management and start to apply RM principles and approaches. I think we are nearing the "tipping point," where we become a movement in making drastic changes to addiction recovery nationally, and even internationally. Recovery Management has been embraced by the United Nations project I've mentioned here.

Finally, I'm excited about the early positive results on research trials on recovery management approaches conducted by Mark and Susan Godley, Mike Dennis, Chris Scott, and others from Lighthouse Institute. The significant impact of Assertive Continuing Care for adolescents and Recovery Management Check-ups are very promising for promoting the outcomes of Recovery Management.

GREAT LAKES ATTC: Mike, what do you see as the next steps for your agency in the coming years?

MIKE BOYLE: I think the recovery concept and the recovery management model are very well ingrained here. I think the next three to five years will entail really finishing the total cross-training of all the staff in evidence-based practices for both mental health and addiction. All staff need to be well versed and well skilled in each of these practices and have their own personal toolboxes of techniques that they can use to support individuals and families in recovery. We're not there yet, even with our supervisors, but we're getting closer every day. I think we will also be increasing our focus on what the community has to offer people in recovery. Let me give you an example. Our staff have put together a list of upcoming events that are free or that cost less than ten dollars, to encourage clients to become engaged in positive social interactions and entertainment in the community. I was reading some case notes the other day regarding an outpatient addiction treatment client who shared how bored he was all weekend. His whole weekend consisted of being bored, with the exception of going to three 12-Step meetings. Part of recovery management is finding ways to make recovery both fun and fulfilling. To do that, we have to get people into the life of the community.

GREAT LAKES ATTC: Your work with the faith community in recent years would seem to illustrate this.

MIKE BOYLE: We've done a lot the last few years to engage the faith-based community to help people become involved in church sampling. Recently, we've established the Peoria Area Alliance for Recovery, which includes many faith-based organizations providing recovery supports. The chemistry is amazing. For example, many women lack the Social Security card and number needed to obtain employment. The churches said they could provide funds to these women to purchase the birth certificates needed for obtaining their Social Security cards. Others in the group suggested the women could volunteer in church activities in exchange, thus empowering and engaging them in positive behaviors.

GREAT LAKES ATTC: How has your relationship with other local community institutions changed in the move toward recovery management?

There are many local organizations supporting recovery, and we realize we need one another to better assist those we serve. For example, the Peoria Area Alliance for Recovery is composed of representatives of organizations providing housing, employment, education, faith-based supports, community development, and other supports that people may need on their journey to recovery.

GREAT LAKES ATTC: Are you providing more services actually out in the community today than you were 10 years ago?

MIKE BOYLE: Absolutely. On the mental health side, 75 percent of our services are community based. On the addiction side, there's probably been less change. We've had our outreach component going for women involved with child welfare for 20 years now, but the recovery coaches are the major change there, moving toward more community-based services. I would love to have more recovery coaches. We did a focus group with people who are involved in our adult drug court in recovery coaching, asking whether or not they would find this beneficial and what types of services they would like from recovery coaching, and it turned out by chance that two of the people who were in the focus group had already been working with recovery coaches. By the end of the group, people in adult drug court programs were saying, "I hope I can stay in this drug court program long enough to get a recovery coach." To hear comments like that from mandated clients is testimony to the potential power of the recovery management model.

PEER-BASED RECOVERY SUPPORT SERVICES:

The Connecticut Experience

An Interview with Phillip Valentine
By William L. White, MA

INTRODUCTION

One of the distinctive characteristics of recovery-oriented systems of care is the elevated role of peer-based recovery support services within such systems and the importance of post-treatment monitoring, sustained support, and early re-intervention. Such systems are pioneering new volunteer and paid roles under such titles as recovery coaches, recovery support specialists, personal recovery assistants, peer helpers, etc. These roles are attached to existing addiction treatment organizations or are emerging from newly conceived grassroots, recovery advocacy, and recovery support organizations. Interest in these roles and in the broader arena of non-clinical recovery support services has been spawned by two Federal programs: the Center for Substance Abuse Treatment's Recovery Community Support Program (http://rcsp. samhsa.gov/) and the White House-initiated Access to Recovery program (http://atr. samhsa.gov/).

One of the most prominent recovery advocacy and support organizations in the United States is the Connecticut Community for Addiction Recovery (CCAR). In December, 2006, I conducted a wide-ranging interview with Phillip Valentine, the Executive Director of CCAR, on behalf of the Great Lakes Addiction Technology Transfer Center. The following interview profiles one of the most successful grassroots recovery support organizations, outlines the kinds of services CCAR provides to support the process of long-term recovery, and describes a new potential component of the addiction treatment service continuum, the recovery community center.

GREAT LAKES ATTC: Phil, briefly describe how you came to be involved in the New Recovery Advocacy Movement and the delivery of recovery support services.

PHIL VALENTINE: Most of the time I think the movement chose me. I received a call back in the Fall of 1998 from a dear friend of mine, Jim Wuelfing, who told me there was an interesting thing happening that I might want to check out. He was involved with NEAAR, the New England Alliance for Addiction Recovery, and told me about the work Bob Savage was doing with the Connecticut Community for Addiction Recovery (CCAR). Both organizations had just received funding from CSAT, and I applied for positions at NEAAR and CCAR. I was offered the position of Associate Director at CCAR and assumed that position in January, 1999.

GREAT LAKES ATTC: How would you describe CCAR's vision and mission?

PHIL VALENTINE: CCAR envisions a world where the power, hope, and healing of recovery from alcohol and other drug addiction are thoroughly understood and embraced. Our mission is to put a positive face on recovery through advocacy, education, and service, in order to end discrimination surrounding addiction and recovery, open new doors and remove barriers to recovery, and ensure that all people in recovery and people seeking recovery are treated with dignity and respect. When people ask me what I do, my "one-liner" is that CCAR organizes the recovery community to put a face on recovery and to build recovery capital.

GREAT LAKES ATTC: How is CCAR organized?

PHIL VALENTINE: CCAR has a central office and four recovery community centers. They evolved out of our chapters. At one time we had six chapters up and running, and their primary purpose was to put a face on recovery. From their needs and desires, we launched the recovery community centers—recovery-oriented anchors in the hearts of the communities, a place where local communities of recovery can design and deliver the supports they need to initiate and maintain their recoveries. Our CCAR staff members constitute an inner circle, and our task is to support, empower, and train the volunteers who form the next circle. Our "target audience" is our volunteers—people in all stages of recovery, family members, interns, friends, and allies. One of our "ideal" volunteers is a retired person in long-term recovery. Our target audience is not people still actively using, or even those seeking recovery or those in early recovery. They are our secondary target audience, and we reach them through our volunteer force. Staff interacts with people at all stages of need, but we're gradually working to have volunteers handle most of the direct peer support. Currently we have 10 staff and 150 trained volunteers. We use this model to multiply our efforts and get the most value for the federal, state, and local dollars we receive.

GREAT LAKES ATTC: What would you consider to be some of the more important milestones in the history of CCAR?

PHIL VALENTINE: There are so many. Receiving funding from CSAT's Recovery Community Support Program laid a financial foundation that was matched by funding from the Connecticut Department of Mental Health and Addiction Services (DMHAS). Our first "Recovery Walks!" held in 2000 was another early milestone and an idea that came from the recovery community. We had never heard of a walk in support of recovery from alcohol and other drug addiction. We did some internet research and found one walk/run for a treatment center in the DC area, so we decided that, if we held a walk and 50 people showed up, we would be successful. Seven hundred showed up for that first walk. Last September walks for recovery were held coast to coast. That's an incredible breakthrough. Recovery is truly becoming more visible. We just held our third Legislative Day, and a few legislators revealed for the first time publicly their own personal recoveries.

We produced a couple videos that are still pertinent and powerful today, "Putting a Face on Recovery" and "The Healing Power of Recovery." We wrote the "Recovery Core Values" in collaboration with mental health recovery advocates that became the cornerstone of (DMHAS Commissioner) Tom Kirk's policy on a Recovery-Oriented System of Care, which has become a national model. Opening our first Recovery Community Center in Willimantic was an important milestone. This was in response to a high-profile series of newspaper articles in the state's largest paper, *The Hartford Courant*, labeling Willimantic "Heroin Town." We like to say that a few years later CCAR had a hand in turning Heroin Town into Recovery Town. Another milestone was starting our Recovery Housing Project that inventoried the state's independently owned, privately operated sober houses; established a coalition; wrote standards; and delivered training. The most recent milestones have been the initiation of our Telephone Recovery Support program, which perhaps we can talk about later; and our purchase of a three-story, character-laden Victorian home in Hartford for our fourth recovery community center, which will also contain our administrative offices.

Great Lakes ATTC: CCAR has developed a very close relationship with the Connecticut Department of Mental Health and Addiction Services, your state addiction agency. How has that relationship evolved over time?

Phil Valentine: The key is that CCAR places a high emphasis on integrity, honesty, and trust. The DMHAS staff trusts us. We will tell them the truth, even if it might mean some temporary "loss" for ourselves. They know we have the best interests of the recovery community at heart. What we will not do is inflate our numbers or exaggerate what we are doing or minimize our struggles to make ourselves look good.

Great Lakes ATTC: How would you describe CCAR's relationship with the treatment community?

Phil Valentine: CCAR has never taken an antagonistic stance with the treatment community. Early on, we were perceived as a threat—a new source of competition for limited dollars. I believe that has changed. Recently, I was meeting with a PhD researcher, and I was talking about working with treatment programs to find better solutions. He was surprised. He wanted to know why I wasn't more angry, or more active, in trying to right ALL the wrongs within the system. I replied that I know a lot of people on the front lines, and have met many counselors with huge hearts trying to move people into recovery, and that I don't have an issue with them. Yeah, there are some bad eggs; there are in every field. But for the most part, we have an incredibly dedicated workforce. Why would I take issue with them? I think it also has to do with another unwritten philosophy that is part of the CCAR culture. I say it this way, "We labor in the light of recovery instead of dwelling in the darkness of addiction." I realize the treatment industry is there; and, yes, there are instances of "harvesting the crop of the addicted for profit"; and, yes, recoverees are usually left to fend for themselves once they're done with their treatment episode. Yet the treatment industry does serve a vital purpose: it is very good at initiating recovery.

Great Lakes ATTC: Describe the recovery values and principles that CCAR helped forge for the State of Connecticut.

Phil Valentine: The State had merged the mental health and addiction services under one new agency. CCAR got together with mental health advocates to discuss what we had in common. We agreed that we had a lot in common when we first entered the "system." Our common concerns are centered around being treated with dignity and respect, that we shouldn't be left to navigate the system on our own, and that the system should reward the providers that are the most recovery friendly and produce the best outcomes. We don't care how many people a provider serves; we care if the people they serve get well. Tom Kirk used these to write Policy #83, a defining document in beginning to design the state's Recovery-Oriented System of Care (see http://www.dmhas.state.ct.us/policies/policy83.htm).

GREAT LAKES ATTC: Describe the evolution of CCAR's involvement in peer-based recovery support services.

PHIL VALENTINE: CCAR was first organized as a pure advocacy organization. Those first four-plus years we did all kinds of cool things to put a face on recovery—posters, website, video, presentations, etc. However, when a member asked a very simple but deep question, "what can I do?" we were often stretched to find something meaningful. They could tell their story (well, what does that mean?), or they could attend a Chapter meeting (and then?), etc. You catch the drift. There was also a segment of our membership that wanted to be of service. They wanted to provide support, give rides, lend a listening ear, mentor, etc., and we didn't have those opportunities available. So when the RCSP switched from Support to Services, we resisted at first and then began to see how this could really be of benefit. We started slowly, and as we've grown into the delivery of support services, they've become more defined.

GREAT LAKES ATTC: Describe the range of recovery support services being provided through CCAR.

PHIL VALENTINE: Our recovery support services range from telephone-based recovery support to offering peer recovery support groups. We were very hesitant to start the latter on the grounds that people should use existing resources, such as AA and NA meetings. But we found a need for an "all-recovery group." Our all-recovery group in Willimantic draws from 20 to 50 people at each meeting. It welcomes 12-Step, Christian-based, methadone, medication-assisted, co-occurring, family members, and community members, but the main theme is to come in and talk about recovery. Such a simple concept, it's brilliant, and it's helped a lot of people. We also are conducting a lot of family-education and community-education activities, as well as family support groups and groups that mix family members and people in recovery. We have a comprehensive recovery housing database that allows us to know up-to-the-minute bed availability and to link people to sober living. And then there's this whole process in the recovery community centers themselves, where people are hooked into jobs or just get support from one another. We serve a broad spectrum of people, but I think we have a special mission of serving people who don't feel fully accepted in mainstream AA or NA. We don't place judgments on people. We say, "You're in recovery if you say you are. Is there some way that you think you might be able to improve your recovery, and how can we help you do that?"

Great Lakes ATTC: How would you describe the relationship between professionally directed treatment services and peer-based recovery support services?

Phil Valentine: I've had a couple knee surgeries that illustrate this relationship. I trusted my doctor to perform these surgeries. They were critically needed, but when he was done he turned me over to a physical therapist. And that's where my recovery would either succeed or fail. If you go regularly to your physical therapy sessions and do the exercises at home like you're supposed to, you can expect your knee to be stronger than ever. Recovery from addiction is the same process. You might need professional treatment to jump-start the process, but recovery is about what happens after treatment. Recovery support services are the physical therapy of recovery.

Great Lakes ATTC: Has your expansion beyond advocacy to providing recovery support services broadened the characteristics of people who volunteer for CCAR?

Phil Valentine: The people who are attracted to CCAR are usually wired one of two ways: they're wired to do advocacy about the big issues—to get out there and speak and fight for the cause—or they're wired for service work with individuals. Recovery support services are a tremendous way for grateful people in recovery to give back. Our advocacy work called for a vanguard of recovering people to offer themselves as living proof that long-term recovery is real. There are many people in recovery who quite frankly aren't comfortable being part of that public vanguard, but who are willing to help offer such testimony to individuals in need. Many of our volunteers know experientially that leaving treatment is like falling off a cliff with no one to catch you. They understand the need for a bridge between treatment and long-term recovery and are willing to serve as that bridge. These are the people who are making the telephone recovery support calls, facilitating groups, facilitating trainings, and getting involved with the recovery housing coalition.

Great Lakes ATTC: Describe your efforts to build a network of recovery community centers.

Phil Valentine: As CCAR evolved, we realized that, in order for local communities of recovery to have a realistic shot at providing support services, they'd need an actual physical location. We put together a loose plan and worked it in Willimantic. The plan follows a theme from the movie Field of Dreams, "build it and they will come."

Willimantic opened. We looked for a site for over a year before we found one in New London. Bridgeport opened after a long search. Last, we've moved into the world of ownership by purchasing a building in Hartford. Our funds are stretched to the maximum now. We'll need additional funding to open more. We've been welcomed wherever we've opened. There has been no NIMBY ("not in my back yard") experience for us (knock on wood). A lesson learned is that the Center will take on the personality of the lead organizer, and that is a good thing. We call the lead organizer a Senior Peer Services Coordinator, and running a Center is more about community organizing than anything else. I think a lot of recovery community organizations lose the organizing piece; they follow a traditional treatment provider model.

GREAT LAKES ATTC: You have recently started providing telephone-based recovery support services to people leaving Connecticut treatment programs. Could you describe the scope of this and what you're learning from it?

PHIL VALENTINE: The Telephone Recovery Support premise is simple: a new recoveree receives a call once a week for 12 weeks from a trained volunteer (usually a person in recovery) to check up on their recovery. We have found, though, that after 12 weeks when we ask the recoveree if they still want to receive a phone call, most times the answer is "yes." We now have people who have been receiving calls for 50 or more weeks, and they're still in recovery. In our first full year of making these calls, CCAR volunteers and staff have made more than 3,100 outbound phone calls. We piloted the project for 90 days out of Willimantic, after meeting with Dr. Mark Godley from Chestnut Health Systems to refine our procedures (DMHAS supported this consultation through a Center of Excellence project). We tweaked the script a bit, and the process works amazingly well. Outcomes have been ridiculously good—our last quarterly report indicated that 88 percent of our recoverees were maintaining their recovery. Volunteers love making these calls; it helps them as well. It's a win-win situation. We have trained dozens of people to make these calls out of all our locations. Anyone is eligible to receive a call—all you have to do is ask.

GREAT LAKES ATTC: Are all of your volunteers people in recovery?

PHIL VALENTINE: We thought the telephone recovery support would best be provided by people in recovery, but we have had some interns who weren't in recovery who have done a great job in this role and have gotten the same results as our recovering people. I think it's just the fact that the agency of CCAR, what we represent, is reaching out to them, and as representatives of CCAR, they really feel and understand that somebody cares for them. It may be more the institution and the relationship with the institution than the particular person who's making that call. And I don't even know if it's the institution as much as the purpose. It's the care, compassion, and love behind the call that seem to work.

GREAT LAKES ATTC: It's hard to estimate the power of such contact.

PHIL VALENTINE: Early in my recovery, I was told to get a long list of names and phone numbers of people in recovery, and I did. I was a good boy. I had probably a couple hundred names. Did I ever call anybody? No. The idea of actually using the phone numbers was foreign to me. I couldn't pick up the phone to call somebody, but when somebody called me, I would talk and talk and talk and talk and felt very grateful for the support.

GREAT LAKES ATTC: What keeps the volunteers coming back?

PHIL VALENTINE: It's fulfilling. I sit here, and I listen to volunteers make telephone recovery support calls. I'm not ever sure who's getting the most out of it, the volunteers or those they're calling, but I see volunteers with eyes lit up, energized on the phone, really glad to hear from this person that they're doing well, praising the person for all the good things they're doing, being able to be a small part in maybe moving that person towards a life of recovery. There is nothing more rewarding in a volunteer position than playing a role in moving someone into a life in recovery.

GREAT LAKES ATTC: How would you distinguish between peer-based recovery support services and treatment services?

PHIL VALENTINE: I associate the terms "treatment" and "clinical" with being cold and sterile. I don't know if that's correct, but maybe that's been my experience. I see treatment as more sterile, professional, hospital-like, staff-focused. Treatment can be real effective in initiating recovery, where recovery support services are more focused on maintaining and enriching recovery. Recovery support services aren't bureaucratically bound—at least not yet—by mountains of rules, regulations, and paper. Recovery support services are more free and unencumbered to sustain a focus on whatever it takes to support recovery. We're trying to escape the coldness you feel when you walk into a place that seems only concerned with forms and money— the feeling that you're just one more person in the assembly line, one more of the addicts or alcoholics coming through the system. It's hard to be seen as a person in such coldness. Recovery support services are the warmth that can heat you back up. They're the antidote to people being paid to be your friend. Frontline counselors are often warm and wonderful people, but they are constrained by the burdens placed upon them.

GREAT LAKES ATTC: Are your recovery support services being provided by people in volunteer and paid roles?

PHIL VALENTINE: The vast majority of our recovery support services are provided by volunteers, and that's they way we hope to keep it. That being said, if a director of a center is a very strong, powerful personality and very visible, people will be drawn to that person for recovery coaching. What we try to do is to get such people to train others so that we can expand the pool of recovery support resources.

GREAT LAKES ATTC: Do you see a danger in the trend toward paid recovery coaches? Might we drift toward that same clinical coldness you described earlier?

PHIL VALENTINE: It's always about the heart. There's a real spiritual component. Some recovery coaches can get paid and handle it well, and others cannot. Getting paid in this role elevates the level of authority and responsibility. I worry about the ego. I worry about coaches aspiring to that kind of life-and-death influence over others. That kind of authority can mess with a person's recovery and humility. The longer I'm in recovery, the less I know. When you're a paid recovery coach for a while, you think you're starting to know all the answers, and that's just not true. There's always gonna be clients who are gonna teach you more than you teach them, and I hope we stay open to the lessons of such people. There are new ways to deal with things. The volunteer piece works in part because you have a whole network of other volunteers that you bounce things off of. With volunteers, the individual is served by a community of people—the volunteers being the welcome wagon of that community. What a difference it makes on the soccer fields! I've had six years' experience as a travel soccer coach. I wouldn't dream of getting paid. I love it, and I do it because the kids are so much fun. The sport's great. I have something to contribute. Why do we think that a recovery coach should be any different than that?

GREAT LAKES ATTC: Could you provide more detail on what you're doing with telephone-based recovery support services?

PHIL VALENTINE: Right now, we're making calls out of all four CCAR recovery community centers in Connecticut: Hartford, Bridgeport, New London, and Willimantic. In a recent quarter (July-Sept, 2006), we had 108 individuals we were calling on our rolls; 95 were in stable recovery, and only 13 had relapsed. The group as a whole included people who were 30, 60, or more than 90 days out of treatment. The services are available to anyone who requests them, even if you haven't been in treatment. Our number-one referral source is the Recovery Housing Coalition in Connecticut. The treatment providers are starting to jump more on board, so we're getting 6 to 10 referrals a day from them.

GREAT LAKES ATTC: You mentioned that many people want to keep up the phone contact after the standard 12-week period. How long are telephone-based services provided?

PHIL VALENTINE: We have people we've called now for more than a year who are still sober and still appreciating our calls.

GREAT LAKES ATTC: Describe a typical recovery support call.

PHIL VALENTINE: We have a set script, but the call really starts on this basic premise: "Hi. This is _____ from CCAR, checking in with our regular recovery support call. How are you doing?" And then the conversation branches from there based on their responses. We use a decision tree to guide those making the calls. "I'm doing well." "What kind of supports are you using for your recovery? Oh great. You're in a 12-Step program. Have you had a chance to get a sponsor yet?" That kind of thing. "You're still clean, but you're not going to any support meetings? Is there some reason why you're not going to meetings? Can I help you find a meeting?" If we find that people have relapses, we explore options with them and try to get them re-linked to recovery support. Our complete script is available for anyone who wants it.

GREAT LAKES ATTC: Describe the orientation and training of those staff and volunteers who provide recovery support services through CCAR.

PHIL VALENTINE: We have this inner circle of ten staff people who know that the best way to multiply our efforts and be good stewards of our funding is to recruit and develop a volunteer force that is highly trained. We modeled our volunteer program on those used at the major hospitals in the New Haven area. There is a formal application, an interview, a background check, an orientation that includes the module "CCAR Ambassador 101," and ongoing training. Our basic orientation covers such areas as crisis intervention, confidentiality, ethics, and relationship boundaries. And then we provide specialty training for the kinds of roles people want to fulfill, such as peer support group facilitation or telephone recovery support. We have a formal schedule for volunteers working, and each volunteer is evaluated at six weeks and again after six months. We spend a lot of time acknowledging and rewarding our volunteers—for example, at reward dinners—to let them know how much we appreciate the contributions they're making. Volunteer management is not easy, and it takes a very skilled person running it.

GREAT LAKES ATTC: Describe the ongoing supervision of volunteers.

PHIL VALENTINE: Volunteer supervision is done by our peer services coordinators, with our statewide Volunteer Manger having a hand in the formal evaluations. Each volunteer is given a clear sense of what we're evaluating them on and how they can improve. The volunteers also get together and talk with each other about situations that are coming up in the phone calls or in the peer support groups. There's not a lot of crisis intervention. We do have situations where people referred to us may come in high or intoxicated, but we're pretty good at responding to them. When people show up at the center high, we understand that they're here looking for something—looking for help.

There is a second tier of supervision that's important that involves the staff who work with and supervise the volunteers. There are always risky situations that can arise in this kind of service work. The key is how we manage it. Our staff meetings are a reporting session, in which we explore these areas of risk. We look at, "What kind of scenarios came up that you struggled with? What did you find most difficult?" We're trying to get the coordinators to always be completely truthful, rather than hide areas of potential vulnerability.

GREAT LAKES ATTC: How are the telephone support services provided by CCAR being funded?

PHIL VALENTINE: We were fortunate in that we worked with the State and their federal Access to Recovery grant to establish our first fee-for-service. We've learned to cope with the complexities and the tedious work of the medical billing world. We also established a case-rate, so for every ATR-eligible recoveree, we receive $151.20 for the first 12-week block of phone calls.

GREAT LAKES ATTC: What are the major obstacles in implementing peer-based recovery support services?

PHIL VALENTINE: One of the potential obstacles is how the treatment providers respond to this growing recognition of the need for non-clinical recovery support services. There is a question of whether they'll jump in and do these services to expand their own service empires, or whether they're going to help the recovery community enhance its own capacities for support. The question is whether treatment agencies will see an "upstart" young recovery community organization as an ally or as a competitor for funds. We are very fortunate in Connecticut that our state leader, Tom Kirk, has promoted a collaborative relationship between CCAR chapters and local treatment programs.

GREAT LAKES **ATTC:** What do you see as the future of funding for peer recovery support services? Is there an ideal way to fund these services?

PHIL VALENTINE: Ideally, the funding will come from the recovery community itself, and I think the recovery community centers will be that vehicle through which people can, through their individual financial contributions, support local recovery support services. State and federal agencies can help seed these programs for a number of years to build a base of support, but in the long term, the recovery community itself must take ownership of these service centers. The problem is that it may take eight to ten years of development work for a center to be fully self-sustaining.

GREAT LAKES **ATTC:** What do you personally feel best about today in terms of CCAR's involvement in recovery support services?

PHIL VALENTINE: I'm a fisherman. I feel good that the recovery support services we provide are a net that's catching a lot of the people who wouldn't have otherwise started and sustained a recovery process. Somebody had to build and maintain that net, and I'm honored and humbled by the enormity of how we have affected people's lives. Counselors in treatment often don't get to see the fruits of their work, but we get to see people and stay involved with people and see how their lives have changed years into the recovery process. We can see how they grow and change. We get to witness the fruits of recovery.

RECOVERY MANAGEMENT AND TECHNOLOGY TRANSFER

An Interview with Lonnetta Albright
By William L. White, MA

INTRODUCTION

The Great Lakes Addiction Technology Transfer Center is one of 14 such Centers in the United States and its territories. The Centers are funded by the Substance Abuse and Mental Health Services Administration, Center for Substance Abuse Treatment (SAMHSA, CSAT) to improve the quality of addiction treatment by enhancing cultural appropriateness, advancing the adoption of new knowledge, developing and disseminating tools, building a better workforce, forging partnerships, and encouraging ongoing treatment system self-assessment and improvement. Each Addiction Technology Transfer Center (ATTC) takes on special initiatives that are of interest to their state constituencies and needed in their regions. In 2005, the Great Lakes ATTC began developing products and training presentations to help their state agencies and regional treatment providers shift from an acute-care model of addiction treatment to a model of sustained recovery management. In the brief interview below, Great Lakes ATTC Director Lonnetta Albright discusses this initiative.

GREAT LAKES ATTC: Briefly describe your history of involvement in the addictions field.

LONNETTA ALBRIGHT: Early in my career I ran a Group Home for adolescent girls. On a number of occasions we would observe what I didn't know at the time were co-occurring disorders. These young women experimented, mostly with drugs, and at least half of them were receiving counseling and/or psychiatric help. Without any

266

background in treatment, we started what were called "Rap Groups," and we reached out to the social service community. We were fortunate to have an organization called South Suburban Council on Alcoholism, which served this population. Their staff would conduct in-services for our team, as well as work with our girls. That early collaboration marks my first involvement in the field of addiction treatment. Following this initial involvement and understanding of the affects of substance use, it became clear that we all (staff, volunteers, and clients) needed to better understand how alcohol and drug use could prevent any progress and/or healing, and why at times it seemed we were spinning our wheels. And now, as I think about it, stigma, denial, shame, and a lack of understanding also perpetuated the problems that our communities faced. The schools, churches, and families all believed that alcohol and drug use were matters of morality and poor judgment. And to be honest, my basic beliefs were in line with that belief, associating stigma and discrimination with people whose problems I didn't understand. The science and the facts about addiction were all but non-existent.

Then (thankfully) during the next decade, my understanding of and education about addiction was developed by professionals in the treatment field who believed that people deserved help with their battle against drugs. As my career continued in the late 80s and early 90s, I became familiar with the TASC agency in Illinois, which exposed me to the criminal justice system and addiction and the nexus between the two. My education, training, and hands-on experience led me to study and take a deeper look at addiction. I was trained in the neurobiological aspects of addiction and in other recent breakthroughs in knowledge that have revealed the tremendous gap between what was being learned in the research arena and what was actually happening on the front lines of addiction treatment. Interest in closing that gap brought me to my current position as Director of this Region's ATTC. As a former educator, I thoroughly embrace the importance of clinician education in elevating the quality and effectiveness of addiction treatment. I was interested in how research could inform us about what works—not just on paper, but in the actual processes of assessment, engagement and retention, treatment planning, and long-term recovery support.

I've spent the past nine years helping systems and the workforce integrate what we're learning from the research and apply it effectively in practice, and this has been no small or easy task. We've learned there are cultural differences and myriad other factors that have to be addressed to effect change. I personally believe that change is good, particularly when it takes the best of what we already have and integrates new knowledge and technologies. These are very exciting and encouraging times for people and communities that have suffered so much. To the extent that this suffering has been exacerbated by the lack of understanding, I feel like we're making an important contribution as a source of healing for individuals, families, and communities.

On a personal level, addiction (primarily to alcohol) has also touched my immediate family. I've lost an aunt, uncle, and cousin to alcoholism and the medical complications brought on by this disease (e.g., hepatitis, kidney and liver failure, and stroke). None of my affected family members ever sought treatment or even acknowledged that they had a problem. They alienated themselves from the family, although the family was always there for them. My dad was what we called a functional alcoholic. When the floor bottomed out for him (a long and touching story), he decided that the drinking was not worth what he stood to lose. Seeing both addiction and recovery close-up intensified my commitment to this field.

GREAT LAKES ATTC: Provide a brief overview of GLATTC's mission and activities.

LONNETTA ALBRIGHT: The ATTC Network's stated mission is: *Unifying Science, Education and Services to Transform Lives.* At our Center's 2006 annual strategic planning and team-building session, we defined our regional mission as one of *Building Bridges That Foster the Advancement of Treatment and Recovery.* We use training, technical assistance, systems change, and technology transfer based on the latest science and evidenced-based and promising practices to: improve the knowledge and practices of substance use disorder (SUD) providers; build culturally competent recovery-oriented systems of care; and develop the SUD workforce in our region. I believe that the success of our regional effort is in large part due to the partnerships, collaboration, inclusiveness, and diversity of our key stakeholders, experts, and constituents. Our activities are driven by significant input from the communities we serve and based on the results of our various needs assessments. Beyond the region, all of our work is disseminated nationally via the ATTC Network.

GREAT LAKES ATTC: How did you first decide to involve the Great Lakes ATTC in the promotion of recovery management?

LONNETTA ALBRIGHT: Well, I've always believed in a comprehensive and holistic approach to care that encompasses medical, psychological, social, cultural, and spiritual dimensions of recovery. My decision to provide full support to the promotion of recovery management is both personal and professional. Several of our colleagues and staff are recovering practitioners. Many of them were embarking upon efforts to serve the people and communities that we work with more effectively. We all agreed that there is so much more to people in trouble—any type of trouble—and that dealing with only one part of the person (e.g., treatment needs) does not at all respect or acknowledge the fact that all people are more than their problems. More important, I personally believe that people can and do get better. I'm an eternal optimist, and I believe that people can change. And if supported effectively, we all have the power within us to continually develop, improve, and heal.

Our colleagues who were engaged in the CSAT-funded Recovery Community Support Program (RCSP) around the country pulled us in a couple of years ago. They believed that the ATTC could assist them in developing various models, and in the development of what I frequently refer to as the recovery community workforce. And then, while GLATTC was involved in this work with the RCSPs, I began reading Bill White's writings and talking with him about Recovery Management (RM). I became a student of RM, and I can't tell you how much excitement this has generated within our team and across our region. As an ATTC, we also look at the science that supports the practices that we promote. The work Dr. Tom McClellan and his colleagues have done in documenting the parallels between addiction and other chronic diseases was also very influential in our decision to take on this initiative. On a personal note, I have first-hand experience observing my dad's eventual healing using these RM principles (another long story with a happy ending)

GREAT LAKES ATTC: What activities have you pursued to-date in the recovery management arena?

LONNETTA ALBRIGHT: To begin our initiative, we first worked to raise awareness about the recovery management model throughout the treatment and recovery field. This first step led us to develop papers and newsletters that were widely disseminated. We wanted to get the word out, to introduce people in our region to the key RM principles, service roles, challenges, and language. Our *GLATTC Bulletin* newsletter was the first publication on RM that was widely distributed across our region and throughout the National ATTC Network. The ATTC National Office has posted this body of work on the home page of the network's national web site. Other ATTCs have produced reprints and disseminated our work in other parts of the country.

The response to the first newsletter was so positive that we followed it with a monograph on RM that included essays by Bill White, Dr. Ernie Kurtz, and our own Mark Sanders. This was the beginning of what we see as an ongoing Recovery Management Monograph Series. We've supplemented these written materials with more than 20 professional presentations, including conference keynote addresses, workshops, and panel presentations.

To-date, we have five significant RM collaborations underway. In Ohio, we're working with the Single State Agency to help them develop a Recovery Management approach for their offender re-entry program. In Michigan, we're working with their Office of Drug Control Policy on a statewide Workforce Development Initiative, and as part of this initiative we're training clinical supervisors in using RM principles and approaches. In Illinois, we've received a request to assist a Hispanic-Latino treatment provider to shift their service orientation toward an RM model. In Indiana, we're just beginning a system-transformation process focused on recovery management. Finally, we're collaborating with two other ATTC regions on projects working with policy makers interested in shifting their state treatment systems to a recovery management model.

I am most proud of our RM Symposium for Policy Makers from the Midwest states in March of 2007. Fourteen states attended, Dr. Clark was our keynote presenter, and our panel of presenters was phenomenal. Not only did our regional single state agencies support and attend the day-long session, but leaders from around the Midwest—including 4 ATTCs and our national ATTC office—were on hand as well. Since that event the past few months have been full of requests from participants who are now pursuing system-change efforts to transform their treatment systems to Recovery Oriented Systems of Care.

GREAT LAKES ATTC: What has been the response from the states and from front-line service workers to this initiative?

LONNETTA ALBRIGHT: To be honest, I've been pleasantly surprised. I'd anticipated some resistance, particularly given the field's track record with change. But it's as if our states and front-line workers had been waiting for this. When we launched our work, the response was overwhelming. We are now challenged to figure out how to keep up with the demand for information, workshops, and more information and workshops. Each of the states in our region decided to include Recovery Management as a major part of its annual conference. Then there are academic institutions that have purchased hundreds of copies of the RM Monograph to use in their Addictions Studies coursework. And our partners and other members from the Recovery Community have embraced this body of work and tell us how pleased they are that we're looking at a long-term or sustained recovery approach that involves the community.

GREAT LAKES ATTC: To what do you attribute such a positive response?

LONNETTA ALBRIGHT: I think the model makes sense, not to mention that the data and science support it. When I first began in the human services field, working with children and families in the child welfare system, these same principles worked. What I mean is that we worked, not only with the client, but also with the family, school, faith community, friends, employers, and anyone else the client believed were important. As a former certified Reality Therapist—a model that also believes in a person's own power, strengths, and assets to deal with and overcome personal challenges—I am not surprised that the field sees the benefit and promise of RM. I also believe that the timing is right. For the past eight or nine years we have been working with the field around adopting evidence-based practices. We have made some great inroads into reducing resistance and helping individuals, organizations, and systems change, not only their practices, but also their attitudes and mindsets. I think we're a smarter field today that is open to new approaches that can positively impact people's lives. That's hopeful and encouraging.

GREAT LAKES ATTC: What do you hope to achieve in establishing the Great Lakes ATTC as a Center of Excellence in Recovery Management?

LONNETTA ALBRIGHT: This Center of Excellence in RM has moved from a vision to an actual plan that we are now implementing. We are especially excited about having a new partner in this effort. The Northeast ATTC has agreed to collaborate on developing and implementing this new Center of Excellence. As with any new model, there will be many different interpretations of principles and variations in practices. We run the risk of lots of misinterpretation and fragmentation of the model. Rather than just raise awareness, we need to facilitate a clear definition of this model and how its core elements can best be implemented. And we want to make sure that we incorporate what we're learning from the research at every step of this process. I frequently quote Dr. Timothy Condon, Deputy Director at NIDA, who says "we want to teach what we *know*, not just what we *think* or *feel*."

This shift is about system change, and there is a process. We intend to follow the appropriate and most effective steps from the ATTCs' perspective. There are many organizations and people who will have a role in helping the field adopt a sustained recovery support approach to helping people with substance use disorders. We have carved out a role for our ATTC that begins with awareness and education. We plan to follow that by helping the field look at service redesign and ways in which the model can be implemented. We plan to use our successful technology transfer strategies to help us develop the workforce, including front-line staff, peer coaches and mentors, clinical supervisors, faith-based providers, and the next generation of leaders and trainers. We will also focus on new professionals (students at academic institutions and other vocational programs).

GREAT LAKES ATTC: What do you see as the future role of the ATTCs in helping shift addiction treatment from a model of acute care to a model of sustained recovery support?

LONNETTA ALBRIGHT: I am continually impressed by the effectiveness and success of the ATTC Network, particularly related to helping the field develop a comprehensive and collective approach that is replicated across the country. The network has a well thought-out strategic approach for harnessing our varied and diverse levels of expertise, abilities, and resources. We have worked hard to "master" the art of collaboration, which as you know is easier said than done. When we started this effort, others joined us. Many partnerships have formed, and new projects are continuing to be formulated. As a network, we are getting the message out across the country and internationally. I anticipate that an ATTC Network response will be developed and implemented at the various levels (workforce development, policy and system change, products, and best practices). We will use all of the tried and proven strategies, and other strategies will be developed by this very creative, responsive, and committed network of professionals who work in partnership with our communities and constituents.

ABOUT THE AUTHORS

Ernest Kurtz is a Harvard-trained historian whose books include *Not-God: A History of Alcoholics Anonymous* and *The Spirituality of Imperfection* (With Katherine Ketcham).

Mark Sanders, LCSW, CADC (*Onthemark25@aol.com*) is an independent trainer and consultant and the author of *Treating the African American Male Substance Abuser* and *Counseling Chemically Dependent African American Women*.

William L. White, MA is a Senior Research Consultant at Chestnut Health Systems. He is the author of many books, monographs, and articles, including *Slaying the Dragon: The History of Addiction Treatment and Recovery in America* and *Pathways from the Culture of Addiction to the Culture of Recovery*. He has also worked with recovery advocacy groups across the country. *Slaying the Dragon* received the McGovern Family Foundation Award for the best book on addiction recovery. He also received the 2003 National Association of Addiction Treatment Provider's Michael Q. Ford Journalism Award. Bill White has a Master's degree in Addiction Studies and nearly 40 years' experience in the addictions field.

Printed in the United States
By Bookmasters